The Essenti

A Guide to Profitable Investing in Real Estate Investment Trusts

By Ralph L. Block

With Appendices by William F.K. Schaff

BRUNSTON

PRESS

Hillside Public Library

Copyright © 1997 by Ralph L. Block

All rights reserved. No part of this publication may be reproduced or transmitted in any form, by any means, electronic, or mechanical, including photocopying, recording or by any information storage and retrieval system, without the prior written consent of the author.

Published in the United States by
Brunston Press
160 Sansome Street, 17th Floor
San Francisco, California 94104

Book Team
Editor: Joe Tarica
Layout: Joe Menkin
Cover Design: Claudia X. Valdes & Craig D. Pollock
Interior Graphics and Illustrations: Craig D. Pollock & Steve Block

Library of Congress Card Catalog Number: 07 -71089

ISBN 0-9657075-0-4

Website address: http://www.bayisle.com

For information on where to purchase this publication, please contact
Brunston Press
at (888) 705-8844

Printed in the United States of America, 1997

ABOUT THE AUTHOR:

Ralph Block is the Executive Vice-President and a Senior Portfolio Manager at Bay Isle Financial Corporation, a San Francisco-based investment advisory firm which manages over $250 million for institutions and individuals. In 1976 Mr. Block started investing in Real Estate Investment Trusts (REITs) personally and on behalf of other individuals. Since then, he has continued to devote much of his time to the analysis of, and investment in, various Equity REIT opportunities. He is currently responsible for analyzing REIT stocks and for managing REIT portfolios at Bay Isle. Prior to joining Bay Isle, Mr. Block was a corporate attorney for almost 30 years and has been a Board member and general counsel to a number of public and private corporations

Mr. Block graduated with a B.A. degree with honors in Political Science from U.C.L.A. in June 1964 and with a J.D. degree from the U.C.L.A. School of Law in June 1967, where he was an Associate Editor of the Law Review and Member of the Order of the COIF. He lives with his wife, her mother and their dog, Beauregard, in Westlake Village, California.

To my father, Jack, who has always been the original "REITman" and without whom this book, in more ways than one, would never have been possible. My only regret is that he was not able to see its completion.

PREFACE

"Writing a book is an adventure — to begin with, it is a toy and an amusement; then it becomes a mistress, and then it becomes a master, and then a tyrant. The last phase is that just as you are about to be reconciled to your servitude, you kill the monster, and fling him out to the public."
— **Winston Churchill**

In 1967, I was a senior at UCLA Law School, and the stock market was in one of its periodic frothy moods. Several of my law school pals and I, believing that we were intellectual geniuses and naively thinking that such talents could easily be applied to the investment world, decided that we could make a financial killing. We bought a few stocks that promptly went up, but, like investors everywhere, we confused "genius" with a bull market. Recently married, with a child on the way and having just left school for a starting law position paying the princely sum of $600 a month, I seized the opportunity for instant riches. Over my wife's objections, I scooped up our entire savings account of $1,800 and opened a brokerage account. I thus launched my investment career and bought, on full margin, U.S. Industries (a high-flying conglomerate) and SMC Investment Co. (an investment company run by a "go-go" investor). As is the nature of things, these "terrific investments" soon crashed and burned and, being on margin, the loss was close to 100%.

Some time later, in the 1970s, I gingerly ventured back into the market's treacherous waters, but now I was smarter. I looked for stocks paying high-dividend yields, which of course "must be" safer than ordinary common stocks. I latched onto Chase Manhattan Mortgage, a "real estate investment trust" that sported an 8% yield. This company, together with several other new REITs recently organized by major banks throughout the United States, lent money to needy developers of office buildings, often providing upwards of 100% financing. That investment was another big mistake and another lesson learned, as most REITs' share prices collapsed under the weight of ill-conceived loans and loose lending standards. "REIT" quickly became, to me and to many others, a four-letter word.

Following that experience, I continued to make occasional forays into the depths of the investment world, trying to avoid the pitfalls and seeking to find the neglected investment gems. Late in 1976 my father asked me to find him a good safe investment, but it had to pay a reasonably good dividend (as he was nearing retirement age). I got out my dog-eared *Standard & Poor's Stock Guide*, and looked for stocks with high yields and reasonably attractive track records of steady growth. After several hours, progressing all the way to the W's, my tired eyes fell upon an odd little company called "Washington Real Estate Investment Trust," which yielded 9% and seemed to be increasing income and dividends at 8-10% per year by investing in real estate in Washington, D.C. "Uh oh, another one of those damn REITs" was my initial reaction. However, after further research, I decided this one looked pretty good and perhaps was worth a shot. I bought Dad 100 shares of "WRIT," as it likes to be called, and moved onto other things.

Several years later I decided to compare the performance of his "WRIT" with the stocks I had bought for myself in the mid-'70s. The results were staggering. His little oddball REIT had gone gangbusters, and I learned two valuable lessons: (1) in the investment world, one must always be humble, and (2) REITs may be worthwhile investments after all.

From that point on, I started buying REITs. And as they consistently delivered great investment returns, I continued to buy. I made it my mission to be a "REIT man" and to buy them at every opportunity. I bought them personally, and in my firm's retirement plans. I bought them for my parents and my in-laws. I funded my children's college education with them. I've recommended them to my friends, and written memos, letters, heck, even poems about them. I've subscribed to the advisory services that have followed REITs over the years, I've talked to REIT managements and I've gone to REIT conferences. More recently, I've become the "resident REIT analyst" for Bay Isle Financial Corp., a San Francisco-based asset management firm. Sure, I've had my share of REIT turkeys over the years; some of the old-timers may remember names such as HealthVest and Consolidated Capital. But after owning REITs for 20 years and buying more whenever possible, I've been able to obtain, at the ripe old age of 53, complete financial independence.

This book will show you how REITs can help you to achieve your own long-term financial objectives. As I will show in Chapter One, REITs' total returns (dividend return plus price appreciation) have pretty well matched those of the S&P500 index over the last 20 years (and for shorter periods as well), with higher current income, lower volatility and generally less risk. Steady and substantial income and growth in one's investments, if begun early enough, provide for a very comfortable retirement; taking significant risks is simply unnecessary.

Why is it that I and other investors have been able to do so well with REIT stocks? In my case, I would not attribute my success to a Warren Buffett-type investment brilliance. Nor have I spent inordinate amounts of time researching the minute operating details of the REITs' assets and visiting managements and properties. What I have done is apply a certain amount of common sense to my task and refined a few investment principles that have stood me in good stead over the years. And I've been patient. I've found that successful REIT investing is 30% common sense and 70% patience; we don't have to be investment or financial wizards to do well with these investment gems. To put it simply, I've done nothing that anyone of average intelligence and using a modicum of effort couldn't do.

The real reason for REITs' outstanding long-term investment performance is two-fold: First, buying and managing well-located properties (and acquiring or building additional properties as the opportunity arises) is not terribly difficult, and managements who have a certain amount of common sense and a bit of imagination can do very well for the REIT and its shareholders as long as they avoid dumb mistakes. And, second, REITs have not been terribly popular investments, having been overlooked during much of their history. It is due to this unpopularity that REITs' shares have traded at bargain prices most of the time; that, in turn, has provided investors the opportunity to earn total returns commensurate with the S&P500 index, all with less volatility and less risk.

So when friends said to me, "A book about REITs? You've got to be kidding," I just smiled. I know that they've been unloved and under-followed (the REITs, that is, not my friends), and that writing this book may not affect that reality. Will REITs ever get the investor following they so richly deserve? Absolutely — they are already becoming increasingly accepted in the investment world and their popularity continues to grow. In the meantime, invest, enjoy the high yields and double-digit returns, and sleep well at night.

Ralph Block
Westlake Village, California
January 6, 1997

P.S. This book is not intended as a scholarly tome, but rather a reflection of one investor's experience and overall assessment of an investment sector that has proven very rewarding to him. I have not had, until recently, access to huge databases of financial information, nor have I had the time to plow through them. Most of my statements and assertions are matters of opinion, based upon my 20 years of experience and reflection relating to the REIT industry and to individual REITs. Accordingly, I have limited, to the extent possible, various footnotes, asterisks and the like, and have avoided bibliographies altogether. Nevertheless, this book could not be written without my purporting to state some things as fact, and to provide examples where appropriate. I therefore have used my best efforts to verify all statements of fact, dates, performance numbers and the like which are contained in the book. Any errors are solely my responsibility.

ACKNOWLEDGMENTS

"No man but a blockhead ever wrote except for money"
— *Samuel Johnson*

I've always been shy. I could never have been a trial or entertainment lawyer, where the skills of verbal persuasion are so important. And I've never liked public speaking; many years ago I gave the "Valedictorian" address at our high school graduation and almost croaked from stage fright. But I love to write, and my friends say I'm good at it. Maybe that's why I went to law school and became a business and securities lawyer in my "first career." Anyway, after many years of drafting agreements, proxy statements and the like, it became essential to the preservation of my sanity to write other things. I started a weird little newsletter for friends and fellow investors called "Chips Off the Old Block," which I provided free of charge (my reward was being able to write about non-legal issues and problems that caught my fancy and to preach the wonders of REIT investing). Several years later, when I joined Bay Isle, I started writing a quarterly column for the firm's newsletter, dealing mainly with REITs. I decided that the next step would be a book devoted to REIT investing. However, the necessary time was never available until the Fall of 1995, when Gary and Bill at Bay Isle gave the book their whole-hearted support. I had no more excuses.

First and foremost, I'd like to express my sincere thanks and gratitude to Gary, Bill, Steve, Libby, Craig, Claudia, Loren and all my friends at Bay Isle, without whose support, encouragement and massive assistance this book would, truly, never have been written. It's almost unbelievable that such highly competent professionals can also be such nice people. Mark Decker, Chris Lucas, Vicki Baker and their associates at NAREIT have provided me with the encouragement, support and REIT data which allowed me to proceed with confidence, and Milton Cooper, a giant of the REIT world and a gentleman in every respect, provided me with the necessary moral support.

I'd also like to express my appreciation to Mike Kirby, Jon Fosheim and their associates at that quintessential research firm, Green Street Advisors, for their outstanding research and analysis on REITs over the years; in particular, I'd like to thank John Lutzius, who has been kind enough to donate many hours of his personal time reviewing the chapters and providing me with his valuable insights. Joe Tarica, my editor, has persistently and tirelessly helped me to massage my meanderings into a more reader-friendly form, for which I'll be eternally grateful. Joe Menkin has done a yeoman's job in getting the manuscript prepared for printing. Thanks, also, to the many REIT enthusiasts I've known over the years who have expressed their belief in REITs with their hard-earned dollars, and to Michael, Dan, Barry, Ralph (of the East), Stephen and my other new REIT friends at Motley Fool who have helped me to sharpen my understanding of the world of real estate and REITs. Finally, allow me to express my gratitude to my lovely wife Paula, who has put up with a great deal of "benign neglect" during the time it's taken me to complete this project.

TABLE OF CONTENTS

FOREWORD

By Mark Decker, President & Chief Executive Officer,
National Association of Real Estate Investment Trusts

I am delighted to have been given the opportunity to say a few words about Ralph Block's new book on investing in Real Estate Investment Trusts (REITs). Ralph has taken what can be a rather technical subject and, based upon his many years of experience in REIT investing, has explained it in such a way that all of us can easily grasp the essence of successful investment in real estate through REITs. Investors of all types and temperaments will find REITs to be one of the most exciting areas of investment over the next several years, and will provide them with the opportunity to earn excellent returns for their hard-earned investment dollars in the next decade and beyond. Let me explain why.

Real estate has historically been a boom and bust industry where fortunes were made and lost by "swashbuckling" entrepreneurs. You generally had to be a very wealthy individual or a large institutional investor to participate in commercial real estate. Simply put, investing in a wide variety of property types has not been an opportunity that has been widely available to the average investor through the public markets the way the automobile, consumer products, steel, technology, chemicals, financials and other sectors have been. Yes, small investors have been able to invest in real estate through REITs for over 30 years, but the REIT industry, until recently, has been a small one, and most REITs owned only apartments and neighborhood shopping centers.

However, the virtual collapse of commercial real estate in the late 1980's and early 1990's changed the real estate industry fundamentally and permanently. Institutional investors who owned, directly, large office buildings and hotels, and small investors who owned apartments and other types of property (directly or in limited partnership form) were hurt badly. But the small REIT industry came away from the carnage virtually unscathed; this was due, in large part, to REITs' quality managements and very conservative use of debt. 1992 ushered in an entirely new world for REITs, as they emerged, Phoenix-like, from the ashes of the real estate collapse. The REIT industry is now leading the securitization of real estate. The potential for REITs has now become reality. Ralph Block has given us a road map to this new and exciting destination. One that will give you great pleasure and satisfaction. A road not taken until now. A road not built until the last few years.

Ralph's book is particularly timely, as it appears at the very time that REITs are assuming their rightful place as the pre-eminent vehicle for investing in real estate. His formula for successful investing in REITs is compelling and straightforward. Every investor will allocate 15-25%, or more, of his or her assets to REIT stocks. Not because I say so; not because Ralph explains why such a percentage is appropriate; but because REITs, as an asset class, comprise the only sector of the U.S. capital markets that remains relatively untapped and under-represented by investors' dollars and because we can achieve consistent, annual double-digit total returns with the ability to diversify our investments among a wide variety of property types. Ralph explains why this is so, and how the average investor can achieve a relatively low risk, high return portfolio utilizing REITs.

Real estate securitization, led by today's REITs, is a dynamic growth industry with tremendous upside, and is changing the face of real estate investment. A sea change has occurred: Investors, whether institutions or individual investors, can now invest large or small amounts in commercial real estate and participate in the greatest wealth producing asset in the history of mankind — real estate.

I know why Ralph Block wrote this book. He understands that the REIT industry today is a new and better mousetrap, and is home to the most forward-looking, dynamic and innovative organizations which have ever owned and managed quality real estate. You will understand why REITs are able to create significant values for their investors. You will invest in REITs as you understand the nature of the investment opportunities inherent in REIT stocks, and why the past isn't prologue when it comes to investing in the U.S. real estate markets using the modern REIT vehicle.

As you read Ralph Block's book, I am confident that you'll see why the REIT industry represents the first, best opportunity to co-invest with the finest U.S. real estate companies in a liquid, diversified manner that has never been so widely available until now.

INTRODUCTION

"The instinct of ownership is fundamental in man's nature."
— **William James**

All of us think we know real estate, and we have all interacted with it in one way or another since our arrival in the hospital delivery room. That building, our earliest impression of the world, is real estate; the residence we were taken home to, whether a single-family house or an apartment, is real estate; the malls and neighborhood centers where we shop, the factories and office buildings where we work, the hotels and resorts where we vacation, even the acres of undeveloped land — all are real estate. Real estate surrounds us. But do we really understand it?

For many years we have had a "love-hate" relationship with real estate. We love our homes and fully expect that they will appreciate in value. We admire real estate tycoons such as Joseph Kennedy, Barron Hilton and the Rockefellers; we find Donald Trump and Leona Helmsley fascinating. Yet we believe real estate to be a risky investment and marvel at how major Japanese companies have spent hundreds of millions of dollars on U.S. hotels, golf courses, major office buildings and other "trophy" properties during the late 1980's, only to see their values plummet in the real estate recession of the late 1980s and early 1990s.

Is real estate a good investment? Real estate investment trusts, or "REITs," own real estate, but to what extent are they dependent upon the fortunes of real estate in general? Can we make money in REITs regardless of how real estate fares?

This book will answer those questions and more. It will not only make a convincing case for investing in REITs, but also provide all the details, background and guidance investors should have before delving into these highly rewarding investments. Here's what's in store:

Opening Part I: Meet the REIT, the first order of business will be to explain why REITs, which are simply corporations (or trusts) that acquire, own and manage real estate, are terrific investments that belong in every well-diversified investment portfolio (Chapter One). From there, we'll explore the "nature of the beast," and obtain a good working familiarity with REITs and their characteristics (Chapter Two). Chapter Three will follow with a description of the types of properties REITs own and the investment characteristics of each.

Upon reaching Part II: History and Mythology, readers should find REITs such an intriguing investment that they'll wonder why these mystery moneymakers have been unpopular for much of their history; Chapter Four will answer these questions, as well as dispel some old myths about REITs. We'll then, in Chapter Five, take a look back to study the history of the REIT world since its inception in 1962, and we'll see what we can learn from the mistakes of others.

Part III: What We Need to Succeed (Chapters Six, Seven and Eight) will provide the basic tools investors need to understand the dynamics of REITs' revenue and earnings growth (Chapter Six), distinguish the blue-chip REITs from their more ordinary relatives (Chapter Seven), and find investment bargains among REIT shares (Chapter Eight). This section may be a bit technical in places, but it's not difficult to follow with a bit of concentration.

Finally, in Part IV: How to Do It and What's Ahead, we'll get into the nitty-gritty of building REIT portfolios with adequate diversification (Chapter Nine), followed by a discussion of the risks investors face as they wend their way through the REIT world (Chapter Ten). At last, in "Tea Leaves" (Chapter Eleven), we'll do some speculating as to the future growth of the REIT industry and how we might profit from future trends.

By the time you finish this book you will have a firm understanding and appreciation of one of the most misunderstood yet highly rewarding investments on Wall Street. Even more important, you will be able to build your own portfolio of outstanding real estate companies that should provide you with attractive current dividend yields and the prospects of significant capital appreciation in the years ahead. By investing in investment-quality REITs, investors large and small have been able to earn total returns averaging at least 12-14% annually, with steady income, low market price volatility and investment safety.

REIT investors today have a much wider choice of investment properties than ever before and can choose from some of the most experienced and capable managements as have ever invested in and operated real estate in the United States. As the title of the book claims, REITs should be an *essential* part of every investor's portfolio; REIT investors have done quite well over the last 30 years, but the best is yet to come!

Part I

Meet the REIT

Chapter One

REITs: Those Unsung Heroes of the Investment World

"How do I love thee?... Let me count the ways."
— **Elizabeth Barrett Browning**

When I first sat down to write this book, I prepared an outline as I learned to do as early as the eighth grade. My "game plan" was to begin by describing what a REIT is (Chapter One), followed by a discussion of the kinds of properties REITs own (Chapter Two) and then a chapter on why virtually all investors should own them (Chapter Three). I quickly realized, however, that unless I cut to the bottom line and made it clear at the outset why these stocks are such good investments, many readers would suffer a bad case of the yawns and never get beyond Chapter One. As a result, the why-all-investors-should-own-REITs chapter has been moved up to the beginning, albeit at the risk of putting the cart before the horse and advocating a type of investment that readers may not fully understand until they've finished the following two chapters. So, with a caveat to all things in good time, let me first count the ways in which I love REITs.

What's your idea of a perfect investment? Here's mine: It must be highly profitable; after all, that's why we forego that new car or vacation home — investing requires us to make sacrifices now in order to enjoy much greater wealth in future years. Next, it must have performed well over significant periods of time; although past success in any endeavor is no guarantee of future success, our odds are better with a proven track record. Also, it must be low-risk; any gunslinger can make lots of money temporarily by taking lots of risks, but the ideal investment is one that will do well without exposing us to a partial or total wipeout.

There's more: It must pay a good current return on our investment capital; receiving significant current income allows us to decide for ourselves whether to continue to entrust hard-earned assets to a company's management, and also provides a source of funds for additional investing. And it must not be highly volatile, as we don't enjoy seeing our investment capital bounce around like a kid on a trampoline. Finally, it must be liquid — if we decide to sell (for whatever reason), we need to know we can find a buyer quickly, and easily get our hands on the sale proceeds with minimal transaction costs.

1

Fortunately, there's an investment that meets all of these criteria: REITs. My twenty-plus years of investing in REITs have more than proven their value to me. Now I'll prove them to you. For over 35 years, REITs have been highly profitable, consistent winners in all types of investment environments, they've rarely dealt investors a major loss of capital, they've paid high and consistent dividend yields, they've enjoyed low volatility in relation to other common stocks and they've been easy to buy and sell. What's more, they're more liquid and profitable and less aggravating than direct real estate investment, they provide better total returns than bonds and other high-yielding investments such as utility stocks, and they give us outstanding diversification in our investment portfolios. Every investor, no matter how aggressive or conservative, simply *must* own a portfolio of high-quality REITs.

Sound too good to be true? It's not.

Still not quite convinced? Read on, and you will be.

REITs' Investment Performance

O.K., let's get into the nitty-gritty. First and foremost, throughout most of their history, REITs have provided terrific investment returns. The National Association of Real Estate Investment Trusts (NAREIT) has kept a record of the stock price performance of all REIT stocks, sorted by several types. "Equity REITs," which *own* property rather than make property *loans*, make up the largest sector (approximately 87%), and have provided the highest total returns in REIT world.[1] NAREIT's figures show that, for the five-, 10-, 15- and 20-year periods ending December 31, 1996, Equity REITs[2] have provided their investors with compound annual total returns of 17.1%, 11.7%, 15.1% and 16.1%, respectively. (Total returns, simply stated, are dividend income plus capital appreciation, before taxes and commissions). When we consider that the total returns of the S&P500 Index — a broader market measure than the Dow Jones Industrial Average — were 15.2%, 15.3%, 16.8% and 14.6%, respectively, over the same time periods, it's clear that Equity REITs have been able to perform on a par with the broader stock market over the last 20 years. In a January 1996 article in Financial World,[3] author Pablo Galarza wrote that "over their 35-year history, equity REITs have averaged an annual rate of total return of 12.5% — 7.5% from dividend yield and 5% from earnings growth — in good and bad years alike."[4]

Finding investments that simply match the performance of a broad index of stocks such as the S&P500 is not all that impressive until we consider several other extremely valuable attributes that REITs enjoy. In view of such attributes (which we'll review below), REITs' performance over the years is truly awesome.

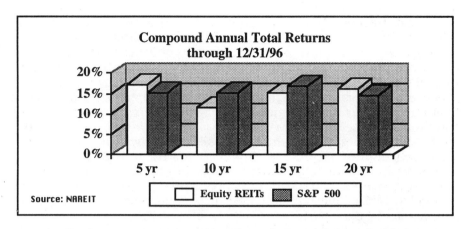

Compound Annual Total Returns through 12/31/96

Source: NAREIT

Equity REITs ☐ S&P 500 ▨

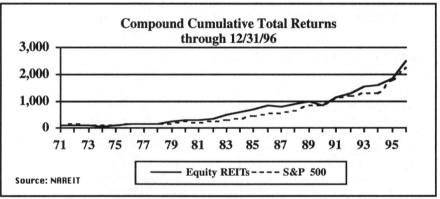

Compound Cumulative Total Returns through 12/31/96

Source: NAREIT

—— Equity REITs - - - - S&P 500

REITs' Attractive Investment Characteristics

We'll now turn to a more detailed discussion of some of the investment characteristics of REITs that, in my opinion, give them major advantages over other stock investments. These characteristics include low "betas," low market price volatility, limited investment risk and high current returns. These advantages are so significant that we could probably justify accepting a smaller total return from REITs than we would demand from ordinary common stocks; yet, as seen above, the total returns have been quite comparable over many years. All right, let's check out these investment characteristics which virtually *require* a place for REITs in every investor's portfolio.

Low "Beta"

The academic term "beta" refers to the extent to which a stock's price moves with an *index* of stocks, such as the S&P500. According to Ibbotson Associates, a stock with a beta of 1.0 "is as

3

risky as the overall stock market and, therefore, will provide expected returns to investors equal to those of the market. The price of a stock with a beta of 2.0 will, on average, rise approximately twice as much as the percentage gained by the overall stock market during periods of rising stock prices, and fall approximately twice the percentage lost by the market in periods of declining stock prices. Stocks with betas less than 1.0 have risk levels and, consequently, expected returns that are lower than that of the overall stock market."[5] Ibbotson seems to be a follower of "modern portfolio theory" (MPT), which equates "risk" in a stock to its tendency to rise or fall more than a broad stock market index such as the S&P500. MPT believers also claim that higher risk stocks provide investors with higher returns (in order to compensate them for the extra risk).

Whether or not one believes in MPT, it is very useful for investors to know what a stock's beta is, if for no other reason than to be able to predict its likelihood of moving "with the market." According to a January 1996 Lehman Brothers publication,[6] the REIT industry beta in relation to the S&P500, using monthly data for the prior 10 years, is 0.59.

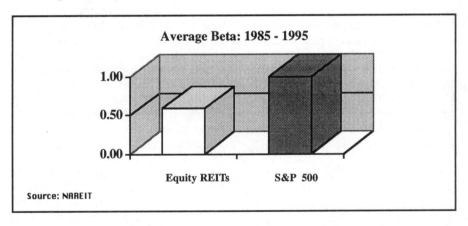

What this would mean, according to "beta theory," is that price movements in REIT stocks will have only a 59% correlation with the broad market, as measured by the S&P500 Index. Is this good? Not when the S&P500 index is consistently rising. In "hot markets," REITs' relatively low beta will normally act as a drag on their performance vis-à-vis the popular broad stock market indices. This occurred in 1995; REIT stocks did quite well in that year (providing investors with total returns of 15.3%, according to the NAREIT Equity REIT Index), but lagged behind the popular indices. (In 1996, however, REIT stocks refused to follow what would be "expected" of them under beta theory and turned in a performance

4

substantially higher than the broader market). Beta theory would also suggest that when the broad market declines almost daily, as it will during bear markets, low-beta stocks such as REITs will provide an anchor to windward and, if included in a broad stock portfolio, will tend to cushion the drop in the portfolio's value.

As noted earlier, many followers of MPT believe that betas are indicative of expected investment returns; thus a high-beta stock would mean that investors demand a high return in order to compensate them for the risk of the stock's greater fluctuations vis-à-vis the broad market, and vice-versa. It's interesting to speculate further and wonder why, if REITs have low betas, and thus expected investment returns which would be lower than those of the broad market, their performance has, over many years, pretty much *matched* that of the broad market, at least on a total return basis. An implication of this could be that, perhaps due to the myths and misperceptions concerning REITs that we'll explore in Chapter Four, REIT stocks are not efficiently priced and, in fact, are priced *below* what one would expect in a perfectly efficient market.

Low Volatility

A stock's "volatility" refers to the extent to which its price tends to bounce around from day to day, or even hour to hour, depending upon the measurement period. A stock with low volatility might just sit there for days, whereas some high-technology stocks are so volatile that they make investors dizzy with their wild price fluctuations. Volatility is different from beta, as a stock may yo-yo wildly intra-day or from day to day, yet its closing price may move pretty much with a market index over slightly longer periods of time. I know of no academic study that has measured the volatility of REIT stocks over any significant period of time. However, my experience in REIT investing over the past 20-plus years has convinced me that REITs are almost as good a soporific as a sleeping pill. On most days the average REIT might be up or down an eighth or quarter, but more likely will be unchanged from yesterday's close; movements of a point or more in a trading day are not common events. Exciting stocks they clearly are not.[7] This low volatility is due primarily to the REITs' high dividend yields, which act as a shock absorber for the vagaries of daily market fluctuations, and to the predictability and steadiness of most REITs' operating and financial performance from quarter to quarter and from year to year — there is simply less worry about major negative surprises.

Is this characteristic of low volatility a good thing? Yes, for two reasons.

First, the psychological. We investors are human beings, whether investing for ourselves or for others. As students of human nature have observed, we are all influenced by both greed and fear.

Therein lies a problem for investors, as during periods of greed we tend to throw caution to the wind and ignore prudence in our investment practices; likewise, we are terribly anxious to dump otherwise sound investments when in the grip of fear. Accordingly, a significant advantage of an investment with low market volatility is that we will often avoid selling a good investment at the bottom of a market cycle. Besides, it's easier to sleep at night when we know that our favorite stock is unlikely, even in a bear market, to open five points lower the next morning.

The second advantage of a non-volatile stock relates to the possible need to sell an investment during a market downturn. While we all should have enough cash on hand to see us through the proverbial "rainy day," we can't be sure that an unexpected financial blizzard won't arrive next week, whereupon our emergency funds won't be adequate and we'll have to do some selling. If a stock is not terribly volatile, the likelihood of taking a real drubbing is much less if we must sell during the occasional bear market.

Low Risk

Let's now turn from beta and volatility and look at pure risk. For purposes of this discussion, I'm making the assumption that investment "risk" is more than just a high beta — that it implies a potential permanent loss of one's investment capital. Real estate ownership and management, like any other business or commercial endeavor, is subject to various risks. Mall REITs are subject to the changing tastes and lifestyles of consumers, apartment REITs are subject to overbuilding and declining job growth in the geographical areas in which they own their properties, and health care REITs are subject to stingy health care reimbursement from federal and state governments, to cite just a few examples.

Yet, despite this, property owners are somewhat insulated from the operational risks of the companies that do business at the property's location. If the underlying real estate value of a store, for example, is sound, how badly can the real estate owner be hurt if the tenant goes belly up? This kind of thing happened repeatedly in 1989-1990 in the retail industry, and the retail REITs came out of it virtually unscathed; they merely found new tenants to replace the losers. This happened again in 1995, and REITs whose managements have structured their leases to provide a reasonable return based upon the underlying values of their real estate will not be badly burned by tenants who self-destruct. (We should note, however, that this "insulation" from risk may not be present where the real property is designed for a single use, in which case a departure by the tenant could make re-leasing difficult for the property owner).

Another way to look at the riskiness of a REIT investment is to examine the history of Equity REITs. Unlike Mortgage REITs, very

6

few of the former have gotten into serious financial trouble over the years. True, a few have encountered major difficulties through the use of excessive debt leverage, some have promised investors performance which they couldn't deliver and others have engaged in questionable transactions with directors or major shareholders (we'll explore such nastiness in Chapter Ten). On the whole, however, the great majority of the REITs that have been around for several years (and which have avoided loading up their balance sheets with too much debt and shunned "insider transactions") have done quite well by their investors. And if we invest primarily in the higher-quality REITs (in Chapter Seven we'll discuss how we determine "high-quality"), the long-term risk in such REIT investments is low in relation to most other common stocks.

There is also another type of risk which shareholders must contend with that relates not to the company's business but to the financial markets. We may own shares in a company whose business is doing quite well but where investors become disappointed and dump their shares, thus causing shareholders potentially significant losses (at least over the short term). Such investor disappointment frequently arises out of quarterly earnings announcements. How often have we seen a stock's price sliced by 20% by an "earnings shortfall" despite a nice increase from the same quarter in the prior year? REIT investors have rarely been victimized by such events. Analysts who follow REITs are normally able to forecast each quarter's earnings to within one or two cents, and significant earnings shortfalls are rare. This may have to do with the stability and predictability of REITs' operating cash flows, including rental rates and real estate operating costs. Whatever the reason, we REIT investors are able to get through the quarterly earnings rituals with a minimum of aspirin and Maalox, as we know that it's unlikely that our favorite REIT stocks will take a major dive as a result of a significant "earnings disappointment."

High Current Returns

It is interesting to note that of the 10%+ average annual total return on stocks since the mid-1920s, approximately 40% has come from dividends. Investors should never underestimate the importance of steady and rising dividend payments upon total investment performance.

In the non-REIT world, corporations are taxed on their net income, and dividends are taxed again when received by the shareholders; this discourages most corporations from paying out, in dividends, a high percentage of their net income. REITs, however, are not taxed at the corporate level, so dividends to shareholders are taxed only once. This makes REITs an ideal vehicle for high payout rates. Over the years, REITs in general have yielded between 6% and 8% for their investors.

7

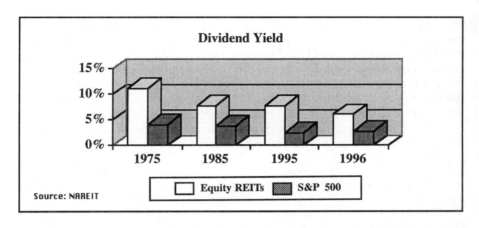

Dividend Yield

Source: NAREIT

Equity REITs S&P 500

The down side to high payout ratios is that the REIT has less retained capital with which to expand the business, which means that the typical REIT may not be able to increase its operating income as quickly as the typical corporation that retains more capital and invests it wisely in new growth opportunities. As a result, to the extent that stock price appreciation results from rapidly rising earnings, a REIT's share price will normally rise at a slower pace than that of a non-REIT stock (but the REIT investor expects to make up the difference through much higher dividend payments). REITs' high payout requirements mean that they must periodically go to the public for additional capital. Yet, there is a very positive aspect to this: The REIT is reviewed closely by investors and is held to a very high standard of returns on new investment. If the shareholders do not have confidence in management or its investment program, it will be denied additional capital. In fact, the very process of having to continually retain shareholders' confidence imposes a discipline on REITs that may not be present at other companies who do not frequently have to seek additional capital.

Another disadvantage of large dividend payments is that, unless the shares are owned in an IRA or other tax-exempt entity, taxes will have to be paid on the dividends received (although, as we will see later in this Chapter, a significant portion of a REIT's dividends may be deferred until the REIT shares are sold); conversely, the holder of shares of a low- or non-dividend paying company generally seeks capital appreciation, and can defer taxation on such appreciation until the sale of the shares. Taxes are paid at that time, often at lower capital gain rates.

Nevertheless, there are certain distinct advantages to owning high-yielding stocks such as REITs. One is that the shareholder, rather than management, can make the decision as to what to do with

8

his or her share of the company's operating income (received in the form of dividends). Additional shares can be bought with the dividend income (albeit on an after-tax basis in taxable accounts), or the funds can be invested elsewhere or spent on personal uses. Shareholders in companies such as Intel (which pay little or no dividends) have no such choice: Essentially all of "their" share of net income is reinvested for them by management.

Furthermore, even well-regarded public companies have been known to fritter away their shareholders' funds in ill-timed business expansions or, as Peter Lynch has said, "diworsifications." In contrast, REITs' requirement to pay a large chunk of income to the shareholders in the form of dividends tends to impose a major discipline upon management.

Many of us may be inclined to panic out of our investments during bear markets, when every day we see our net worth slowly but steadily melt away. Having something tangible to show for our investing efforts in the form of significant dividend income helps to put the occasional bear market in perspective and may keep us invested at bear market lows when our natural instincts are to bail out.

Finally, there's a certain psychological value in seeing significant dividends roll in each month or each quarter. Personally, I've had to work most of my life for the salary I've earned, and seeing a check come in for several hundred dollars without having to show up at the office to earn it somehow gives me a very warm feeling, whether I spend it or reinvest it.

While I don't advocate putting all of one's investment dollars in REITs, from an overall portfolio perspective the high yields they generate raises the overall yield of the portfolio and tends to minimize volatility while providing stability in major bear markets.

REITs' Investment Competitors

Many years ago while I was in law school, I took a course on antitrust law. Our professor always had us wrestle with the concept of the "relevant market." Suppose Nestle wanted to acquire Hershey Foods, for example. In order for us to determine whether this might create an antitrust problem resulting from one major competitor acquiring another, we had to figure out whether the "relevant market" was simply chocolate bars, a wider market such as "candy" or a still wider market such as "snack foods." There might or might not be an antitrust problem, depending upon which market was the "relevant market."

A similar issue arises when we compare the merits of REITs to those of other investments. Much depends upon the nature of the investments we compare them to. Is it appropriate to conclude that REITs compete with *all* common stocks for investors' attentions, or do they compete in the more narrow "market" of high-yielding investments? Up to this point we've been assuming the former; after all, REIT shares are common stocks, and they trade actively in the stock market just like other stocks do. However, many investors see them as somehow different from stocks such as Merck, Ford, Disney or Intel — and they really *are* significantly different. This is true for many reasons, one of the most important of which is their very high dividend yields and lesser capital appreciation prospects.

So, if we narrow the field, how do REITs match up against other securities investments with which they share similar characteristics: Utility stocks, preferred stocks and bonds? These popular securities are sought out by investors who, whether due to their need for significant investment income or because they just feel more comfortable with high steady income, normally invest in higher-yielding investments. The principal competition here is utility stocks, as they are closer to REITs than preferreds and bonds in two major respects: Their yields are more comparable and, even more important, they offer the prospects of dividend growth and capital appreciation. Non-convertible preferreds and bonds offer no dividend growth and, unless they are bought at a discount from "par" or redemption value, no capital appreciation prospects.

REITs vs. Utilities

Back in 1994 I did an informal study of REITs' popularity in relation to the utility stocks. According to a Barron's mutual fund section (April 1994), 71 mutual funds were specifically designed to invest in utilities and only 11 to invest in real estate securities. The aggregate asset value of these utility funds was $25.3 billion vs. only $1.27 billion for the REIT funds. Five utility funds *each* had assets greater than all 11 of the REIT funds combined. If just 20% of the assets in the utility funds were shifted into REIT funds, $5 billion of additional capital would be available to REIT fund managers, or four times their combined asset value as of the date my survey.

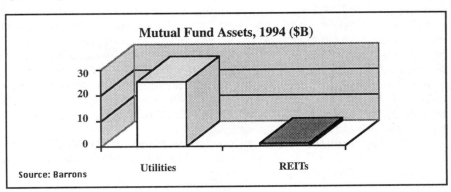

What does all this prove? Simply that utilities have been much more popular than REITs among income-seeking investors. Do they deserve to be? I will argue definitely no; in fact, while utilities have different investment characteristics than REITs and perhaps should have a place in some portfolios, REITs are clearly superior investments in most respects, and a large portion of an individual's funds now invested in utilities should be re-allocated to the REIT world. Here's why:

Growth Prospects. REITs have much better growth prospects. Their annual total returns to shareholders for the five year period ended December 31, 1996, as seen earlier, was 17.1%. Utilities, on the other hand, have not grown anywhere near as fast, particularly in recent periods, and most analysts do not expect the average utility to grow earnings beyond the 2-3% per year implied by forecasted inflation rates. Utilities' average total return over the five year period ended December 31, 1996, as measured by the Dow Jones Utility Average, was only 7.0% per year.

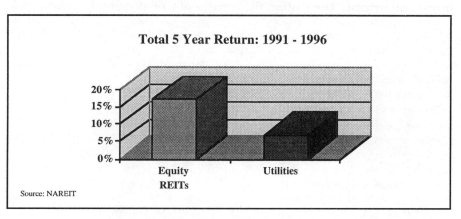

Total 5 Year Return: 1991 - 1996

Source: NAREIT

Growth is difficult for electric, gas and water utilities. Being highly regulated, most utilities can charge customers only what state regulators will allow them. They are normally locked into one geographical area, and expansion is problematical. Many, if not most, efforts by utility company managements to expand into other businesses, most likely in response to their poor growth prospects as regulated companies, have been dismal failures. Will the current efforts by some utilities to expand internationally turn out any better? Don't count on it. In view of these obstacles, its unlikely that even the most ardent supporters of utility stocks would predict future growth rates in excess of 3%.

Managements. While there are certainly some REITs being run by "caretaker" managements, the good ones are run by

11

extremely capable individuals who have had many years of experience in the successful ownership and management of real properties. They are energetic and entrepreneurial, and quick to seize new opportunities. Perhaps most important, many REITs are managed by persons who have most of their net worths invested in the shares of their REIT. Although the managements of some of the utilities may be very capable, most are not known for their vision and innovation; further, unlike most REIT managements, most do not own significant amounts of stock of the company they manage.

Regulation. Ah, the bugbear of every utility investor! For the regulatory commissions of most states, rate regulation is a "heads we win, tails you lose" proposition. If management makes a major decision that, with 20-20 hindsight, was a mistake, such as building an unneeded power plant, the regulators (being beholden to the politicians who appointed them and who, in turn, must answer to the voters if electricity or gas rates rise) will simply stick the shareholders with the costs. On the other hand, if things go well, lots of luck in getting the regulators to reward the company and its shareholders with healthy rate increases. Other thorny issues include the recovery of costs spent to build nuclear power plants, the costs and environmental issues involved in the disposition of spent uranium, "acid-rain" legislation and the costs to install expensive scrubbers. REITs, on the other hand, are largely unregulated.

Competition. Until recently, the power companies have had a Faustian bargain with the regulators. "You tell us what we can charge our customers and how much we can make, but in turn we get a monopoly on supplying all the power in our area" has been the position of the utilities and largely accepted by the regulators. How much longer will this be true? Utility investors should be wary now that words such as "co-generation," "deregulation" and "wheeling" are being bandied about, as they suggest that the areas in which their utility had long had an absolute monopoly are going to be opened to new competition. It appears to be just a matter of time.[8] These new competitors, whether upstart co-generation companies or other major power companies, are siphoning off large commercial electricity users, causing the local company to seek to impose significant rate increases upon the consumer to make up for the lost revenue. What are their chances of success against tight-fisted and politically-appointed regulators? To make matters worse, power company managements are not used to competition. How will they fare as they try to defend their turf? REITs, on the other hand, have always been exposed to substantial competition from a myriad of competing real estate companies, merchant builders and knowledgeable private investors.

Inflation. At the time this book was written, that old bear inflation was in his cave and didn't seem to be ruining anyone's

12

picnic. Nevertheless, this will not always be the case; although no one can consistently predict future inflation rates, it's inevitable that a nasty bout of it will come around some time in the not-too-distant future. Utilities are singularly ill-equipped to cope with this challenge, as they are prodigious borrowers, and interest rates will rise significantly in the face of a new inflationary environment. And while the regulators may allow them to pass onto the user much of the higher borrowing costs and the increased costs of power generation, it's problematical whether they will be able to recover all their costs and whether they will be able to do so within a reasonable time period. Furthermore, as most utility stocks trade in the market much like fixed-income securities, significantly higher interest rates will likely translate into large price declines for the utility stocks.

REITs also borrow significant amounts to fund development of new projects, to make acquisitions and to carry their real estate, and would be hurt by rising interest rates. Nevertheless, the costs of building competing properties would become substantially higher, thus perhaps increasing the underlying value of existing real estate. Furthermore, investors could decide to treat REIT shares like those of the oil companies during the last Arab oil embargo: They may be bought as inflation hedges, which could offset any price decline resulting from rising interest rates. REITs will clearly be affected less than utilities in the event of a major increase in inflation.

Increasing Investor Interest. The investment merits of utility stocks are widely known. Either one loves them or hates them, but it's unlikely that there will be a major surge of new investors who suddenly discover their virtues. REITs, on the other hand, have been largely ignored by investors since their arrival approximately 35 years ago. Despite their burst of popularity in 1992-1993, by 1994 many investors lost interest in them. (A later chapter, on REIT history, gets into all of this). The point here is that there are hundreds of thousands of potential REIT investors out there looking for excellent yields with reasonably good growth prospects, both individual and institutional, who are not now invested in them. Will they ever become REIT persons and, if so, when? No one knows. REITs have, however, enjoyed a new burst of popularity in 1996, and the prospect of substantial new funds coming into the REIT universe is yet another advantage of REITs over the utilities. Supply and demand forces do tend to move markets.

Yields. At the time of this writing, excellent quality REITs available in the U.S. markets could be bought at current yields in the range of 6-7%, and offered growth prospects of at least 6-8% annually, over the next five to 10 years. On the other hand, the most widely regarded utility companies were yielding between 5%

and 6%, and were expected to grow at perhaps 3%. Which would you rather own?

An April 1996 article in the Los Angeles Times[9] titled "Safe Widow and Orphan Utility Stocks May Be History" made the point that electric, gas and telephone utility stocks, which for many years have been regarded as one of the safest investments around, may no longer be so. The author, Tom Petruno, states that "as many utility-stock owners have painfully discovered in the 1990s, times have changed, and generally not for the better ..." He cites, as possible causes, utility deregulation, increased competition and poorly executed diversification. Of the five California utility stocks listed in the article, only Pacific Telesis was up substantially (115%) between December 1989 and March 31, 1996; Pacific Gas & Electric was up only 6%, Enova was virtually unchanged and Edison International and Pacific Enterprises were down 17% and 47%, respectively, during that time period, while three of the five have cut their dividends since the beginning of 1990.

So, what we seem to have with electric utilities are yields of close to 6%, 3% earnings growth at best and lots of risk arising from legislation, regulation and deregulation and other imponderables. On the other hand, with REITs we get yields of 6-7%, a like amount of growth and (for those REITs which haven't taken on excessive debt) much less risk. REITs *deserve* to be valued more highly than electric utilities but, as the curtain came down on 1996, REITs were being priced in the market much more cheaply than were the electrics, at least on a total return expectation basis. Is it any wonder than investors have traded over $2 billion of utility mutual funds for REIT mutual funds in 1996 (as I'll highlight below)? In fairness, the pendulum of history swings widely, and some day the electric utilities may be priced very low vis-à-vis REITs. This could come about as a result of excessive pricing discounts of the "utes" (or REIT stocks being too richly priced), a major shift in risk profiles between the two types of investments, a shift in their relative growth outlooks or other presently unknown factors. But today, in my opinion and that of many others, there's no contest

Summary of REITs vs. Utilities

	REITs	Utilities
Yield	6% - 8%	5% - 6%
Appreciation/growth	6% - 8%	3% - 4%
Risk Level	Low	Moderate to substantial
Management	Capable	Caretaker
Regulation	Low	High
Competition	High	Moderate/High (in Future)
Inflation Sensitivity	Moderate	High
Investor Flow	Increasing	Stagnant to declining

Putting all this in perspective, utility stocks are not worthless investments. They do have a place in many portfolios, and a few of them offer good yields and modest growth prospects with moderate risk. The point here is that every income-oriented investor should own REITs and perhaps some utility stocks as well; the relative percentages of each will depend upon one's own comfort level. But, as this book maintains, investors would do better, as a rule, to invest significantly more of their money in REITs than in their utility counterparts. A shift of this type is already occurring. According to mutual fund cash flow analyses provided weekly by AMG Data Services[10], at the end of November 1996, mutual fund flows for real estate funds for 1996 (through November 26) increased by $2.0 billion, compared with a *decrease* of $2.58 billion for utility mutual funds. Total assets at that date were $4.6 billion for REITs and $20.3 billion for utilities.

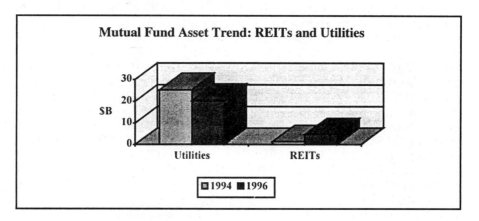

REITs vs. Bonds and Preferreds

While REITs compete with utilities for the funds of yield-oriented investors, their competition with bonds and preferred stocks is more tenuous. Except for their convertible cousins (which will be discussed briefly below), bonds and preferreds frequently provide higher yields than the best-quality REITs, but the investor gets nothing beyond the interest coupon; there is absolutely no growth potential. Bonds do offer something that REITs cannot provide: Repayment of principal at maturity, so that in the absence of bankruptcy or other default, the investor will always get back his or her investment. Because of this major feature of bonds, REITs don't compete with them directly. Thus, if absolute safety of capital is paramount, by all means do *not* buy REITs, toss this book in the trash can and have a nice day.

But wait; let's take a step or two back. This is a book about REITs, and this chapter discusses why investors should own them.

More specifically, investors should consider whether they are better investments than bonds. The problem is, as was mentioned earlier, REITs are *different* from bonds because of bonds' promise to pay a fixed amount at a specific maturity date in the future. It's like trying to figure out whether a filet tastes better than ice cream.

Nevertheless, for those shareholders who don't insist upon the absolute certainty of the return of capital at a specified payment date, REITs are better investments. Let's assume that Beauregard T. Canine invests $10,000 in a bond that yields 8%, payable in 10 years. At the end of 10 years, Beauregard will have $10,000 in cash plus the cumulative amount of his interest payments (10 x $800), or a total of $18,000, less taxes on all of his interest. If, however, he'd invested the $10,000 in a REIT, his probable total return would calculate as follows: Mr. C. buys 1,000 shares of a REIT trading at $10 per share, which yields 6% (or $.60 per share). Let's also assume that the REIT grows "funds from operations" ("FFO" — which, as will be explained in more detail in Chapter Two, essentially means cash flow) at 6% annually, and increases the dividend by 6% annually. Finally, let's assume that the shares will rise proportionally with increased FFO and dividend payments. Ten years later, the REIT will be paying $1.01 in dividends, and Beauregard's total investment will be worth $24,803 ($7,908 cumulative dividends received plus $16,895 in value of the shares at that time), less taxes on his dividends. This does compare rather well with the bond investment, doesn't it? (Even if we analyze these two types of investments taking into account the "time value of money," the conclusion is still the same). The following table breaks down the hypothetical REIT returns:

Year	Price	Dividends
1	$10.00	$0.60
2	$10.60	$0.64
3	$11.24	$0.67
4	$11.91	$0.71
5	$12.62	$0.76
6	$13.38	$0.80
7	$14.19	$0.85
8	$15.04	$0.90
9	$15.94	$0.96
10	$16.89	$1.01
		$7.91
X 1,000 shares	$16,894.79	$7,908.48
	Total Investment	$24,803.27

"Unfair," you say, "REITs *should* provide a higher total return because they are much riskier than bonds." Well, maybe and maybe not. It is true that, unlike bonds, they offer no specific maturity date and there is no certainty at what price they can be sold for in the future. But unlike bonds, if history is any guide, they will appreciate in value as their real estate assets rise in value (as Will Rogers once said, "buy land — they don't make it any more") and as they earn more income from their tenant leases over the years. Take a look at the following chart showing the FFO and stock price of United Dominion Realty, a long-established and very well-run apartment REIT, over the last 10 years. There doesn't seem to be a lot of risk here, other than the normal price fluctuations (which we experience with bonds also).

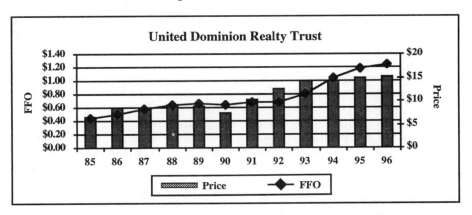

Further, investors get absolutely no inflation protection with bonds. When bonds pay their face amount at maturity some years down the road, only God knows what the purchasing power of a dollar will be at that time (and He doesn't write books or investment letters). In fact, the odds are stacked against the bond investor: If inflation rises, so generally will interest rates, which reduces the market value of the bond while it's being held (and which will result in an actual loss if the bond is sold prior to maturity). On the other hand, if inflation slows, resulting in lower interest rates, bonds are often called before their stated maturity, which deprives the investor of what, with hindsight, has been a very attractive yield and places upon him the burden of reinvestment while interest rates are low. So, for the bond investor, it can be a case of "heads the borrower wins, tails the bond investor loses." (U.S. Treasury bonds are generally not callable prior to maturity and entail no repayment risk; however, their yields are lower than those of corporate bonds and they, too, will fluctuate with interest rates.)

What about preferred stocks? Do they provide tougher competition against REITs? Unlike bonds, they do not represent the promise of the issuer to repay a specific amount at a specific date in the future, and in the legal pecking order their claims against the corporation are below those of every other creditor. Unless the terms of the preferred provide for the right of the holder to demand redemption, preferred shares enjoy the worst of all possible worlds: They have no fixed maturity date and they don't confer on their holders the status of creditors. They do, however, provide relatively high yields; in today's market, many preferred stocks yield 9-10%. But what you see is what you get: pure yield and very little else. While the high dividends are enticing, unlike REIT (and even utility) *common* stocks, preferred stocks (of the non-convertible variety) offer little in the way of price appreciation potential nor any hedge against rising inflation. Their prices are also, like bonds (and, to a lesser extent, REITs and utility stocks), very sensitive to rising and falling interest rates.

Finally, there are *convertible* bonds and preferreds to be considered. These investments do in fact provide competition for REITs. They offer pretty good yields (comparable to REITs), appreciation potential (if the common stock into which the convertible bonds or preferred may be converted rises substantially) and, with respect to convertible bonds, a fixed maturity date if the underlying common fails to appreciate in value. Convertibles can be relatively attractive investments; a principal drawback, however, is that not every company issues them — in fact, most do not. The yield-hungry investor just has to keep an eye out for these "hybrids" from time to time; if (and only if) the underlying common stock appears to be a good investment, then the convertible may also be a good investment.

REITs: The Best Real Estate Investment

There isn't an intelligent financial planner alive who doesn't recommend that individuals (and institutions, too, for that matter) own a well-diversified mix of investments. Obviously, this means real estate as well as common stocks of various types, bonds, money market funds, foreign stocks and perhaps even exotic investments such as art, precious metals or collectibles. And when they talk about "real estate," they don't just mean the family home. (While home ownership has been a great investment during many periods in the past, it's been a poor one in the 1990s, and no one can say whether it will, as an "investment," regain its former stature).

Is "real estate," as an asset class, a good investment? A well-situated investment property may grow in value over the years, if well-maintained and well-located, and rental rates charged to tenants who occupy it may grow apace. While buildings may depreciate over time (*e.g.*, a "Class A" building may become a "Class B" building), only a finite amount of land exists upon which an apartment, store or building can be built, and if we own such a facility in the right area, it can be, if not a gold mine, a cash machine whose value is likely to increase over the years. Particularly when inflation rates are high, new buildings will not be built unless rents are high enough to justify the development costs. These higher rental rates may establish a new prevailing level of market rents, which would enable the owners of older buildings to increase rents as well.

Yet inflationary trends don't necessarily mean that real estate, per se, will rise in value; one real estate observer[11] has concluded that, based upon a study of real estate performance data between 1978 and 1993, the net operating income of the properties studied did not even come close to keeping up with inflation. (See also Chapter Four regarding the extent to which real estate values are tied to inflation.) Nevertheless, well-maintained properties located in geographical areas that are economically healthy and have barriers to an influx of competing properties (perhaps due to the lack of available land, stringent zoning requirements or other reasons) are likely to rise in value over time.

It may well be the case that buying real estate at cheap prices is much more profitable to real estate investors than merely owning it for long time periods. If investors can buy properties at the "right time" from distressed sellers, they may earn much more on their invested capital than those who simply buy at fair prices and earn steady rental income. If this is true, buying REITs that are managed by wise and opportunistic real estate professionals who frequently find and take full advantage of buyers' markets will provide much greater returns to investors than merely owning real estate directly. The importance of a REIT's management will be discussed in Chapter Seven.

Assuming that investors are convinced of the wisdom of putting a portion of their assets in real estate (other than their home), the next issue is how best to own real estate. And here the answer is quite clear: REITs! There is no other form of real estate ownership that provides better all-around advantages than the REIT.

Let's first consider four typical ways in which real estate is owned: One, direct ownership by an individual; two, with others in private partnership form; three, as an owner of publicly traded limited partnership interests; and four, indirectly through the ownership of shares of a publicly traded real estate company such as a REIT.

Although direct investment can be very profitable, as the owner need not share his or her returns with anyone else, it is clearly the most risky. Most individuals simply do not have the financial resources to buy enough properties to obtain sufficient diversification, either by property type or by geography. The economic effects of real estate ownership are quite often determined by local conditions; at any given time, apartment buildings may be doing very well in Atlanta but very poorly in Los Angeles, or vice-versa. If an investor owns just one or two apartment buildings in one location, he or she may do very poorly indeed if economic growth migrates to a different region, if the neighborhood "goes downhill" or for a host of other reasons. Just as we want a diversified investment portfolio, our real estate portfolio should also be diversified, and we just can't get enough variety if our real estate is owned by just ourselves. Illiquidity is another major disadvantage of individual ownership; a single piece of real property may be very difficult, time-consuming and costly to sell, and selling or exchanging is the only way the investor can cash out of the investment. I won't even mention, except in passing, the inability or unwillingness of most individuals to undertake the very substantial efforts needed to manage a property well in order to obtain its highest economic benefits.

Option two, ownership through a private partnership with two, 10 or 20 partners really isn't much better. Here, the investor gets to delegate to others (either a general partner or an outside company) the tasks of property leasing and management, which is clearly an advantage. However, most private partnerships of this type own only one or very few properties, and they are rarely diversified as to property types; thus there is still inadequate diversification. The problem of illiquidity may not be quite so bad, depending upon how the partnership is drafted and the financial solvency of the investor's partners. As a result, it may be possible for an investor to sell a limited partnership interest to his or her partners without the underlying property being sold. Nevertheless, getting out of an investment owned in private partnership form is usually problematical. Conflicts of interest often abound in private partnerships, usually between the general partner and the limited partners, and often with regard to compensation or the desirability of selling or refinancing partnership property. Finally, individual partners can have some pretty serious personal liability if the partnership gets into financial trouble; this has happened often in recent years.

How about acquiring the advantages of some (albeit limited) diversification, tax benefits and liquidity by owning interests in publicly-traded limited partnerships, option three? This was the pitch of many limited partnership sponsors in the 1980s, as they plucked billions of dollars from investors seeking the benefits of real estate and liquidity. Most of the publicly traded limited partnerships that they passed off to unsuspecting investors did very poorly, and many such investors were lucky to recover 10 or 20 cents on the dollar. These investments failed for several reasons: For one, fees, in many cases, were so high that the ultimate owner (the investor) could not possibly make any money. Also, the partnerships often grossly overpaid for the properties they were buying, and the sponsors frequently hired mediocre managers to operate the properties, having failed to recognize that, particularly in the 1990s, real estate is a very management-intensive business. In addition, many of these limited partnerships had extensive conflicts of interest with the general partners—to the detriment of the investors. (The differences between real estate limited partnerships and REITs are discussed in more detail in Chapter Two).

Unlike the other forms of real estate ownership discussed above, option four, investing in publicly-traded companies such as REITs, offers diversification, liquidity, competent management (which normally owns a significant amount of the REIT's shares) and, in most cases, relatively few conflicts of interests between management and the investor. These companies are large enough so that each will normally own 20, 50 or hundreds of properties; by buying as few as six or eight REITs, we can get substantial diversification by property type and geographical area. Most REITs' shares trade on the New York Stock Exchange; while institutions have complained about the lack of market depth in REITs' shares, most individual investors can easily buy or sell meaningful positions very quickly.

Management, as will be shown later, is often a very key element in the success or failure of a real estate-owning company, and here is where REITs really shine. As in the overall stock market, there are some REITs with mediocre management; nevertheless, most of them are blessed with experienced and motivated real estate professionals who own a significant stake in the REIT, thus aligning their personal financial interests with those of the investor. (See Chapter Seven for a more detailed discussion of the ownership of a REIT's shares by management and other insiders.) Furthermore, a tremendous amount of United States commercial real estate is owned by amateur and part-time investors. Experienced REIT managements frequently compete against these investors for the purchase of real estate and to attract the highest quality tenants; the professional managers at many (if not most) REITs are usually able to compete very well against their amateur competitors. Finally, most REITs are organized with independent boards of directors and other structural safeguards designed to prevent conflicts of interest between management and the shareholders in the REIT. While it's important to be aware of conflicts that can arise (see Chapter Seven), a large number of REITs have pretty much designed conflicts out of the organization.

To summarize, all investors should own real estate along with their other investments and only REITs offer the complete package of advantages: diversification, liquidity, quality of management and the absence of conflicts of interest.

	Direct Ownership	Private Partnership	Limited Partnership	REITs
Profit Potential	High	Moderate	Moderate	Moderate
Risk	High	Moderate	Moderate	Low
Capital Needs	High	Moderate	Moderate	Low
Diversification	Low	Low	Moderate	High
Liquidity	Low	Moderate	Moderate	High
Effort	High	Moderate	Moderate	Low
Personal Liability	High	High	None	None
Conflicts of Interest	None	High	High	Low
Competent Management	?	?	Low/ Mod.	High

Tax Advantages: Return of Capital

There is yet another important advantage in owing REITs. Because of the effects of real estate depreciation upon a REIT's net income, very often a significant portion of the dividends received each year from a REIT are not fully taxable as ordinary dividends are. As will be explained later, REITs base their dividend payments on "funds from operations" (FFO), not net income; FFO, simply stated, is a REIT's net income but with real estate depreciation added back. As a result, many REITs pay dividends to their shareholders in excess of "net income" as defined in the Internal Revenue Code, and a significant part of such excess may be a "return of capital" to the shareholder and not taxable as an ordinary dividend. It has been estimated that the "return of capital" component of a REIT's dividend is typically 25-30%.[12] This non-taxable portion reduces the shareholder's cost basis in the shares, and defers the tax on this portion of the dividend until their ultimate sale (assuming the sale is made at a price exceeding the adjusted cost basis). However, if held for at least 12 months, the gain is taxed at long-term capital gain rates and the shareholder has, in effect, converted dividend income into a deferred capital gain. See Appendix A for further discussion and an example of how this works in practice.

If the shareholder is lucky enough to die while holding the shares (I've often been accused of having a weird sense of humor), the heirs get a "step-up in basis," and no tax is ever payable with respect to that portion of the dividends that was classified as a return of capital. Finally, if a REIT realizes long-term capital gain from a sale of some of its real estate, it may designate a portion of the dividend paid during the year of the sale as a "long-term capital gain distribution," upon which the shareholder will pay taxes, but at capital gain rates.

None of the foregoing tax advantages will induce a non-believer to run out and buy REITs. However, these tax considerations are often very valuable to REIT investors, and are thus additional reasons to own REIT stocks. For a further discussion of the taxation of REIT dividends, see Appendix A.

REITs' Batting Average

Considering all that's been said so far, several conclusions can be drawn about investing in good-quality REITs.

First, on a total return basis, REITs have performed on a level pretty much on a par with that of the broad stock market. As they must pay out most of their income in the form of dividends, they do not retain much capital and therefore will not normally expand their business as fast as many non-REIT companies. A large component of their total return to shareholders (approximately 50%) will be in the form of high dividend payments which, while (to a large extent) immediately taxable, nevertheless offer certain significant advantages (not the least of which is that the investor, and the investor alone, can decide to either spend the dividend portion of the total return or reinvest it in the same or any other company — or in Florida swampland, baseball cards, Elvis Presley shirts, whatever).

Second, because REITs own and manage (and sometimes develop) properties, the risk profile of their business is significantly lower than that of most businesses. Competition is limited to neighboring properties (and nearby vacant land), government regulation is not much of a problem and well-located and well-managed properties (whether apartments, retail stores, office buildings or other property types) are not normally subject to rapid obsolescence or to major changes in technology.

Third, good-quality REITs are well-run by professionals who have had years of experience in both the acquisition and management of real estate and who generally own a significant stock interest in the REIT. They are highly motivated to make the REIT a success for themselves and their shareholders.

Fourth, REITs own many different properties — up to several hundred for the largest of them, and this diversification produces less risk. No single problem property can have an overwhelming effect upon the entire portfolio. Many REITs are also diversified geographically by owning properties in several different regions of the U.S.

Adding it all up, shrewd investors should come to one conclusion (which matches my own personal REIT investing experience over the last 20-plus years): We never hit home runs with REIT investments, but we get lots and lots of singles; our batting average is very high, we rarely strike out and we score lots of runs. Accordingly, those investors (speculators?) who like to swing for the fences shouldn't own REITs, nor should savers who insist on absolute safety. But for the rest of us, who either want to

23

get rich continuously or to build up a retirement fund for our later years, REITs are a great place to put a significant portion of our investment dollars.

---

[1] Because of the more stable price performance, larger market caps and lower risk level of Equity REITs, I have focused on them rather than "Mortgage" or "Hybrid" REITs.

[2] NAREIT defines its Equity REIT Index as "an index comprised of the common stocks of all publicly-traded REITs which have 75% or more of their gross assets (at book) invested in the equity ownership of real estate." The Index is market weighted. For more on this (and other) REIT and real estate indices, see Appendix E.

[3] "The Reit Stuff," by Pablo Galarza, Financial World, dated January 2, 1996.

[4] Some observers of the REIT investment scene do not believe that statistics relating to REITs' total returns prior to 1992 are very meaningful, given the relatively small number of REITs in existence prior to such year. It's my belief, however, that these statistics are highly relevant, as they generally reflect the returns which were available to most REIT investors who bought shares in such widely-available REITs as Federal Realty, New Plan Realty, United Dominion, Washington REIT and Weingarten Realty, all of which have been public companies for many years. Further, there is no reason to think that REITs' total returns will be lower after 1992; indeed, due to the quality of many of the newer REITs, one could make the argument that pre-1992 statistics understate the kinds of total returns that REIT investors might reasonably expect throughout the rest of the decade and into the next century.

[5] Ibbotson Associates, "Stocks, Bonds and Inflation: 1995 Yearbook".

[6] Lehman Brothers, "1996 - Annual Review and Outlook for REITs," dated January 1996.

[7] However, as institutional investors become more active in REIT investing and the volume of trading increases, we could see more volatility in REIT stocks; indeed, towards the end of 1996, this was already starting to happen. Such increased volatility, however, is not a foregone conclusion. Michael Giliberto, who has done significant research on REITs for JP Morgan Investment Management, believes, based upon his findings, that "there is no systematic relationship between institutional ownership and REIT share price volatility." See The Journal of Real Estate Investment Trusts, November 1996, p. 43-45.

[8] According to a December 17, 1996 article in the Wall Street Journal (p. A24), in July 1996, Rep. Dan Schaefer (R. Colo.), Chairman of a House Commerce subcommittee, "introduced legislation that would give all consumers the ability to choose their own electricity service by December 15, 2000."

[9] Los Angeles Times, April 7, 1996, Section D, p. 1.

[10] Data provided by AMG as set forth in PaineWebber's "Real Estate Research" for the week ending November 29, 1996, p. 3.

[11] "The Handbook of Real Estate Portfolio Management," by Joseph L. Pagliari, Jr. (Irwin, 1995).

[12] Robert A. Frank, interviewed by Barron's for the issue of December 18, 1995, stated that the figure was close to 30%. David Kostin, at Goldman Sachs, calculated the figure for his group of REITs at between 23-28% between 1993 and 1995.

Chapter Two

What Are These Creatures Called "REITs"?

"Our clients are not so much __risk__-averse as they are __loss__-averse."
— Gary Pollock

The above quotation pretty well summarizes the investment manager's lament: Investors don't seem to mind investing in a risky stock until it goes down in price and depletes their capital — then they become irate! As a result, it's essential to most investors' peace of mind that they invest a significant portion of their assets in such a way that significant losses will be avoided. Most REITs are very conservative investments and therefore belong in the portfolios of long-term investors. In the first part of this chapter, we'll review just what a "REIT" is; we'll learn that it's merely a legal structure having certain tax and operating privileges and restrictions under which various types of real estate-related companies do business.

In the second part of the chapter, we'll review some of the investment characteristics that separate REITs from other common stocks and even limited partnerships. Despite their peculiarities, it's important to keep in mind that, in many respects, investing in a REIT is just like investing in, say, IBM or Johnson & Johnson. Investors have certain expectations when they invest in a company, and most of them come down to one simple thing: When I sell the stock, am I ahead and by how much? We shouldn't be distracted by the fact that a company happens to be structured as a "REIT"; when we invest in a REIT, we expect our investment to grow, just as we would for any other stock. True, certain investment characteristics are different with REITs (the high yield, for example), but by and large REITs today primarily are operating companies with active managements, whose main business is real estate rather than computers, cars or any of the myriad of products available in our society. From the investors' perspective, we want to see the company's profits grow from year to year, which provides the fuel for dividend increases and price appreciation, just the same as we would for *any* of our stock investments.

The Book on REITs

Just as corporations are "creatures of the state," real estate investment trusts are creatures of the U.S. Congress. They were authorized by the Real Estate Investment Trust Act of 1960 (the first REIT was formed in 1963). The purpose of the legislation was to provide investors with the opportunity to participate in the benefits of owning significant commercial real estate and to engage in mortgage lending, all on a tax-advantaged basis.

One of REITs' essential characteristics is that they are not subject to corporate tax; however, as we will see, they must pay out most of their net income to their shareholders, and such shareholders must pay income taxes on all or most of their dividend income, unless of course the REIT shares are held in an IRA or pension plan. This avoidance of "double taxation" is one of the key advantages to the REIT structure.

To Be a REIT

To become a REIT, a corporation (or business trust) must meet several statutory requirements, the most important of which are:

- The REIT must distribute to its shareholders, through dividends, at least 95% of its taxable income (excluding capital gains) each year

- At least 75% of the REIT's assets must be invested in real estate, mortgage loans, shares in other REITs, cash or government securities

- At least 75% of the REIT's gross income must come from rents, mortgage interest or gains from the sale of real property, and at least 95% must come from these sources, together with dividends, interest and gains from securities sales

- The REIT must have at least 100 shareholders, and more than 50% of the outstanding shares may not be concentrated in the hands of five or fewer shareholders

- No more than 30% of gross income may come from the sale of real estate held for less than four years (except for foreclosed properties) or from the sale of securities held for less than six months

In 1986, the Tax Reform Act relaxed certain prior restrictions on REITs by allowing them to render normal and customary maintenance and other services for real estate tenants, which eliminated the need for REITs to hire and retain outside agents to perform property-related services such as property management. The significance of this cannot be overstated, as one of the key attributes of the best REITs today is that they are fully integrated operating companies that can handle *internally* all aspects of real estate operations, including acquiring properties, managing them on-site, finding and replacing tenants, completing tenant improvements and, where appropriate, developing new properties and selling existing properties.

What's an "UPREIT"?

We will sometimes hear or see the term "UPREIT" used by REIT investors and analysts. The UPREIT, an acronym for "Umbrella Partnership REIT," was created by imaginative investment bankers in 1992 as a way for long-established real estate operating companies to take advantage of the REIT structure while avoiding the payment of significant capital gain taxes on their low-basis investments (which could be incurred if such companies' properties were *sold* to the new REIT entity). An UPREIT is merely a REIT that is structured in a more complicated form than the normal REIT. In the typical UPREIT, the REIT itself doesn't own any properties but owns a controlling interest in a limited partnership which, in turn, owns the real estate. Other limited partners in the real estate-owning limited partnership normally include management and private investors who indirectly owned the organization's properties prior to its becoming a REIT. The "units" in the limited partnership are convertible into shares of the REIT, give their holders the right to vote as if they were shareholders, are entitled to the same dividends as the publicly traded shares, and generally enjoy the same attributes of ownership as the REIT's outstanding shares.

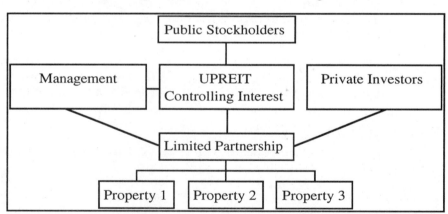

Although the UPREIT concept was devised as a tax deferral device, the UPREIT format is well suited to making acquisitions. Through the issuance of "operating partnership" units in the UPREIT to the holders of the property being acquired, such persons can defer the payment of taxes while at the same time obtain a more diversified form of investment. This could give the UPREIT an advantage over its vanilla-variety REIT brethren in making attractive acquisition deals with sellers who would like to defer the payment of taxes.[1]

It should be noted, however, that the UPREIT format often creates conflicts of interest. Management normally owns units in the UPREIT's partnership rather than (or in addition to) shares in the REIT. Such management usually will have a low-cost basis in such units, and the sale of a property could trigger taxable income to the holders of the units (but not to the shareholders of the REIT). Accordingly, management may be reluctant to sell a property despite its lack of future growth potential, or may ignore a very generous offer made for the property (or, indeed, the REIT itself) by a third party. We'll discuss these conflicts in a later chapter. It's too soon to tell whether being an UPREIT is a plus or a minus for investors; much may depend upon how management handles the conflicts issue and the extent to which operating partnership units are used to finance attractive property acquisitions.

More recently, some REITs have been organizing "DownREITs," which is a variation of the UPREIT structure. In a DownREIT, a new operating partnership is formed, having the existing REIT as its general partner. Real estate assets that would otherwise be acquired by the REIT are, instead, acquired by the new operating partnership in exchange for limited partnership interests which are normally convertible into shares of the REIT. This type of structure, being formed subsequent to the REIT's organization, does not normally result in the issuance of limited partnership interests to the existing REIT management and thus is less susceptible to conflicts of interest problems.[2]

What Makes REITs One-of-a-Kind

As we'll see in Chapter Four, REITs have not been given the recognition and respect in the investment world that they deserve. One of the reasons for this, which will be addressed in *this* chapter, is that REITs are in some respects different from other common stocks, just as they are different from limited partnerships and other forms of direct property investment. REITs blend property acquisition and management skills with real estate ownership in a manner which makes them truly unique investments.

What REITs are Not: The Infamous Limited Partnerships of Yesteryear

Today's REITs are *not even remotely* like the notorious real estate limited partnerships of the late 1980s. Comparing the two is like comparing a fine filet mignon with a fast-food burger: They're sliced from the same source, but one's a prime cut and the other's griddle gristle.

Objectives. The differences in these two types of investments stem from the very purpose for which they were created. The real estate limited partnerships of the '80s were designed by syndicators and brokerage firms in response to the investing public's desire to own real estate assets whose values were "sure" to appreciate and, at the same time, to provide a tax shelter to the investors. In many cases, the tax savings were designed to be so large that it didn't matter if the economics worked — a sure prescription for disaster, or at least an I.R.S. audit. And when the tax laws were changed in 1986 to, among other things, reduce the amount of depreciation that could be taken on a property, most of these older partnerships were in hot water.

There is nothing inherently evil about the limited partnership structure, nor in syndicators and brokerage firms making money by fulfilling the desires of the public investor. However, these limited partnerships were frequently laden with excessive fees and massive conflicts of interest. Even more important, they typically owned just one or a handful of properties that were bought or brokered by the sponsor and bundled together for sale to the small investor. On the other hand, most of today's REITs are dynamic and growing real estate organizations managed by experienced, motivated real estate professionals whose inventory or "stock in trade" is real estate. For REITs, neither the appreciation potential of the real estate nor tax savings are emphasized; rather, the REIT's success is measured by its ability to grow its funds from operations and dividend payments to its shareholders, all of which will increase the value of the REIT's shares.

Management. The limited partnership, whose mission was simply to own a portfolio of properties, was often burdened with mediocre management. Most properties were managed by an outside advisor who hired caretakers to run the properties. The advisor was often paid a fee based upon the dollar amount of the assets under management, so there was a strong incentive to add properties for the sake of the fees generated rather than for their potential to attract quality tenants and increase rents. Today's well-regarded REITs employ their own experienced executives who generally have a significant stake in the company. Such persons tend to have long-term track records of successful real estate management and development before forming their REITs (Kimco Realty and Post Properties are two good examples).

Growth Prospects. The difference in management quality leads to another important difference: growth dynamics. Limited partnerships, burdened by mediocre management, high fees and limited fund-raising abilities, have not had many avenues for growth. They could add properties if new capital could be found, but the format and illiquid nature of the limited partnership vehicle made this option problematical. Growth was often limited to rental

29

increases and appreciation of the properties owned. Conversely, the quality and track record of a well-run REIT's management allow it to raise capital by selling new shares or debt securities in order to purchase additional properties at cheap prices from "motivated" sellers. Further, capable management will look to refurbish and upgrade newly acquired properties and find quality growth-oriented tenants, and can develop new properties or expand a property where the economics justify additional tenants.

Liquidity. Most of the limited partnerships were creatures of brokerage firms or other syndicators. And, as disappointed investors learned, there were no public markets in which units in these limited partnerships could be traded; thus there was no way to get rid of them. For many years owning a limited partnership interest was worse than a bad marriage — you could never get rid of it and its trailing stream of "K-1s." A few years ago, narrow trading markets for limited partnerships were created, but the "bid-ask" spreads have been large enough to make a pawnbroker blush. REITs, on the other hand, are very actively traded, usually on the New York Stock Exchange. The investor can generally buy or sell several thousand shares quickly.

Yield vs. Growth. Brokers promoting limited partnerships often touted high-dividend yields. After all, a 9-10% payout with appreciation "potential" is nearly irresistible. In reality, the limited partnership units offered little or no appreciation potential unless real estate inflation continued spiraling upward (it didn't), and they rarely produced the hyped income. This illustrates another distinguishing factor between the two investments. REITs offer lower dividend yields, but these dividends are more reliable and total returns are higher. The savvy investor prefers 6% in dividends and another 7% in growth, with excellent management behind the investment, rather than a promised 9-10% yield with minimal growth prospects and lots of risk. (A high-quality REIT retains part of its funds from operations for growth opportunities rather than paying it all out in dividends, as we'll discuss in Chapter Seven).

When you get down to it, the only significant similarity REITs share with limited partnerships is that they both invest in real estate. And yet, that factor alone has been influential enough to make investors once burned by limited partnerships unjustifiably wary of REITs. This "guilt by association," however, is wholly unmerited, and shrewd investors will realize that there are many more differences than similarities between the two types of investments. The bottom-line difference is that REITs have succeeded in a domain where limited partnerships have failed.

Lending REITs vs. Ownership REITs

Nothing in the legislation authorizing the REIT requires it to *own* real properties. It is sufficient if the REIT merely lends funds on the strength of the collateral value of real estate by originating, acquiring and holding real estate mortgage loans. These could be in the form of mortgage loans secured by residential or business properties, health-care facilities, or other properties. ("Hybrid" REITs own properties and also make loans secured by real estate. They were popular many years ago but, except to the extent that certain health-care REITs may be regarded as hybrids, they have long since faded into obscurity.)

In the late '60s and early '70s, lending REITs were the most popular type of REIT, as many large regional and "money-center" banks and mortgage brokers formed their own REITs. Almost 60 new REITs were formed back then, all lending funds to property developers at high interest rates. In 1973, interest rates rose substantially, new developments couldn't be sold or leased, non-performing loans spiraled way out of control, and most of these REITs crashed and burned, leaving investors holding the bag. A decade later, a number of REITs sprang up to invest in collateralized mortgage obligations and they didn't fare much better. Today, while many lending REITs have been successful, they generally occupy specialized niches of the REIT world.[3]

The vast majority of REITs now own real property rather than make real estate loans. The real money in real estate comes from owning and efficiently managing it, together with buying good properties at cheap prices. With the possible exception of small segments of the health-care REITs' portfolios that are represented by mortgage loans to health-care providers, the REITs that most investors want to own invest in real estate and do not make real estate loans. Throughout the rest of this book, then, "REIT" will generally refer to REITs that *own* real estate of one type or another.

The Reach of REITs

So, we now know what a "REIT" is. It's authorized by Congress, pays no corporate income taxes if certain requirements are met, and in most cases owns real estate. But what kind of real estate? Not that many years ago, until the REIT initial public offering (IPO) boom of 1993-1994, REITs owned a very limited number of property types. These included neighborhood shopping centers, apartments, health-care facilities (including hospitals and nursing homes) and, to a very limited extent, office buildings. If you wanted to invest in another sector, such as shopping malls, you were out of luck.

However, by the end of 1994, the REIT industry had mushroomed in size as a result of a huge increase in the dollar amount of new IPOs and secondary offerings in 1993 and 1994. According to NAREIT statistics, the total dollar amount of such offerings in those years was $18.3 billion and $14.7 billion, respectively, constituting approximately 117% and 46% of the total

31

REIT market capitalization at the time. By the end of 1995, REITs' total book assets had grown to more than $88 billion, held by approximately 220 publicly traded companies, including Equity REITs and Mortgage REITs.[4] Looking back, the 1993-1994 REIT IPO boom revolutionized the REIT industry, and there are now a great many well-managed and highly regarded REITs owning properties of numerous types from which the investor may choose.

Today, in addition to the types of REITs mentioned above, we can invest in mall REITs, factory outlet center REITs, manufactured home community REITs, industrial property REITs, self-storage REITs, hotel REITs and even a golf course REIT. Each of these property types, which we'll discuss in Chapter Three, has its own set of investment characteristics, including its own economic cycle, risk factors, competitive threats, growth rate and other considerations affecting one's investment. As we'll consider in Chapter Nine, the wise REIT investor will be fairly well-diversified among the different property types, perhaps skipping only those where the economic cycle creates a very unfavorable risk/reward ratio (assuming such can be determined ahead of time). As always, the quality of management is a key consideration in REIT investing; it is therefore fortunate that virtually all property types are represented by one or more REITs that can boast of a strong management team with an established track record of successful real estate ownership and management.

What's the Scoop on FFO (and Why Should We Care)?

Rising earnings are to a stock what an all-star quarterback is to a football team. It's possible, but unlikely, for either to do well without their driving force. The same principle holds true in the REIT world; nicely rising earnings normally indicate that the REIT is increasing rents faster than its expenses and making favorable acquisitions or completing profitable developments. Furthermore, higher income each year is a precursor to dividend growth and, on a longer-term basis, generally propels the stock price upwards. However, instead of the "net income" used by common stock investors, REIT investors use "funds from operations," or "FFO," as a measure of a REIT's operating success.

"Net income" has a clearly defined meaning under GAAP (generally accepted accounting principles), and audited financial statements filed with the Securities and Exchange Commission by all publicly traded companies (including REITs) must comply with all its technical requirements. The problem is that "net income" under GAAP is not very meaningful as a measure of a REIT's operating success because real estate "depreciation" is always treated as an accounting expense, but most well-designed, well-maintained and well-located properties have generally retained their value over the years and many have *appreciated,* perhaps due to rising land values, property upgrades and increasing construction costs to build new competing properties. Accordingly, REITs' reported *net income* includes large expenses for "depreciation" that, in most cases, distort the picture of how the REIT has fared operationally. The higher the depreciation expense (as when additional properties have been recently constructed or acquired), the more distorted the picture becomes.

For example, when Weeks Corp. reported its results of operations for its second quarter of 1996, we saw in the newspaper that net income per share was flat, at $.28 vs. $.28 for the comparable quarter in 1995. However, Weeks' FFO didn't appear in the newspaper, as REITs cannot "report" FFO — that is not a term accepted by GAAP. When, however, we reviewed Weeks' press release for the second quarter, we learned that Weeks' FFO per share actually *increased* by 13% over the comparable quarter in 1995. Thus, what we might have thought was a mediocre quarter turned out to be an outstanding one, as Weeks had bought and developed a large number of properties between the two quarterly reporting periods, and depreciation expense significantly held down the reported earnings per share.

Thus the concept of FFO was created to enable both REITs and their investors to correct the depreciation distortion by looking at net income *before* the deduction of the depreciation expense (or, which amounts to the same thing, adding back depreciation expense to net income). Other adjustments are usually made as well, such as subtracting from net income any "income" recorded from the sale of properties. (The REIT can't have it both ways — it can't ignore depreciation, which reduces the cost at which a property is carried on the balance sheet, and then include in FFO the capital gain which results from selling such property in excess of its carrying value). Some REITs have included in funds from operations an add-back of amortization charges of items such as organization or IPO expenses, costs to "buy-down" or cap the interest rates on existing or new debt or goodwill incurred in certain acquisitions. Furthermore, GAAP net income is normally determined after "straight-lining" rental income (smoothing out rental income over the term of the lease); in the real world, rents are frequently not received in this manner, so some REITs, when determining FFO, adjust "rent" to reflect the rental revenues actually received.

FFO has, over the years, been defined in different ways by different REITs at different times, which has added confusion to an already confusing subject. To address this problem, NAREIT has attempted to standardize the definition of FFO so as to level the REIT playing field. Commencing in 1996, NAREIT has stated that the term "funds from operations," when used by REITs, should mean "net income (computed in accordance with GAAP), excluding gains (or losses) from debt restructuring and sales of property, plus depreciation of real property, and after adjustments for unconsolidated entities in which the REIT holds an interest." That definition may sound like a lot of legal mumbo-jumbo, but it is a significant step forward, and enables investors to more easily compare the FFO of one REIT with that of another.

Before we leave the concept of FFO, a caveat is in order. Not all property retains its value year after year, as some properties actually do depreciate (even when the underlying land is considered). One might say, therefore, that adding back depreciation to net income to determine FFO provides a distorted (and overly aggressive) picture of operating results. There is probably some truth in this observation, but FFO is nevertheless a much more realistic picture of a REIT's operating performance than is net income under GAAP

Unfortunately, another murky but important area still remains. What happens, for example, when a REIT installs in its apartment buildings new carpeting that is expected to have a life of five years? The cost of such carpeting is often not expensed for accounting purposes; instead, it is capitalized and depreciated over the carpeting's useful life. However, including such "real property" depreciation in funds from operations can give a misleading picture and artificially inflate FFO: Carpeting, in fact, really *does* depreciate over time and does not significantly increase the value of the real estate to which it becomes attached. The most complete and accurate picture of FFO should take into account investments of a "capital" nature, such as carpeting and similar furnishings, that are not immediately expensed but that do not improve or prolong the life of the real property that "houses" it. Similarly, leasing commissions paid for the rental of offices are usually capitalized and then amortized over the term of the lease. These commission amortizations, when added to net income to derive FFO, can similarly inflate FFO artificially. The same can be said about tenant improvement allowances such as those provided to office and mall tenants, many (or even most) of which do not increase the long-term value of a property. Thus, costs incurred merely to maintain the value of a property or its tenant base should be subtracted from FFO to give the most accurate picture of a REIT's operating performance. Finally, many REITs, when determining FFO, do not adjust for the "straight-lining" of rents. GAAP accounting requires companies to "straight-line," or smooth out, the expected lease payments over the life of the lease; smaller amounts are usually received in the early years and greater amounts are received in the later years. Most REIT analysts believe that this "smoothing" should be eliminated when determining a REIT's operating results and thus adjust for such straight-lining when determining AFFO.

Unfortunately, although most REITs provide information in this area, there is no uniform policy for reporting an "adjusted" FFO to take these types of expenditures and adjustments into account. Most investors and analysts, however, do adjust FFO to take into account capitalized expenditures which do not enhance the value of a property and to adjust for rent straight-lining (FFO, as adjusted in this manner, will sometimes be referred to in this book as "AFFO," meaning "adjusted funds from operations"). Thus, while FFO is clearly more useful to REIT investors than net income under GAAP, AFFO is truly the most accurate measure of a REIT's operating performance. The best explanation I've seen regarding the difference between FFO and AFFO (and how AFFO should be calculated) is contained in an article written by Mike Kirby, principal and co-founder of Green Street Advisors which appeared in The Journal of Real Estate Investment Trusts.[5] Such article should be required reading for all serious REIT investors.

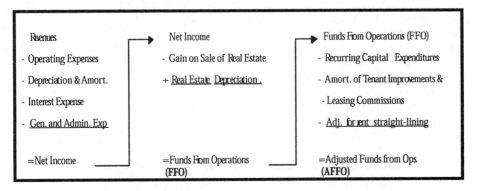

To summarize this rather complex but important concept, when we discuss a REIT's earnings, we will use the term "funds from operations" or "FFO," or "adjusted funds from operations" or "AFFO." Similarly, when we discuss the price/earnings ratio of a REIT's common stock, we will use either the price/FFO ratio or the price/AFFO ratio. We must, however, be aware of how these substitutes for net income are calculated by or for each REIT in order to be as consistent as possible.[7] Appendix B contains an example of how AFFO (as well as other cash flow measurements which are occasionally used, such as Cash Available for Distribution (CAD) or Funds Available for Distribution (FAD)) can be determined for a particular REIT.

Dividend Pay-outs

A final notable peculiarity of REITs (as opposed to garden-variety common stocks) stems from their requirement to pay to their shareholders at least 95% of their net income each year. As we've seen, FFO, which is invariably higher than net income, is a more

35

realistic measure of a REIT's earning power. Therefore, most REITs pay dividends that substantially exceed "net income" and usually range from 80% to 90% of FFO.

Thus, the *good* news is that REITs pay very high dividends, which generally produce yields of between 5% and 9% on their stock prices (some yield even more, but in such instances there is often some doubt as to the REIT's ability to continue paying the current dividend). These high current yields mean, as a practical matter, that fairly low rates of growth in FFO can produce excellent total returns (dividend yield plus capital appreciation). For example, if we own a REIT that yields 7% and if it can increase its FFO at a rate of 6% per year, the 12-month total return from such an investment will amount to 13% (assuming that the stock price 12 months later is selling at the same price/FFO ratio as it sold at initially). See the example in the accompanying chart. As we have seen earlier (Chapter One), total returns of this size have enabled REITs' long-term performance to be very competitive with that of the stocks comprising the S&P 500 Index.

Evergreen REIT	Beginning	End	Return
FFO	1.00	1.06	
P/FFO Multiple	10.0	10.0	
Price	$10.00	$10.60	6.0%
Dividends		$0.70	7.0%
Total Return			13.0%

There is, however, a *bad* news downside to generous pay-out rates. All companies need capital in order to expand; REITs are no different. Because REITs pay out most of their earnings (or, more accurately, their FFOs) to their shareholders, growth-oriented REITs must continually raise additional capital in order to expand their businesses. Such capital will be necessary if the REIT intends to build or acquire additional real estate and must be obtained through additional stock or bond offerings, or through private equity placements or bank or insurance company borrowings. Such dependence upon the capital markets exposes REITs to the possibility that, in certain periods, such capital may not be available or, if available, can be obtained only by paying high interest rates or issuing additional equity at prices that are dilutive to existing shareholders. It is for this reason that, when selecting REITs for investment, we should emphasize those with excellent reputations in the investment community, as such REITs should normally be able to attract additional capital and are likely to do so on terms favorable to the existing shareholders. In Chapter Seven we'll discuss the importance of keeping dividend pay-out ratios low in relation to a REIT's FFO or AFFO.

Summary

Investors often make more of the peculiarities of REITs than is merited by the facts; whether this is due to laziness or fear of the unknown is a question for a psychologist. When we sum it all up, most of the meaningful differences between REITs and other common stocks are straightforward and easy to understand: Most REITs are operating companies which own and manage real estate rather than other types of businesses, and they must pay to their shareholders most of their net income — which keeps their dividends high but requires them to raise capital more frequently than most other companies. Yes, REITs must comply with several unique technical rules but, as they don't ordinarily affect our REIT investments, investors need not worry about them. Finally, operating success is measured by FFO or AFFO, rather than net income; beyond the brief discussion here, this concept can be mastered with an informative Annual Report to Shareholders and an hour or two of concentration.

Although REIT stocks can perform poorly during the occasional bear market (*i.e.*, 1990), there just aren't many bad things that will happen to a well-run REIT. Those investors who are willing to take the time to understand REITs will find them to be conservative investments which pay high current returns, offer significant capital appreciation and entail very limited risk — these are stable investments which will truly appeal to the loss-averse.

---

[1] However, some REITs are now forming "DownREITs" for a similar purpose; see the discussion of DownREITs later in the chapter.

[2] For more information on DownREITs, see "DownREITs Now Everyone Can Do Tax-Free Exchanges" by Glenn L. Carpenter and Gary B. Sabin in "The REIT Report", Spring 1996, p. 9, and "The DownREIT as a Substitute for Cash" by John H. Kuhl and Samuel Gruenbaum, in "The REIT Report," August 1996, p. 32.

[3] By the end of 1995, Mortgage REITs and Hybrid REITs comprised only 5.9% and 7.3%, respectively, of the REIT industry. See NAREIT's "The REIT Industry Summary," dated January 1996.

[4] NAREIT, "The REIT Industry Summary," dated January 1996.

[5] "Capital Expenditure Requirements: The REIT Sector's 'Crazy Aunt in the Basement' ," The Journal of Real Estate Investment Trusts, November 1996, p. 8.

[6] REIT investors may ultimately have to discard the FFO and AFFO concepts altogether. NAREIT is exploring the possibility of causing a change to be made in the definition of depreciation as it relates to income-producing real estate. Should such changes occur, a redefined net income under GAAP would replace FFO and AFFO. However, any real progress on this front is likely to be years away.

Chapter Three

What Types of Properties Do We Want to Own?

"A rose is a rose is a rose."
— **Gertrude Stein**

If Ms. Stein is correct — that a rose is simply a rose — is it also true that real estate is just real estate, and that we can think about various types of real estate in pretty much the same way? Commercial real estate does have many characteristics in common; it's value and profitability depends, to a large extent, on its location, and its being well-maintained and stocked with reliable tenants, together with various "macro" forces such as the strength of the local, regional, national and even world economies, prevailing interest rates and the level of inflation.

Yet there are many ways in which property types differ. The owner of a large, amenity-laden apartment complex, for example, has far different financial concerns than does the owner of a neighborhood shopping center, or, for that matter, a downtown office building. And those are just three of the more common property types. With today's REITs we can pick and choose among the types of real estate (and real estate businesses) we want to invest in. If you like, you can invest your money in nearly any real estate imaginable. How about self-storage facilities? Hospitals? Maybe golf courses? Would you believe, prisons? Well, that REIT isn't available yet, but it's been considered. The accompanying chart, based upon data compiled by NAREIT, provides a glimpse of the diversity within the world of REITs.

The point is, the options are as vast as the differences that distinguish various property types and businesses. It's necessary for investors to understand the importance of these differences — the particular "investment characteristics" that set property types apart — before selecting a particular REIT. While REIT investors need not be experts on apartments, malls, or any other specific type of property, some familiarity with the short- and long-term economics and characteristics of each type is very helpful.

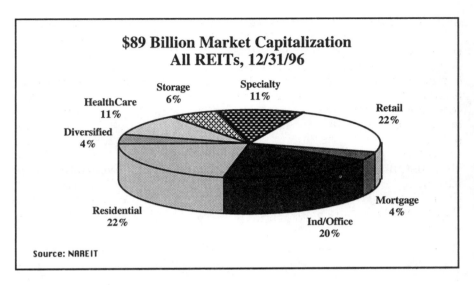

**$89 Billion Market Capitalization
All REITs, 12/31/96**

HealthCare 11%
Storage 6%
Specialty 11%
Diversified 4%
Retail 22%
Residential 22%
Ind/Office 20%
Mortgage 4%

Source: NAREIT

Ups and Downs

Before we begin our journey into REITs' various property types, we should step back a bit and take a look at the cyclical nature of real estate investment. Real estate does tend to go through cycles, and at times these can be rather violent. As REIT investors, we may decide to buy and hold our REITs even as their properties move through their inevitable down cycles; nevertheless, we should at least be aware of them, as they can dramatically affect the ability of a REIT to grow earnings from its existing properties. Furthermore, more aggressive investors may want to plan their REIT investments in accordance with the cycles' patterns.

At the bottom or "depression" phase of a cycle, real estate prices are, understandably, depressed, rental rates are soft, vacancies are high and many properties (perhaps financed with excessive debt) are in foreclosure or are being repossessed by lenders for resale at bargain prices. There is virtually no new construction, as properties change hands at prices well below replacement cost.

Eventually, tenants are found for some of the vacant space, and demand starts to catch up with the previous over-supply. Rents stabilize and slowly start to increase as occupancy rates rise. At this point, the number of property bargains begins to dwindle and prices stabilize; there is still little or no new building during this "recovery" phase.

After a while, most vacant space has been absorbed, allowing property owners to boost rents rapidly. High occupancy and rental rates produce excellent returns for landlords, and property prices rise apace. Rents and profitability are high enough to justify new construction, and developers flex their muscles. Investors (and even lenders) feel that they must join the party and provide all the

40

necessary financing. During this "development" or "boom" phase, we hear lots of reasons why "this time it's different," and why this property sector is "no longer cyclical."

After the boom has rumbled for a bit, an overbuilt condition occurs, perhaps exacerbated by overly aggressive estimates of demand for space or by weakening demand caused by an economic recession. The newly built properties need tenants, and their owners reduce rents in order to fill the buildings. Competing property owners either suffer occupancy loss or cut their own rents to retain tenants. Property buyers shy away under these circumstances, and real estate prices decline. Eventually, this "declining" phase may turn into a depression phase, depending upon the severity of the overbuilding or the economic recession. Now we've gone full circle, only to start a new cycle after the current phase has exhausted itself.

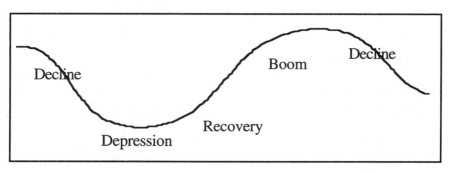

Why do these cycles occur? Commercial real estate is tied closely to the national economy, as well as the economies in the specific area where the property is located, and the relative strength or weakness of these economies will affect the profits available to the owner of the real estate. When business is booming and job growth is expanding rapidly in Atlanta, for example, industrial properties and apartments located there will tend to enjoy boom-like conditions; rents, profits and property prices will rise, and new properties will be built, thus pushing up and prolonging that phase of the cycle.

If the influence of national, regional and local economies were the only determinant, real estate cycles would probably be rather mild; however, this is not always the case. Property cycles are often more pronounced, with depression-like conditions eventually evolving, over several years, into manias. The primary cause for this is simply, in the words of John Maynard Keynes, man's "animal spirits." Today we might just call it old-fashioned greed.

We see this occur from time to time in the stock market: During bull market conditions, investors often throw caution to the wind while forgetting how quickly that wind can shift. New York

City's shoeshine boys and taxi drivers hand out stock tips during these periods, and cocktail party chatter and Internet discussion groups are replete with details of the latest killing on Wall Street. The same phenomenon occurs in real estate, except that it's not limited to investors. Developers, syndicators, venture funds and even lenders want a piece of the action when real estate prices, rents and operating income rise rapidly, and the debt leverage traditionally available on real estate investments exacerbates the situation.

This scenario was played out in the apartment market as well as other sectors in the mid-'80s; investors bought up apartments at furious rates, individually and through syndications and limited partnerships, developers built them everywhere, and the banks and savings and loans provided all the necessary liquidity to drive the boom ever higher. Even Congress got into the act, passing legislation that provided major tax breaks for owners of real estate in the form of rapid write-offs.

These types of excesses usually sow the seeds of their own destruction, which is what occurred in the late '80s and early '90s. Most of the nation rapidly became overbuilt in apartments, as well as office buildings, shopping centers, offices and other property types, and property owners had to contend with depression-like conditions for the next several years.

The bottom line is: Real estate cycles will always be with us, at least until we are able to quell human emotions such as greed and fear. While we can hope that greater discipline and better access to information may help to moderate these cycles (see Chapter Ten), investors must be mindful that every boom has its peak and every bust has its valley, and in the case of each extreme, "this, too, shall pass."

A Smorgasbord of Property Types

So you've got a fistful of dollars, and you're ready to invest. Now you're just wondering, where? As mentioned above, the opportunities are numerous. Apartments... Shopping centers... Industrial parks... Factory outlet centers... Health-care facilities... to name just a few. All are real estate and all have specific features, quirks, idiosyncrasies — cycles included — that set them apart from the others. The difficulty for the investor is deciding which to emphasize. The pie chart at the beginning of this chapter shows the percentages of the REITs' aggregate market value represented by the types of properties held by REITs as of December, 1996. Welcome to the banquet. Let's dig in.

Apartments

Recent history has been witness to a virtual explosion in the number of publicly traded apartment REITs. Before the 1993-1994 binge of new REITs going public, there were four major apartment

REITs (United Dominion, Merry Land, Property Trust of America and South West Property Trust). By October 1996, that number had swollen to at least 30 major Equity REITs, each with market caps of in excess of $100M. These REITs own and manage apartment buildings in geographical areas throughout the United States; some have properties located only in very specific areas, such as Evans Withycombe (in Arizona and Southern California) or Associated Estates (in Cleveland and Akron, Ohio), while others own units scattered across the country, such as Equity Residential and Apartment Investment & Management. Some managements have specialized development skills that enable them to build new properties in healthy markets where rents and occupancy rates are rising quickly.

Well-run apartments have, over the years, been able to generate 8-10% yields for their owners, and many such investments offer the prospects of substantial property value appreciation. Today, most "cap rates" range from 7% to 10% (a "cap rate," generally speaking, refers to the unleveraged return expected by a buyer of an apartment building or any other property, expressed as the anticipated cash flow return (before depreciation) as a percentage of the purchase price. For example, paying $1 million for a 9% cap rate property should produce an initial unleveraged cash return on the investment of $90,000 per year).

Apartment owners do well when the economy is expanding because of the resulting new job creation and rise in the formation of new households; conversely, renters tend to "double up" or live with parents and relatives when unemployment is high and job prospects are poor or when they are pessimistic about the economy. A rule of thumb is that every five new jobs creates the demand for one additional apartment unit. Another very important factor for apartment owners is the rate of construction of new units in the local area. Such competing properties, if built when demand for apartment space is slowing, can force the owners of existing units to reduce rents or offer concessions, and often result in lower occupancy rates.

Inflation is also important in determining an apartment owner's economic fortunes. Inflation causes higher operating expenses for everything from maintenance to insurance to loan interest (if the units have been financed with variable rate debt). However, owners have been able to increase rents to offset the effects of inflation in areas that are not overbuilt. Existing units compete for tenants with new apartment buildings, and inflation increases the cost of building the latter, which in turn increases the rent required by the new owner in order to justify the project. The higher rent charged on new units can act as a "price umbrella" that enables the owner of existing units to increase rentals. Eventually, the process runs its course when new construction is no longer profitable. In 1994-1995, land and construction costs increased rapidly, which made many new apartment projects on the drawing board economically unfeasible; this cut down the number of potential new units that could have acted as a drag on rental rate increases for existing units.

Apartments compete to some extent with single-family residences (SFRs). For many years a part of the "American Dream" has been to own one's own home, close to but detached from the neighbor's adjoining residence, surrounded by a white picket fence and having a private backyard. While the availability of affordable SFRs nearby will clearly affect the economics of apartment ownership, the SFR threat is often overstated, particularly in major metropolitan areas. This is due primarily to the fact that in such areas the monthly payments, plus maintenance expenses and property taxes, associated with owning an SFR are high relative to the cost of renting a good-quality apartment unit, and the down payment is often hard to come by.

Several new factors also tilt the balance of choice toward apartment rental for a large percentage of the population. The 1991-1995 residential real estate slump has reminded us, yet again, that rising home prices are no longer a "slam-dunk," and many members of the middle class no longer automatically assume that home ownership is the road to riches. Furthermore, the population seems to be more mobile, and lay-offs, downsizings and relocations seem to be a fact of American life today; moving from an apartment in Tucson to one in Atlanta is obviously less of a hassle (or an expense) than selling a home and purchasing a new one. Finally, there seems to be a recent trend toward building larger, more luxurious apartment units containing amenities such as weight rooms, business and computer centers, putting greens and security features, and these types of units are capable of attracting the "renter-by-choice" — the more affluent citizen who might otherwise opt for home ownership.

Life — and investing — is not always rosy, however, and apartment REIT investors need to be mindful of certain risks. Even if the national economy is doing fine, the regional (or even local) economy can go into a recession, or worse. A recessionary environment could cause occupancy declines and flat rental rates, at best. Or there could be a significant increase in new apartment construction in the area, which might occur during the "boom" phase of the apartment cycle. Or management could fall down on the job and fail to make the expenditures necessary to maintain the overall quality of the apartment units. Fortunately, these adverse developments rarely happen overnight, so apartment REIT owners will often have sufficient time to spot negative trends before they become too pronounced. And, even then, the well-diversified REIT owner will normally own several apartment REITs so as to spread the risk among several geographical areas.

Earning reasonable returns on apartment buildings was difficult in the late '80s and early '90s, due to the substantial overbuilding of apartments that occurred in the mid- to late '80s. Such overbuilding was, in a large part, a function of the loan largesse of the banks and S&Ls, together with the real estate limited partnerships and other syndications that sprang up like garden pests in the '80s and that collected billions of dollars from hapless investors for the construction of large numbers of new units — many of which found their way into the hands of the Resolution Trust Corporation. Rents flattened (and even declined in many areas), occupancies fell, and market values declined. However, the supply-demand imbalance righted itself in 1993-1994, as the economy strengthened and very few new units were built. By 1994, rents were rising once more, and by the end of the following year occupancy levels were back over 90%.

Assuming a reasonably healthy economy, apartment ownership looks as though it will be rewarding for at least several more years. New construction has been increasing, but remains well below the levels of the '80s, and few markets appear to be in danger of becoming substantially overbuilt. Apartment owners in most areas should be able to get annual rent increases of at least 3% annually while keeping expenses well under control.

In summary, apartment ownership and operation continues to be a good business, particularly if the owner has the skills and disciplines to maintain the units properly, attract quality tenants and keep them there. Good management is particularly important in this sector, as most apartment units may fairly be regarded as "commodity"-type products. When markets are in equilibrium (*i.e.*, supply and demand are in balance), rental rates should be able to grow at a rate equal to or exceeding inflation and provide apartment owners with stable and rising investment returns. Many apartment REIT managements have these skills, and the shares of these REITs will provide high and growing returns to patient investors.

Pros	Cons
Capitalizes on expanding economy	Weak economy can depress occupancy and rents
Normally a stable business	Subject to overbuilding in boom cycles
Benefits from mobile population trends	Needed capital expenditures may not be made
Home ownership no longer a must	"Commodity"-type business

The following list provides certain relevant information concerning the publicly-traded apartment REITs as of October 31, 1996:

45

REIT	Stock Symbol	Market	# of Properties /Units	Primary Locations	Approx. Market Cap
Equity Residential Properties Trust	EQR	NYSE	219/57,190	USA	1,851
Security Capital Pacific Trust	PTR	NYSE	NA/54,329	W	1,561
Post Properties	PPS	NYSE	55/14,642	SE	857
United Dominion Realty Trust	UDR	NYSE	141/34,224	SE	798
Merry Land & Investment Company	MRY	NYSE	81/22,296	SE,E,MW	784
BRE Properties	BRE	NYSE	22/9314	W	730
Avalon Properties	AVN	NYSE	40/11,255	E,NE	722
Summit Properties	SMT	NYSE	47/10,727	SE	466
Irvine Apartment Communities	IAC	NYSE	43/13,841	W	393
Camden Property Trust	CPT	NYSE	59/16,742	SW	392
Gables Residential Trust	GBP	NYSE	46/13,929	SE,SW	392
Wellsford Residential Property Trust	WRP	NYSE	75/18,296	SW,W	392
Evans Withycombe Residential	EWR	NYSE	41/11,053	W	377
CRIIMI MAE	CMM	NYSE	NA/NA	NA	346
Oasis Residential	OAS	NYSE	41/12,298	SW	345
Bay Apartment Properties	BYA	NYSE	22/6,450	W	338
Walden Residential Properties	WDN	NYSE	55/17,205	SW,SE	325
South West Property Trust	SWP	NYSE	39/13,361	SW,SE	311
Redwood Trust	RWTI	OTC	NA/NA	NA	303
Apartment. Investment & Management Co.	AIV	NYSE	56/14,453	NA	287
Associated Estates Realty Corp.	AEC	NYSE	70/15,289	MW	279
Mid-America Apartment Communities	MAA	NYSE	71/18,660	SE,SW	271
Charles E Smith Residential Realty	SRW	NYSE	36/14,150	E	267
Amli Residential Properties Trust	AML	NYSE	34/2,245	SW,SE,MW	260
Berkshire Reality Co.	BRI	NYSE	NA/9,434	SE	251
Columbus Realty Trust	CLB	NYSE	28/4,542	SW	250
Paragon Group	PAO	NYSE	54/13,240	USA	239
Town & Country Trust, The	TCT	NYSE	NA/13,631	E,SE	225
Ambassador Apts	AAH	NYSE	36/10,636	SW	198
Pennsylvania REIT	PEI	AMEX	20/7,337	E,SE	196
Essex Property Trust	ESS	NYSE	24/5,040	W	161
Home Properties of NY	HME	NYSE	NA/5,650	NE	132
ASR Investments Corp.	ASR	AMEX	24/4,121	SW	63
CRI Liquidating REIT	CFR	NYSE	NA/NA	NA	53
Presidential Realty Corp. (Class B)	PDLB	AMEX	NA/575	NA	21
American Real Estate Investment Corp.	REA	AMEX	NA/2,142	SW	9
					14,845

Retail: Neighborhood Shopping Centers

For many years, before the advent of major regional shopping malls, shoppers bought everything locally, at the small stores on Main Street or "down on the boulevard." Whether it be a bottle of aspirin, a hammer or a new shirt or dress, local merchants had garnered most of consumers' spending dollars. But buying patterns have been changing. Over the last 20 years, major malls have sprung up from Maine to California, equipped with piped-in music, elevators and enclosures to ward off the elements and offering

46

everything from Italian inlaid music boxes to $5 bars of soap scented with essence of tangerine oil. In an even more recent trend, the country is now becoming "Wal-Mart-ized," with consumers able to satisfy nearly all their shopping needs at one gigantic store at bargain-basement prices.

The neighborhood shopping center has had to contend with these new trends, and has lost lots of business to its new competitors. Nevertheless, Americans love their conveniences, and being located just three minutes from home gives the local merchant a significant advantage. How many of us want to drive 30 minutes to the local mall or 15 minutes to the nearby discount store to pick up a movie videotape or a mouse trap? Not to mention our service needs such as dry cleaning or shoe repair, which (so far) are not readily available at the major stores.

The neighborhood shopping center is usually "anchored" by one or two major stores — usually a supermarket and a drug store — and contains a large number of additional stores that offer other basic services and necessities. As a result, these centers tend to be "recession-proof" and not significantly affected by national or regional slow-downs. The property owner charges a minimum rent to the tenants, and the lease is often structured to contain fixed "rent bumps" that increase the tenants' rental obligation each year. In addition, or in lieu of fixed rent bumps, the lease may contain "overage" rental provisions, which result in increased rent if annual sales exceed certain minimum levels. Often "triple-net" leases are signed, which impose upon the tenant all obligations for real estate taxes and assessments, repairs and maintenance, insurance and the duty to restore the property in the event of casualty or condemnation.

Many real estate investors believe that retail properties are in the declining phase of their cycle. Such astute REIT men as Milton Cooper (Kimco) and Steven Roth (Vornado) observed in early 1995 that retail stores were rapidly becoming overbuilt, and recent events have borne them out. Today a significant number of major retailers have either filed bankruptcy proceedings or otherwise closed stores; by the end of 1995, these problems were particularly severe in the apparel sector. Consumers don't seem to want to shop as they did in the 1980s. As a result, retail store owners must contend with the prospects of rising vacancies and minuscule rental increases. Norman Kranzdorf, CEO of Kranzco Realty Trust, has stated that between 15% and 20% of the space in neighborhood shopping centers is obsolete.[1] Furthermore, the neighborhood shopping centers are having to contend with competition not only from the malls, but also from the large discount chains. So why would investors want to buy any REITs that specialize in this sector?

The answer to this question demonstrates an important irony of REIT investing. Throughout many, if not most, periods in REITs' history, very strong property markets have caused trouble while poor markets have proven a boon. This is because strong markets can eventually lead to overbuilding, which heightens competitive conditions and depresses operating income for up to several years in the future, whereas weak and troubled markets depress the market prices of existing properties. Because most REITs have access to reasonably priced capital that may not be available to other prospective buyers, they have the ability during weak markets to snap up properties with good long-term prospects at very favorable prices.

The overbuilt conditions in the neighborhood shopping center market and their perceived mediocre prospects for healthy income growth have enabled opportunistic REITs (such as Bradley, Federal, Kimco, New Plan, Regency, Vornado and Weingarten) to buy properties "on the cheap," fill vacancies with stronger tenants, upgrade the facilities and significantly increase rents and operating income. A REIT's management and its access to capital, while always important, are critical during depressed or overbuilt market conditions, and the astute REIT investor will insist on these requirements when considering a REIT during such a phase in the property cycle. Chapter Seven will examine these aspects in more detail.

Pros	Cons
Not significantly affected by economy	Subject to overbuilding
Many leases contain built in rent increases	Sensitive to retail spending
Strong REITs buy properties "on the cheap"	Competition from discounters and malls

The following list provides certain relevant information concerning the publicly-traded neighborhood shopping center REITs as of October 31, 1996:

REIT	Stock Symbol	Market	# of Properties /Sq. Ft. (MM)	Primary Locations	Approx. Market Cap
New Plan Realty Trust	NPR	NYSE	168/18.0	USA	1,280
Kimco Realty Corp.	KIM	NYSE	253/25.4	USA	1,051
Vornado Realty Trust	VNO	NYSE	56/9.9	E,NE	1,046
Weingarten Realty Investors	WRI	NYSE	151/15.4	SW	982
Federal Realty Investment Trust	FRT	NYSE	72/11.9	NE,MW,E	769
Developers Diversified Realty Corp.	DDR	NYSE	111/24.2	USA	726
Glimcher Realty Trust	GRT	NYSE	92/11.8	USA	421
Excel Realty Trust	XEL	NYSE	120/4.5	USA	320
Bradley Real Estate Trust	BTR	NYSE	31/7.5	MW	313
JDN Realty Corp.	JDN	NYSE	42/5.0	SE	274
Price REIT (Class B)	RET	NYSE	19/4.6	NA	270
IRT Property Co.	IRT	NYSE	NA/7.8	SE	245
Regency Realty Corp.	REG	NYSE	32/4.0	SE	235
Western Investment Real Estate	WIR	AMEX	62/25.0	W	212

Trust					
Burnham Pacific Properties	BPP	NYSE	20/2.2	W	207
Alexander Haagen Properties	ACH	AMEX	40/6.5	W	173
Saul Centers	BFS	NYSE	32/5.6	E	172
First Washington Realty Trust	FRW	NYSE	32/3.2	E,SE,NE	159
Kranzco Realty Trust	KRT	NYSE	38/5.7	NE,E	157
Ramco-Gershenson Properties Trust	RPT	NYSE	NA/NA	NA	118
Mark Centers Trust	MCT	NYSE	39/7.2	NE,SE	95
HRE Properties	HRE	NYSE	21/1.8	NE	81
Mid-America Realty Investments	MDI	NYSE	19/3.2	MW,SE	79
Agree Realty Corp.	ADC	NYSE	23/2	MW	63
Mid-Atlantic Realty Trust	MRR	AMEX	27/3.0	E	61
Malan Realty Investors	MAL	NYSE	52/5.7	MW	49
					8,369

Retail: Regional Malls

If neighborhood shopping centers provide the "necessities of life," the large regional malls provide the "un-necessities." Where else can you find a cut crystal clock in the shape of a heart, or a cute little duck with a "welcome" ribbon around its neck? The concept of the mall is that shopping is an enjoyable adventure. For many of us, mall shopping has become a social event or, at the least, something interesting to do in our spare time; we can't quite say the same thing about buying a package of nails at the local hardware store.

The economics of malls are very different from those of neighborhood shopping centers. Rent payable by the tenant is higher, but so are the dollar volumes of sales per square foot. Even with higher rent, a retailer can do very well in a mall, due to the high traffic and larger sales potential per store. Stores that can't generate substantial sales, however, can quickly run into trouble (due to the higher overhead of operating in a mall), so there is a premium on the mall owner finding and signing leases with the "hottest," most successful retailers. Some mall REITs own nationally renowned malls, where rental rates are high (close to $40 per square foot) and sales per square foot approach $400. Others emphasize smaller malls, which are usually located in less densely populated cities, where rental rates are in the low $20s and sales per square foot don't get much above $200-$250. Malls are truly in the retail business, and success depends upon leasing to successful retailers who can attract the fickle and demanding customer, as well as the overall strength of the national, regional and local retail economies.

Mall REITs are relatively new on the investment scene. Prior to 1992, malls were owned only by large real estate organizations and by institutional investors; there was no way a REIT investor could own a piece of the great "trophy" shopping properties of America. However, between 1992 and 1994, the large shopping mall developers such as Messrs. Taubman, Simon and DeBartolo "REIT-ized" their empires by going public as REITs. Skeptical investors wondered, in view of the lackluster mall sales in the early '90s, whether these large and sophisticated owners were simply forming REITs as a vehicle for foisting large chunks of mall properties on the public at inflated prices. Others were more trusting, maintaining that bank financing had been difficult to obtain since 1992, and that by forming a REIT an organization would have much better access to capital. Regardless of their motives, these owners took their organizations public, and there are now 10 REITs that own and operate regional shopping malls, almost all of which have gone public just since 1992. As of October 1996, their collective market capitalization made malls one of the largest sectors in the REIT world.

Are malls and the REITs that own them good investments? Before we tackle this question, let's first take a quick look at the past. The 1980s were the "golden years" for the regional mall. Wives were launching their own careers and buying clothes for the workplace, and the Baby Boomers were spending their double incomes like giddy teen-agers. America was malled from coast to coast, and "shop till you drop" became the national motto. Tenant sales rose briskly, the major retailers *had* to have space in all the malls, and mall owners could increase rental rates almost at will. Malls were truly attractive investments, and most large property-investing institutions wanted to own them.

By the early 1990s, however, this great era of consumerism ended, hastened by the same recession that knocked President Bush out of office and created waves of corporate "restructuring." As downsizings and intense global competition took hold in the United States, wage gains grew hard to come by, fears of layoffs were rampant and consumer confidence declined. "Deep discount" became the American consumer's rallying cry. Further, on a longer-term basis, the Baby Boomers became concerned about their future retirements and decided to buy mutual funds rather than Armani suits.

These developments and trends have taken their toll on mall owners and their tenants. Apparel sales, for years the stock-in-trade of most mall retail establishments, have been in the dumps for quite some time, and no one is predicting a major rebound in the near future. The "over-storing" of apparel retailers has resulted in bankruptcy for many of them. This has been a significant problem for the mall owners; according to Barry Vinocur, editor of the Realty Stock Review, between 30% and 35% of mall gross leasable area is tenanted by apparel (including footwear) retailers.[2] Another effect, which could have been caused by consumers' preference for discount shopping, has been a shorter duration in mall shopping trips. According to consultants Stillerman Jones & Co., the amount of time that shoppers spend in the malls has declined from 90 minutes per shopping trip in 1982 to 68 minutes in 1995.[3] Reflecting these problems, after years of healthy sales growth, the malls' same-store sales have been sluggish since 1990.[4]

Another problem for mall REITs has been the lack of good external growth prospects. There simply have been few opportunities for them to grow by acquisition (few malls have been available for purchase) or by development (just exactly where do we need another mall?). As a result, mall REITs have had to rely primarily upon revenue improvements within each mall (*i.e.*, increasing rental rates to tenants, increasing occupancy levels, and replacing underperforming tenants) in order to create meaningful FFO growth.

Due to all of these factors, mall REITs have not, until recently, been very popular with investors, and their investment returns until 1996 were lackluster. Shall REIT investors therefore just shun the mall REITs and look for better prospects elsewhere?

Not so fast; to paraphrase Mark Twain, reports of the malls' demise have been greatly exaggerated, and they are not without comeback potential. Unlike many property types, malls do not normally run the risk of competitors springing up several blocks away. The cost of building a new mall can amount to $100 million, and overbuilding within a given geographical area is unlikely. These barriers to entry give the malls a substantial edge over most other property types.

Another key advantage to mall ownership is that most major retailers continue to rely upon the malls for a very large portion of their total sales. It's significant that, despite the widely heralded problems of most retailers over the last several years, malls' occupancy rates have been holding steady. For example, the occupancy rate at the malls owned by Taubman Centers was 87.6% at the end of 1991 and 88.0% at the end of 1995. Furthermore, despite the belief of many that DeBartolo Realty's former management did not do a particularly good job of managing its properties, occupancy rates fell just slightly from 88.7% at the end of 1991 to 84.4% at the end of 1995, and this drop is overstated due to the new management's pro-active program of recapturing and reconfiguring unproductive space (DeBartolo has since been acquired by Simon Property Group).

While the apparel retailers' poor performance in recent years has had a negative effect on overall mall sales, such events are not unusual in the mall business. Mall owners historically have been able to reconfigure retail space to reposition themselves to meet ever-changing consumer demands. The mall owners are now emphasizing home accessory, gift and other "lifestyle" retailers and seeking to attract new types of tenants to replace many of the poorly performing apparel stores. Simon has been very active in adding

51

entertainment locations to many of its malls. DeBartolo Realty (prior to merging with Simon) set up an "Entertainment Leasing Division" with the intent of attracting such new tenants as theaters, "lifestyle" restaurants, family entertainment and other special attractions. These strategies may now be working; sales of home accessories, gifts and children's clothing at Taubman Centers increased by 44% over the past six years, as compared to 1% for apparel sales; the former represented 37% of revenues in 1995, up from 29% six years earlier.[5]

To the extent that the mall owners are successful in these endeavors, mall traffic will increase, tenant sales will rise and rental rates will increase (somewhat surprisingly, most mall owners have been able to increase rental rates in recent years despite sluggish same-store sales, as older leases negotiated at lower rental rates have come up for renewal). Occupancy rates will start to improve with successful tenant repositionings, and rents from the newly leased space will flow almost directly to the bottom line. It's quite possible that investors who have dumped mall REITs in the expectation that income growth will be dismal will be proven wrong, and that the better-managed mall REITs will be able to report 5-7% FFO growth (aided by selective acquisitions and developments), which would be pretty much in line with the long-term FFO growth of the entire REIT industry. Finally, cap rates on malls have begun to rise (thus increasing their returns to mall buyers) and more malls are becoming available for purchase, as institutional investors are now becoming more willing sellers. This, combined with the malls REITs' reduced cost of capital, could make external growth (through acquisitions) more likely. Mall REITs could be solid performers in the years ahead.

Pros	Cons
Lack of nearby competition from other malls	Competition from discount shopping in U.S.
Very stable business	Shorter duration of shopping trips
Retailers' reliance on malls	Market saturation throughout U.S.
Malls are repositioning to meet changing lifestyles	

The following list provides certain relevant information concerning the publicly-traded shopping mall REITs as of October 31, 1996:

REIT	Stock Symbol	Market	# of Properties / Sq. Ft. (MM)	Primary Locations	Approx. Market Cap
Simon DeBartolo Group	SPG	NYSE	185/128	USA	1,545
General Growth Properties	GGP	NYSE	68/53	USA	672
Taubman Centers	TCO	NYSE	19/22	USA	496
CBL & Associates	CBL	NYSE	16/10.9	SE	484
Macerich Company, The	MAC	NYSE	17/12.4	W, MW	442
JP Realty	JPR	NYSE	44/5.0	W,SW	365

Urban Shopping Centers	URB	NYSE	12/8.2	MW,W	354
Mills Corp.	MLS	NYSE	11/6.0	E	351
Crown American Realty Trust	CWN	NYSE	24/13.3	SE,NE	206
Arbor Property Trust	ABR	NYSE	1/1.6	NE	97
					5,012

Retail: Factory Outlet Centers

Neighborhood retail centers provide the necessities at reasonable prices, and malls provide non-necessities, often at higher prices, so what's left? Americans, inventive souls that we are, have developed another type of retailer that provides non-necessities at cheap prices: "factory outlet centers." These centers are normally located quite a few miles from major population areas and are tenanted by major manufacturers such as Bass Company, Van Heusen, Corning Revere, Jones New York, Geoffrey Beene, London Fog and the like. While most of these companies are manufacturers and generally sell to the major retailers, in these factory outlet centers they sell direct to the public at cut-rate prices. The concept is that they sell over-stocked goods, odd sizes or fashion ideas that just didn't click, and that these goods are priced to move quickly. Advertising is limited, due to the manufacturers' desire that the outlet centers not appear to be competing head-on with their major retail customers. They sometimes deliver what they promise, as consumers can often get fashionable or quasi-fashionable items at 25-35% below retail.

The outlet industry has been around for a long while but has been growing rapidly in recent years; industry sales have more than doubled from 1990 to 1995, and now exceed $11 billion. From January 1988 to January 1996, the industry's GLA (gross leaseable area) increased from 13.9 million to 50.7 million square feet.[6] While still normally located far from "civilization" (primarily to protect the manufacturers' normal retail channels but also to utilize cheap land), the typical outlet center contains 40 to 60 stores. The size of the centers has become larger; 15 years ago they averaged approximately 50,000 square feet but now the average size is closer to 250,000 square feet. There are more than 300 outlet centers in the United States, where more than 500 manufacturers operate close to 12,000 individual stores.[7] While this sector has experienced considerable growth, there is still room for more: According to Montgomery Securities,[8] outlet industry sales represent only 3% of the $350 billion of U.S. general merchandise sales, and outlet square footage represents only 1% of the 44 million total U.S. retail square footage.

Sales per square foot for 1995 for two representative publicly traded outlet centers, Chelsea/GCA and Tanger Factory Outlet Centers, were $313 and $226, respectively, which compares well with that of the typical regional mall ($270).[9] A very important measure of a retail store's operating costs and a key factor in determining that store's profit margins is occupancy cost *as a percentage of sales*. The lower the figure, the more of each sales dollar is available to pay other operating costs or to bring down to the bottom line. While sales per square foot at outlet centers are very close to those at the malls, occupancy costs have been estimated at only 8-9% of sales, based upon data provided by these outlet center REITs, which compares very favorably to almost 12% for regional malls.[10] These statistics help to explain the attractiveness of the outlet centers to the manufacturer-as-retailer.

Five major developer/owners of outlet centers went public between May and December of 1993 to very enthusiastic receptions, as investors expected these new REITs to grow much faster than the REITs who own more traditional retail properties such as neighborhood shopping centers and regional malls. However, early in 1994 the shares of these REITs ran into rough weather. McArthur/Glen, at the time one of the most highly regarded outlet REITs, suddenly announced that instead of completing the one million square feet of new outlet center space that was promised to investors at the time of its initial public offering, it would deliver only 175,000 square feet.[11] Factory Stores of America (since renamed FAC Realty Trust) also fell out of favor, due to its perceived overly rapid expansion and high debt levels.

Investors then began to see the glass as half-empty rather than half-full, and began worrying about over-development of outlet centers, market saturation and disappointing same-store sales. In mid-1995, McArthur/Glen was acquired by Horizon Outlet Centers (which was subsequently renamed Horizon Group, Inc.), thus putting what was, at that time, one of the poorest performers out of its misery. By the end of 1995, Factory Stores of America announced it would have to cut its dividend. Nevertheless, despite these problems and worries, both Chelsea/GCA and Tanger are trading above their IPO prices and they continue to show significant growth in funds from operations.

After witnessing such an exciting beginning, many REIT investors are trying to determine whether the outlet center REITs are unloved and misunderstood growth companies poised to deliver outstanding total returns, or are merely accidents waiting to happen. And it's certainly true that outlets face particular challenges. The typical outlet center has no anchor tenants, and the land on which it is situated usually has little underlying value apart from its use as an outlet center. These properties are normally bought and sold in the private real estate market at cap rates significantly higher than other retail properties, indicating a higher level of risk. Same-store sales, like other retail sectors, have (with the exception of Chelsea/GCA) been flat during the last two years. Over-development in certain geographical areas remains a risk.

Also, many manufacturer-tenants offer products that are specially made for the outlet store, rather than normal products that are over-stocked or slightly out-of-date; this could cause consumers to wonder whether they are really "getting a deal."

Shoppers may also become less inclined to travel 60 miles out of their way than they were earlier when the outlet centers were a major novelty, especially if tenanted by hum-drum retailers who offer less-than-exciting products. These issues may have been responsible for a recent slow-down in the number of new stores opened and the number of manufacturers participating in this sector. Finally, there is the problem of new competition from the regional malls, which are advertising "sales" much more often, and from the new "Mills-type" retail format pioneered by Mills Corp., which offers value-retailers such as traditional outlet stores in combination with "category killer" retailers (such as T.J. Maxx, Burlington Coat Factory, Target, etc.), discount department stores (such as Off Fifth) and entertainment centers containing multi-screen theaters, water slides and other novelty attractions.

These uncertainties make the outlet center REITs controversial investments. Yet they also have certain advantages going for them: Their small market share (which may allow for rapid growth through additional development, assuming the centers continue to appeal to both manufacturers and consumers), impressive sales per square foot in relation to lease rates, high property occupancy rates that frequently exceed 95%, high tenant retention, and increasing rental rates on new leases being signed (which seems to be a good portent for future demand).

What investors should look for in an outlet REIT investment is management that emphasizes leases with high-end, high-quality tenant manufacturers. These are the types of tenants that can draw shoppers away from the malls, traditional stores and major discounters in hopes of getting good values on "designer-type" products. Names such as Polo, Barneys New York, Burberrys and Donna Karan come to mind. Equally as important is finding REITs whose strategy is to locate new centers as close to densely populated areas as possible or in proven tourist spots, where shoppers do not have to travel miles out of their way to find attractive shopping. These types of centers will also tend to have and hold value as real estate, and will (due perhaps to zoning laws and regulations) discourage competition from new outlet or other retail stores. In this sense, a well-located and well-tenanted outlet center may, in the future, become an "open-air mall" or "horizontal department store" that offers discount pricing in all stores virtually all the time.

Outlet center REITs appeal to the "contrarian" and value-oriented REIT investor as, similar to the mall REITs until 1996, they are an unloved sector selling at cheap prices. The key to making money in these stocks is to determine whether consumers will

55

continue to find outlet centers an attractive place to shop. If they do, the factory outlets will report increasing same-store sales, and the stocks of the outlet REITs will do well.

Pros	Cons
Small market share = substantial growth potential	No anchor tenants
High sales per square foot	Land frequently has little value
Low vacancy rates	Same store sales have been flat
Increasing rental rates on new leases	Potential overbuilding
High tenant retention	True values to customers?
Appeal to value oriented shoppers	Competition from discounters

The following list provides certain relevant information concerning the publicly-traded outlet center REITs as of October 31, 1996.

REIT	Stock Symbol	Market	# Properties / Sq. Ft. (MM)	Primary Locations	Approx. Market Cap
Horizon Group	HGI	NYSE	35/8.5	USA	442
Alexander's	ALX	NYSE	9/1.4	NE	366
Chelsea GCA Realty	CCG	NYSE	16/2.9	W	338
Prime Retail	PRME	OTC	17/4.3	USA	158
Tanger Factory Outlet Centers	SKT	NYSE	27/3.6	USA	156
FAC Realty Trust	FAC	NYSE	NA/NA	SE,MW,SW	99
Angeles Participating Mortgage Trust	ANM	AMEX	4/NA	N, SE	25
					1,584

Offices and Industrial Properties

Office buildings and industrial properties are often grouped together when discussing REIT sectors. While their economic characteristics are very different in some ways, they are the only types of properties leased to businesses that do not cater to individual consumers in one form or another; in that respect they are very different from apartments, retail stores, self-storage facilities or even health-care institutions. In addition, many of the REITs in this sector own both office buildings and industrial properties.

Office Buildings. Office buildings have had their own set of overbuilding problems in recent years, and they have been doozies. While apartments were greatly overbuilt in the late 1980s, the office overbuilding problem has been far worse as vacancy rates rose into the 20%-plus zone in some major markets and "see-through" buildings have been the bane of office owners and lenders. And this sector has been much slower to turn around, due perhaps to the depth of the office sector depression and the major corporate "downsizings" of the 1990s, where "lay-offs" and "early retirement" have been the names of the competition game in U.S. industry. To exacerbate the problem, office leases normally have fixed rental rates during their terms (with perhaps a small annual rental step-up, determined by the Consumer Price Index or a contractual formula) and run for much longer terms than do apartment and retail leases. As a result, the problem of declining rental rates upon lease renewal is late to appear. During the last few years, as older higher-rate leases have expired, many building owners have continued to see their cash flows diminished by the newer and lower lease rates, even apart from the rental loss due to higher vacancy rates. A problem unique to the office sector is the long time between obtaining building permits and final completion; this makes it more difficult to stop the development process should the builder or lender realize that there is insufficient demand for yet another office building. For these reasons, the office property sector has truly been a "deep cyclical" type of business.

As if these problems weren't bad enough, office building owners have had to contend with the drift of the office-using population to the suburbs and other outlying areas (and even to states not previously known for significant central business districts), perhaps to get away from the problems of decaying inner cities. (Gangs, graffiti, smog, congestion and declining educational standards have hardly been conducive to encouraging businesses to take on new space in many major population areas). Tenants have been lost to such "hot" areas as Oregon, Idaho, Utah, Arizona, New Mexico, North Carolina, Tennessee, Florida and some parts of Texas not only to improve the executives' and employees' "quality of life" but also in order to take advantage of low taxes, low operating costs and cheaper labor. Furthermore, some wonder whether it's truly necessary to put all of one's employees in a big box; while telecommuting may not presently be worrying building owners, it does seem to be a rising trend. Finally, building owners must expend significant sums on tenant improvements, lobbies and other amenities in order to keep the buildings competitive.

Should we therefore conclude that office building REITs are to be shunned like the plague? Not at all. Rental space and the prices that can be charged for it are, like most things, governed by the laws of supply and demand. Even during the 1990-91 economic slump when office jobs declined, net office space absorption, nationwide, has been positive. Thus it's quite likely that the problems in the office building sector resulted primarily from an over-supply of space. There has been very little development of new office buildings over the last few years, and rents in many markets started to rise in 1994, initiating a new cycle that looks as though it will continue for several years. As a result, office properties appear to be early in the "recovery" phase of their real estate cycle.

If a desirable building is located in a growing area, has attractive amenities, is well-maintained and is not subject to competitive building by developers, both occupancy and rental rates can rise quickly and generate very healthy returns for the building owner. For example, the office building occupancy rate in the "research triangle" around Raleigh and Durham, N.C., was approximately 93% at the end of 1995, and rents were scaling up nicely. (Highwoods Properties has significant holdings in this area. Its unleveraged returns from office buildings acquired since it went public in June 1994 have been in the 10-11% range, and until recently there has been little new development in most of its areas.)

Office REITs which own properties in higher-growth areas and which have access to cheap capital (which allows them to make attractive acquisitions) have excellent growth prospects. While office markets continue to improve across the board, there seems to be a trend for businesses to relocate in suburban areas. Suburban office vacancy rates are declining faster than those for offices located in metropolitan areas. However, at least in the near term, office markets seem to be recovering almost everywhere, and office REITs which are expanding rapidly on a nationwide basis (such as Beacon, CarrAmerica, Crescent and Prentiss) should do as well as those (such as Cali, Cousins, Highwoods and Reckson) which are concentrating in more localized areas, regardless of the specific location. Investors should be mindful, however, that due to the very cyclical nature of the office market, office building REITs should be bought well before significant new development ruins the party and should consider selling their shares if and when it becomes apparent that such ills will occur. Nevertheless, it's my guess that this sector will do well for at least the next few years

Pros	Cons
Insignificant development in recent years	Overbuilding has often been a problem
Rental growth accelerating	Corporate downsizing may reduce absorption
Positive spread investment opportunities	Possible "flight" to suburbs and telecommuting
Recession insulation resulting from long-term leases	Ownership requires continual upgrading & tenant improvements

The following list provides certain relevant information concerning the publicly-traded office REITs as of October 31, 1996 (the list excludes Arden Realty, Kilroy Realty and Prentiss Properties, which went public after such date):

REIT	Stock Symbol	Market	# of Properties / Sq. Ft (MM)	Primary Locations	Approx. Market Cap
Crescent Real Estate Equities	CEI	NYSE	47/8.8	SW	979
CarrAmerica Realty Corp.	CRE	NYSE	36/6.3	SW	866
Beacon Properties Corp	BCN	NYSE	26/6.7	NE	805
Cousins Properties	CUZ	NYSE	NA/4.6	NA	643
Highwoods Properties	HIW	NYSE	41/17.3	S	570

Reckson Associates	RA	NYSE	90/6.4	NE	499
Cali Realty Trust	CLI	NYSE	40/3.9	NE	452
Koger Equities	KE	AMEX	21/7.7	SE	282
G&L Realty	GLR	NYSE	14/0.5	W	65
Brandywine Realty Trust	BDN	AMEX	4/0.3	E	9
Nooney Realty Trust	NRTI	OTC	3/0.2	MW	8
Realty ReFund Trust	RRF	NYSE	NA/NA	NA	6
					4,685

Industrial Properties. Industrial properties include distribution centers, warehouses, service centers, light manufacturing facilities, research and development facilities and adjacent small office space suitable for sales and administrative functions. The buildings can be free-standing or situated within landscaped industrial parks. A building can be occupied by only a single tenant, or by several tenants. It has been estimated that the total square footage of all industrial property in the U.S. is approximately 9.5 billion square feet, of which about half is owned by the actual user; ownership is highly fragmented, and the public REITs own only about 1% of all industrial real estate. Leases normally have terms ranging from one year up to 15 years (most are for five or ten years), and the tenant typically pays for increases in taxes, operating costs and insurance over a "base year." Some "build-to-suit" facilities are leased on a "triple-net" basis and require the tenant to pay for *all* taxes and operating costs. Many industrial property leases also require the tenant to pay increased rents each year or at other specified intervals during the term of the lease, based upon a predetermined formula.

Ownership of industrial properties has generally provided stable and steady returns, particularly in relation to office properties. According to a research report published by Apogee Associates, LLC[12], approximately 80% of the tenants renew their leases, which provides for low tenant turnover, and default rates are low. Further, such report states that demand for industrial space has, since 1981, exceeded the demand for office space and that rents have generally grown slowly but steadily at a rate equal to or better than office properties (and declined, overall, only during the early 1990's, when this sector had its own overbuilding problem). Vacancy rates, according to the report, have historically been lower than those of office properties, and were at 7% at the end of the first quarter of 1996, which is close to the long-term norm for industrial property.

Fortunately, due in part to the relatively short time period required to construct and lease an industrial building and the small size of most buildings, the industrial property market has had a good track record of being able to quickly shut down the supply of new space when markets become saturated with new space. Furthermore, there generally has not been excessive space built on

59

speculation; most new space is built in response to demand by new users, and tenant expansions provide attractive business opportunities. Another key advantage to the industrial property owner is that, unlike the office sector, significant capital expenditures are not required in order to keep the building in good repair, and tenant allowances which must be given to new tenants or upon re-leasing are much less significant on a square foot basis than is required for office properties. The industry is currently well along in the "recovery" phase of its real estate cycle, and investors need to watch for signs of possible overbuilding in some markets.

Major risks applicable to industrial properties include declining economic and business conditions in the area in which the properties are located (which would increase vacancies and depress rental rates), dependence upon the financial health of the tenants of the properties, and (as is the case in almost all property sectors) the possibility that the area in which the properties are located could become overbuilt. While the cost of developing an industrial property is not insignificant (between $2 million and $10 million), it is not so large that "merchant developers" cannot engage in speculative development that could quickly result in an overbuilt situation with its attendant negative consequences.

REITs that specialize in industrial-type properties can be very good investments, particularly if their managements have long-standing relationships with major users of industrial space and if they concentrate on healthy geographical areas where business is growing rapidly. Weeks' properties are concentrated in Atlanta, Nashville, the "Research Triangle" of North Carolina and Florida. Highwoods' industrial properties are held primarily in the Piedmont area of North Carolina, and Spieker's are located in the Silicon Valley and other West Coast areas. Security Capital Industrial, the largest of the industrial property REITs, seeks to build long-term relationships with America's largest companies, and to provide for all their industrial property needs; their properties are in major markets in most areas of the U.S. All four of these REITs, together with several other industrial property REITs which I haven't mentioned specifically, are likely to provide growing funds from operations and increasing dividends for their shareholders as long as the areas in which they operate do not become overpopulated with new industrial buildings.

Pros	Cons
Low tenant turnover and default rates	Highly sensitive to economy
Modest real estate cycles	Overbuilding may occur due to "spec" development
Low capital expenditures	Modest NOI growth at the property level
Steady demand	Possible obsolescence of some property types
Building is quick to adjust to market	

The following list provides certain relevant information concerning the publicly-traded industrial property REITs as of October 31, 1996:

REIT	Stock Symbol	Market	# Properties / Sq. Ft. (MM)	Primary Locations	Approx. Market Cap
Security Capital Industrial Trust	SCN	NYSE	950/67.5	USA	1,582
Duke Realty Investments	DRE	NYSE	NA/25.0	MW	1,016
Spieker Properties	SPK	NYSE	128/16.2	NW	978
Liberty Properties Trust	LRY	NYSE	208/16.7	E,SE	657
First Industrial Realty Trust	FR	NYSE	314/27.6	MW	626
CenterPoint Properties	CNT	NYSE	78/13.0	MW	359
Weeks Corp	WKS	NYSE	144/9.6	SE	318
Meridian Industrial Trust	MDN	NYSE	70/7.4	NA	210
Bedford Property Investors	BED	NYSE	30/2.6	W	95
Monmouth Real Estate Investment	MNRTA	OTC	12/1.0	MW/NE	21
American Industrial Properties REIT	IND	NYSE	14/1.4	USA	17
Meridian Point Realty Trust '83	MPTBS	OTC	1/0.06	USA	6
Meridian Point Realty Trust VIII Co.	MPH	AMEX	24/2.6	USA	4
					5,889

Health Care

Health-care REITs were launched in the late '80s and, despite a few hiccups along the way, have enjoyed an outstanding track record. Health-care REITs specialize in purchasing and leasing to health-care providers various types of health-care facilities, including nursing homes, "congregate" and assisted-living facilities, hospitals, medical office buildings, and rehabilitation/trauma centers. These REITs don't generally operate any of their properties, and thus maintain a very low overhead. They have generated strong returns for their shareholders over the years. According to information published by NAREIT, Equity REITs in general provided their investors with a total return during the five- and 10-year periods ending December 31, 1995, of 17.2% and 10.3%, respectively. However, if health-care REITs are excluded, these total returns dip to 16.9% and 8.4%, respectively (similar figures for the five- and 10-year periods ending December 31, 1996 are not available, as NAREIT discontinued the "Equity REIT without Health Care" category during 1996 — see Chapter One regarding the total return performance of Equity REITs over various time periods ending December 31, 1996.) These figures alone are testament to the success of the health-care REITs.

Health-care REIT properties are, in most cases, bought by the REIT and leased back to health-care companies who use the facilities for patient care, although many of them provide mortgage loan financing; new property development has been limited. The REITs' revenues come from lease payments from the operators; there is generally a base rent (or, for mortgage loans, interest payments), together with additional payments if revenues from the facility exceed certain pre-set levels (in this respect, the leases (or mortgages)

61

are similar to percentage rent on retail properties) or based upon an inflation index such as the CPI.

The most widely respected health-care REITs have easy access to the capital markets, which allows such REITs to increase their investments by purchasing additional health-care facilities or making additional mortgage loans. As lease and mortgage income received by the particular REIT exceeds the REIT's cost of funds (whether debt or equity), each new facility adds to funds from operations and enables the REIT to increase dividends. In recent years, with banks shying away from health-care lending, the health-care REITs have pretty much had this business to themselves. Competition is starting to increase, but the REITs have an edge due to their successful track records, low cost of capital, deep knowledge of the business and valuable contacts within the health-care provider industry.

The highest-quality health-care REITs are well-diversified as to their lessees (a large number of which are public companies) and the geographical location of their facilities. Tenant defaults are much less common than with other Equity REITs, due to the fact that, unlike office buildings and certain other property types, supply and demand for most health-care facilities has been pretty much in balance over the last 10 years. Another positive factor for investment in this sector is that the health-care industry is much more recession-resistant than other industries and property types.

In addition, overbuilding has not been a problem with respect to nursing homes, due in large part to the fact that in most states a "certificate of need" is required before a new facility is approved, which significantly reduces the danger of overbuilding. However, investors should be mindful that overbuilding could become a problem as numerous new investments are being made by the health-care REITs in assisted-living and congregate care facilities, which cater to healthier (and often wealthier) senior citizens These facilities are not nearly as regulated as nursing homes, and generally do not require certificates of need before being developed. Manor Care and Marriott, as well as several smaller companies that have recently gone public, are building assisted-living facilities quickly in response to rapidly increasing demand. This bodes well for these types of investments, and the health-care REITs should be able to find lots of opportunities; investors must, however, be a bit more careful due to the overbuilding risk.

Potential investors in these types of REITs also need to worry about health-care reform; the current cost-containment environment can put a significant squeeze on certain health-care providers. Market pressures from employers and insurers are forcing the health-care delivery system to operate more efficiently, and this is a fact of health care life whether or not Congress passes health-care legislation or reduces Medicare payments. Those REITs with heavy emphasis on nursing homes, congregate care and assisted-living facilities are largely immune to these cost containment pressures, as these types of facilities are the lowest-cost providers of health care, and are benefiting by shorter hospital stays as well as by their diversification into efficient delivery of various post-operative recovery services. Nationwide Health and LTC Properties are REITs with large percentages of their properties in these sectors; MediTrust, Health Care Properties, Health & Retirement Properties and Omega Healthcare Investors are also well-situated in this respect.

Another potential concern for investors is the health-care providers' reliance upon government reimbursement programs to cover their costs and to enable them to earn a reasonable profit (and which, of course, allows the provider to pay lease payments to the REIT, as owner of (or lender to) the facility). Medicaid payments from the states and, to a lesser extent, Medicare payments from the federal government, are very important, especially to nursing-home owners, as most patients in such facilities are not covered by private insurance at the present time and do not normally have the personal assets with which to fund the substantial expenses (which can run $35,000-$40,000 annually).

Stingy state reimbursement policies have been a problem in the past, but since the passage by Congress of the Boren Amendment in 1981 and reinforced by a 1990 U.S. Supreme Court decision, nursing home operators have had the ability to file lawsuits against states on the grounds of inadequate reimbursement. Medicaid reimbursement rates have also risen in recent years due to court victories won by several health-care service providers. Nevertheless, investors must be mindful of the fact that, to a large extent, the REITs and the providers are very dependent upon reasonable reimbursement policies of federal and state governments.

The long-term prospects for health-care REITs depend upon the stability and growth prospects for the U.S. health-care industry, and in particular the segments served by their lessees. Demand for health care should be no problem: The average age of the U.S. population increases every year, with the over-80 group now the fastest growing segment, and the 60-80 age group will be expanding at a rapid rate as well. New drugs will prolong lives, but (let's face it) we have more health problems at 80 than at 50. It's been said that nearly 75% of the average person's total lifetime health care expenses are incurred in the last six months of his or her life. *Someone* must provide health care for those in need and, in view of Congress' inability to agree even on cost containment, it's not likely that the government will be taking on the responsibility of delivering health-care services to our citizens. Accordingly, privately owned health-care companies will continue to provide the necessary services, and government will have to provide reimbursement rates high enough to keep these companies in business.

What we want to look for in health-care REITs are those companies that have conservative balance sheets (which facilitate additional capital-raising at rates that will generate profits from new investments), emphasize nursing homes and related facilities such as congregate care and assisted-living, enjoy good diversification as to both facility operators and geographical location, can boast impressive past growth in funds from operations (both internally and externally), adhere to conservative dividend pay-out ratios, and retain and motivate highly capable management teams.

Pros	Cons
Good business knowledge and industry contacts	Uncertainties of health care reform
Tenant defaults low	Government reimbursement issues
Recession resistant	Single use facilities with questionable real estate value
Overbuilding usually not an issue	Possible overbuilding in assisted living facilities
Good demographics	Increasing competition from lenders

The following list provides certain relevant information concerning the publicly-traded health care REITs as of October 31, 1996

REIT	Stock Symbol	Market	# Facilities / Beds	Primary Locations	Approx. Market Cap
Meditrust	MT	NYSE	406/36,105	USA	2,176
Health & Retirement Properties Trust	HRP	NYSE	165/20,000	USA	1,208
Health Care Properties	HCP	NYSE	202/22,075	USA	992
Nationwide Health Properties	NHP	NYSE	210/25,798	USA	924
National Health Investors	NHI	NYSE	227/NA	USA	752
Omega Healthcare Investors	OHI	NYSE	188/17,417	USA	527
American Health Properties	AHE	NYSE	33/4120	USA	502
Health Care REIT	HCN	NYSE	NA/10763	USA	344
LTC Properties	LTC	NYSE	256/26,164	USA	328
Health Realty Trust	HR	NYSE	65/1274	USA	320
Capstone Capital Corp	CCT	NYSE	NA/NA	USA	236
Universal Health Realty Income Trust	UHT	NYSE	13/NA	USA	170
					8,479

Self-Storage Facilities

Everyone's seen those ubiquitous self-storage facilities on the edge of town, perhaps near the railroad tracks or even next to that new industrial park. These providers of storage space offer units normally ranging from 5 by 5 feet to 20 by 20 feet, are rented by the month and allow the renter to store items such as business and personal files, sofas and chairs and even large RVs and boats.

These facilities were developed experimentally during the 1960s, and have slowly but inexorably spread throughout the nation. Most users are individuals, who rent approximately 70% of the available space; commercial users account for about 20%, and the balance is comprised of students and members of the armed forces.[13]

Self-storage was a mediocre investment in the late 1980s, due to the same overbuilding problems that so bedeviled apartment, office and other real estate owners at that time. Such excess capacity probably resulted from the mega-millions raised by limited partnership syndicators, who earned fat commissions, built anywhere and everywhere and had no meaningful stake in the continuing profitability of each facility.

The industry's health, however, has recovered substantially since 1990, as occupancy and rental rates have improved significantly. This was primarily due to a reduction in the number of new units built in recent years and the increasing popularity of this type of facility. From a longer-term perspective, these properties may be benefiting from such recent trends as a more mobile workforce (which involves more frequent moves of household items), businesses' desire to reduce costs (by using storage facilities in place of additional office space), and the increase in the number of "renters-by-choice" who are less inclined to own their own home and more apt to seek a new luxurious apartment (but which contains much less storage space). According to the Self-Storage Almanac, an industry publication, occupancy rates nationwide have increased from 78% in 1987 to 81% in 1990 and 88% in 1995, and monthly rental rates for the typical 10-by-10-foot storage space have improved steadily over that time, from $45.07 in 1988 to $51.70 in 1990 to $56.02 in 1995.[14] The self-storage industry appears to be rather late in the recovery phase of the real estate cycle and may soon be entering a development phase.

The investing public has been offered investments in self-storage facilities for many years, either through limited partnerships or small REITs closely related to the Storage Equities organization. However, the industry gained substantial credibility with experienced REIT investors only recently, as four new high-quality REITs were formed between February 1994 and June 1995 (in chronological order, Shurgard, Storage USA, Storage Trust and Sovran Self-Storage). Public Storage, the former "Storage Equities" organization and which is now the largest self-storage REIT, became a REIT in 1980 and in 1995 completed a complicated reorganization which has greatly simplified its corporate structure.

Notwithstanding the entrance of these major players, the industry is still highly fragmented, and is dominated by many "mom-and-pop" owners. The Self-Storage Almanac (1994-1995) notes that 66% of all self-storage facilities are owned by only one person or company, and only 17% are held by persons or entities that own four or more. This, of course, presents substantial opportunities to the publicly held REITs that have more sophisticated management and significant access to capital with which to make frequent (and profitable) acquisitions. Not only can properties be acquired at attractive returns, but the acquiring REIT can target certain metropolitan markets and increase its marketing effectiveness. And these REITs are, in fact, taking full advantage of the situation. Storage USA, for example, has bought 116 properties for an aggregate of $370 million just in the period between the date of its initial public offering (in March 1994) and December 31, 1995.

Recent trends in the industry include building new facilities or retrofitting existing properties with climate control, computer-controlled access gates, more sophisticated computer-based financial controls and advanced marketing and sales techniques. The more technologically advanced units can, of course, command premium prices and perhaps higher profit margins for their owners.

A good case can be made for the argument that the self-storage industry is recession-resistant. In recession, renters will often seek smaller apartments or even "double-up" with friends or other family members, homeowners may sell their homes and seek to rent apartments or condominiums, and businesses may give up some of their existing office space. All of these events tend to increase the demand for "temporary" outside storage facilities, thus largely offsetting the negative effects resulting from economic downturns.[15] Many operators were able to increase rental rates even during the 1990-1991 recession.

As with any investment, though, self-storage REITs aren't a sure thing. What can go wrong? The largest risk is overbuilding, which hurt this type of real estate as well as most others in the late 1980s. Self-storage facilities are not expensive to build (only $3 million to $5 million per facility), and (as we've seen in the '80s) supply could exceed demand within a few years, depressing rents and increasing vacancy levels. This could easily occur in certain parts of the country where population growth lags behind projections or where developers become overly aggressive. Another risk is that non-REIT investors (or even a large number of competing REITs) could become such aggressive purchasers that they push property prices so high that property acquisitions at positive spreads would become problematical; to some extent, this is what happened to some apartment REITs commencing in 1995. The disappearance of "positive-spread investing" would hamper many of the self-storage REITs' FFO growth and could result in lower stock prices.

That being said, well-managed self-storage REITs that have access to attractively priced capital should continue to do well. Growth prospects are favorable, from both internal and external standpoints, and this situation is unlikely to change in the near

66

future. And national or regional economic recessions may be much less of a problem for this industry than others. As always, however, investors should avoid paying a price for a REIT's stock based upon estimated future growth rates that are overly optimistic. (This subject will be addressed in further detail in Chapter Eight.)

Pros	Cons
More mobile workforce = greater storage needs	Overbuilding will always remain an issue
Businesses reducing warehousing costs	No barriers to entry
Many acquisition opportunities	Low cost of new construction
Recession resistant	

The following list provides certain relevant information concerning the publicly-traded self-storage REITs as of October 31, 1996:

REIT	Stock Symbol	Market	# Properties / Sq. Ft. (MM)	Primary Locations	Approx. Market Cap
Public Storage	PSA	NYSE	1,000/61	USA	1,630
Storage USA	SUS	NYSE	159/10.7	USA	679
Shurgard Storage Centers	SHU	NYSE	265/11.8	W	603
Storage Trust Realty	SEA	NYSE	137/5.7	MW,E,SE	216
Sovran Self Storage	SSS	NYSE	82/4.4	N, SE, S	199
Partners Preferred Yield (I)	PYA	AMEX	19/1.3	USA	57
Partners Preferred Yield (II)	PYB	AMEX	24/1.3	USA	62
Partners Preferred Yield (III)	PYC	AMEX	9/0.6	USA	26
					3,472

Other Property Types

REIT investors should not overlook other property types that could generate attractive total returns. They range from commercial hotels to manufactured housing communities to, believe it or not, golf courses. Long-time REIT analyst Bob Frank has said that there are even serious entrepreneurs who want to create a prison REIT! Still other REITs are very diversified as to the types of properties they own and, despite the unpopularity of this strategy, a few of them have done well for their investors over the years. The success of each REIT type will depend not only upon the economic strength of the geographical areas in which their properties are located and the supply-demand relationship applicable to that type of property, but also upon management's ability to successfully manage the properties, to take advantage of growth opportunities (both internal and external), and to avoid financing problems and other pitfalls. Let's take a quick look at the hotel REITs, the manufactured housing community REITs and the diversified REITs.

Hotel REITs. The hotel sector has been a star performer in the REIT world recently, as this type of property is still fairly early in its

67

recovery phase following a horribly overbuilt condition that lasted throughout much of the '80s; hotel companies returned to profitability in 1993 following many years of operating losses. Room rates and occupancy rates have been rising steadily since 1991. Between August 1993 and the end of September 1996, 10 hotel REITs have gone public, raising almost $1.1 billion, and follow-on offerings have raised significant additional proceeds. Nevertheless, while the prospects continue to look good for this property type, some observers are concerned about the prospects of overbuilding, especially in the "limited-service" subsector where some properties are being bought at prices exceeding replacement costs and where large numbers of new properties are being built. A major concern regarding the hotel industry is that its cycles can be very deep and violent; these are not investments for the faint-of-heart.

Another difficulty for investors in this area is finding hotel REITs without major conflicts of interest. Operating a hotel is a very management-intensive business, and the owner's success comes, in a large part, from the popularity of the hotel with business and individual consumers. "Operating" or "business" income cannot be received legally under the laws pertaining to REITs,[16] which means that the hotels must, in most cases, be leased to a third party which provides the management services. A REIT's owners might prefer the lessee to be an entity in which one or more affiliates of the REIT's management is actively involved (so that, at the least, a "known commodity" is operating the hotel and keeping an eye on operations). Such a situation creates obvious conflicts of interest between the REIT management's obligations to the REIT's shareholders and its ability to earn substantial management fees outside the REIT.

Two companies, however, have arrangements designed to avoid these conflicts. Starwood Lodging is structured through a "paired shares" arrangement which allows the REIT to own the hotel properties and a "sister" corporation (whose shares are owned by the REIT's shareholders) to manage the hotels. Patriot American Hospitality has recently agreed to acquire another corporation which, like Starwood's predecessor, has been "grandfathered" the right to operate on a paired share basis, and expects to complete such merger in 1997; the deal would allow Patriot, like Starwood, to manage its hotels through a sister corporation. These two REITs may be of interest to investors who would like to participate in the hotel sector but wish to avoid the major conflict-of-interest issues.

Pros	Cons
Early in the cycle (for luxury hotels)	Very cyclical business
RevPar is growing rapidly	Many hotel REITs have major conflicts of interest
Demand exceeds supply in some sectors	Inability to manage owned hotels
Attractive acquisitions still available	Overbuilding concerns

68

The following list provides certain relevant information concerning the publicly-traded hotel REITs as of October 31, 1996:

REIT	Stock Symbol	Market	# Facilities/ Rooms	Primary Locations	Approx. Market Cap
Patriot American Hospitality	PAH	NYSE	NA/7,392	NA	802
FelCor Suite Hotels	FCH	NYSE	34/4,880	USA	756
Hospitality Properties Trust	HPT	NYSE	82/11,700	USA	679
Starwood Lodging Trust	HOT	NYSE	50/11,600	USA	675
RFS Hotel Investors	RFS	NYSE	52/6,667	USA	395
Equity Inns	ENN	NYSE	27/4,444	USA	278
Boykin Lodging	BOY	NYSE	NA/NA	NA	223
Winston Hotels	WINN	OTC	21/2704	E,SE	214
American General Hospitality Corp	AGT	NYSE	NA/NA	NA	190
Innkeepers USA Trust	KPA	NYSE	21/2,411	USA	136
Sunstone Hotel Advisors	SSI	NYSE	13/2,009	USA	92
Jameson Inns	JAMS	OTC	39/1,935	SE	42
Host Funding	HFD	AMEX	NA/382	NA	12
Americana Hotels and Realty Corp	AHR	NYSE	1/192	W	7
					4,278

Manufactured Housing REITs. A number of years ago, an enterprising landowner brought a number of trailers, together with their owners, to a remote spot in the boonies, semi-affixed them to foundations and called the project a "mobile-home park." Many of today's modern "manufactured housing communities," however, bear little resemblance to yesterday's mobile-home park. The homes are now manufactured off-site, rarely leave their original home sites and many have the quality and appearance of site-built homes. According to an article in Barron's on the manufactured housing industry,[17] they accounted for more than one-third of all new single-family homes sold in the U.S. in 1996 (up from 25% in 1991), and about 370,000 manufactured homes were shipped that year; that amounted to $14 billion in total sales. Particularly in view of rapidly-rising rents in some parts of the U.S., manufactured homes clearly help to satisfy America's need for "affordable housing" (particularly for first-time home buyers).

The quality manufactured home community today looks something like a blend of a single-family home subdivision and a quality apartment building. The residents own their own home (the average price is about $40,000, compared with a nationwide median price of $120,000 for a site-built home) but lease the underlying land (typically at $150-300 per month) from the owner of the community. The home owners partake of such "community services" and amenities as a main entrance with attractive signage, clubhouse, pool, tennis courts, putting greens, exercise room and laundry facilities. Perhaps most of the communities cater to the elderly or retirees, but many are attracting younger couples who cannot afford to purchase more expensive site-built homes or who enjoy the extra amenities. According to the Manufactured Housing Institute, there are now more than seven million manufactured homes in the U.S., in which more 18 million people reside.

Owners of manufactured-home communities enjoy certain advantages not available to owners of apartment buildings. Tenant turnover is very low, due to the low monthly rental obligation (even assuming amortization of the loan incurred to buy the home) and the difficulty of selling the home or moving it elsewhere. The business is very recession-resistant, in a large part because of the low turnover rate. Capital expenditures required of the community owner are relatively small and are limited to upkeep and modest upgrading of the grounds and common facilities. And last, but certainly not least, overbuilding has rarely been a problem, due to the difficulties of getting land zoned for this type of property and the long lead time involved in filling a new community with tenant/owners.

The disadvantages experienced by owners and operators of manufactured-home communities include the periodic pressures for rent control in some states and localities and the difficulty and time-consuming nature of developing new communities or expanding existing communities.

All things considered, this is not a very glamorous business but is a very consistent and profitable one. Rental increases, even at 3-4% annually, together with modest debt leverage, provide for healthy growth in net income due to the low turnover rate and the absence of any requirement of the community owner to maintain the homes (which remains the responsibility of the home owner). Furthermore, because of the fragmented nature of manufactured-home community ownership throughout the U.S., profitable acquisitions can add an additional avenue for growth.

Four manufactured-home community REITs went public between February and November 1993, including Sun Communities, Manufactured Home Communities (led by the well-known real estate investor, Sam Zell), ROC Communities and Chateau Properties. Chateau and ROC, as this book went to press, had just completed a hotly-contested merger. Investors in these REITs should expect higher-than-average safety, dividend yields of close to 6% and steady (albeit unspectacular) profit and dividend growth.

Pros	Cons
Low tenant turnover	Periodic pressures for rent control
Stable & recession resistant business	Long lead times to complete new developments
High barriers to entry	Acquisition opportunities scarce
Low required capital expenditures	
Lack of overbuilding	

The following list provides certain relevant information concerning the publicly-traded manufactured home community REITs as of October 31, 1996:

REIT	Stock Symbol	Market	# Sites / Units	Primary Locations	Approx. Market Cap
Manufactured Home Communities	MHC	NYSE	66/26,284	USA	482
Sun Communities	SUI	NYSE	NA/18,200	MW,SE	417
ROC Communities	RCI	NYSE	71/21,041	NA	303
Chateau Properties	CPJ	NYSE	44/19,594	MW,SE	148
United Mobile Homes	UMH	AMEX	21/4,920	NE	76
					1,426

Diversified REITs. Some REITs are diversified as to property type, owning several different types in either the same geographical location or scattered throughout the U.S. This approach has not normally been conducive to success, but the REIT world is filled with exceptions and a well-managed, highly diversified property-type portfolio can be successful (particularly if concentrated in one geographical area). For many years, under the direction of the almost-legendary Franklin Kahn, Washington REIT provided outstanding returns to its investors despite owning apartments, office buildings, shopping centers and "business centers" (all located in the Washington, D.C., area). A newcomer to the diversified format is Colonial Properties, which has done quite well since going public in late 1993. All of this is proof-positive that in REIT investing, the quality of management is much more important (measured over meaningful time periods) than the nature of the specific property the REIT owns. (For more on what to look for when investing in a REIT, see Chapter Seven).

The following list provides certain relevant information concerning the publicly-traded diversified property REITs as of October 31, 1996:

REIT	Stock Symbol	Market	Primary Locations	Approx. Market Cap
Washington Real Estate Investment Trust	WRE	AMEX	E	496
Colonial Properties Trust	CLP	NYSE	SE	461
Allied Capital Commercial Corp	ALCC	OTC	USA	309
MGI Properties	MGI	NYSE	NE	221
Pennsylvania REIT	PEI	AMEX	E,SE	193
PMC Commercial Trust	PCC	AMEX	USA	180
Value Property Trust	VLP	NYSE	W	132
First Union Real Estate Investments	FUR	NYSE	N	125
Chicago Dock and Canal Trust	DOCKS	OTC	MW	118
EastGroup Properties	EGP	NYSE	SE,SW	117

CV REIT	CVI	NYSE	SE	102
Pacific Gulf Properties	PAG	NYSE	W	91
Property Capital Trust	PCT	AMEX	USA	89
Glenborough Realty Trust	GLB	NYSE	USA	79
Sizeler property Investors	SIZ	NYSE	SE	77
Commercial Assets	CAX	AMEX	NA	64
Franklin Select Realty Trust	FSN	AMEX	W	64
BRT Realty Trust	BRT	NYSE	E, MW, SE	46
National Income Realty Trust	NIRTS	OTC	NA	46
Banyan Strategic Realty Trust	VLANS	OTC	MW,SE	45
Continental Mortgage & Equity Trust	CMETS	OTC	NA	45
Metropolitan Realty Corp	MET	AMEX	MW	40
Trancontinental Realty Investors	TCI	NYSE	NA	40
Boddie-Noell Properties	BNP	AMEX	SE	38
Vanguard Real Estate Fund I	VRO	AMEX	USA	34
Angeles Mortgage Investment Trust	ANM	AMEX	USA	25
California REIT	CT	NYSE	W	22
Arizona Land Income Corp.	AZL	AMEX	SW	16
Income Opportunity Realty Investors	IOT	AMEX	NA	15
EQK Realty Investors I	EKR	NYSE	MW,SE	13
HMG/Courtland Properties	HMG	AMEX	NE,SE	7
				3,350

Mortgage REITs. Mention Mortgage REITs to most investors and their first reaction will be to string a garland of garlic around their necks. Nor do they garner much more respect from Wall Street Equity REIT analysts or their operating REIT peers. After all, many of the old, and now nonexistent, Mortgage REITs were responsible for dragging down REITs' investment returns in the 1970s and early 1980s. However, the few that have survived are much better run and have become market leaders within their defined niches. The difference between fact and perception, here as elsewhere in the investment world, can result in investment opportunities.

Unlike almost all of the *Equity* REITs, Mortgage REITs invest in financial instruments secured by real estate. Some examples would include federally backed or sponsored debt obligations such as Ginnie Mae, Fannie Mae and Freddie Mac securities or corporate sponsored commercial paper of the type issued by GMAC or GE Capital. To fully understand the underlying debt obligations and the potential financial implications of repayment schedules, credit risks, and different securitization options would require a serious lesson in fixed income analysis. However, we can simplify the analysis greatly by looking at three main points that generally apply to the Mortgage REIT industry today: (1) Mortgage REITs generally offer higher yields but less appreciation prospects than their Equity REIT peers, and they are much more interest rate sensitive —they can be excellent investments when interest rates are declining or stable such as in 1996 (and vice-versa); (2) managements have improved, over time, their ability to manage interest rate and portfolio risk; and (3) most importantly, management has been focusing more than ever before on building profitable businesses instead of just buying and selling paper — otherwise, investors could just as easily buy a bond fund. For example, Capstead Mortgage Corp., now the largest Mortgage REIT, has added a sophisticated loan servicing business to enhance shareholder returns. CWM Mortgage Holdings has created a home construction lending business; and CRIIMI MAE has developed a full commercial mortgage business, including origination and securitization capabilities. As you can see, to look upon all Mortgage REITs as merely bond surrogates does not do them justice. This sector of the REIT world, although highly specialized, should not be ignored. It can offer investors very substantial returns if shares are bought at the right time.

Pros	Cons
High dividend yield	Lower long-term appreciation potential
High returns during declining interest rate cycles	Highly sensitive to increasing interest rates
Improved interest sensitivity risk	No property appreciation potential
Adding new businesses	Still regarded as financial intermediaries

The following list provides certain relevant information concerning the publicly-traded Mortgage REITs as of October 31, 1996:

REIT	Stock Symbol	Market	# Properties / Sq. Ft. (MM)	Primary Locations	Approx. Market Cap
CWM Mortgage Holdings	CWM	NYSE	NA/NA	NA	923
Capstead Mortgage Corp	CMO	NYSE	NA/NA	NA	896
Resource Mortgage Capital	RMR	NYSE	NA/NA	NA	539
CRIIMI MAE	CMM	NYSE	NA/NA	NA	346
Redwood Trust	RWTI	OTC	NA/NA	NA	303
Thornburg Mortgage Asset	TMA	NYSE	NA/NA	NA	284
Imperial Credit Mortgage Holdings	IMH	ASE	NA/NA	NA	136
Asset Investors Corp	AIC	NYSE	NA/NA	NA	90
TIS Mortgage Investment Co.	TIS	NYSE	NA/NA	NA	6
					3,523

In the "old days" of REIT investing (prior to the 1993-1994 REIT IPO boom), REIT investors had little choice with respect to the property types in which they could invest. There were a few apartment REITs, several which invested in neighborhood shopping centers and a handful of others. Today's REIT investor can own apartments, malls, neighborhood shopping centers, outlet centers, offices, industrial properties, health-care facilities, self-storage properties, hotels, manufactured-housing communities and golf

73

courses, owning properties in many different locations. The choices are vast; the challenge is to buy and own the right ones.

[1] As quoted in "The Ground Floor," by Barry Vinocur, Barron's, March 11, 1996.

[2] Realty Stock Review, January 31, 1996, p. 1.

[3] "Oversupply Opens Opportunities," Forbes, April 8, 1996. Notwithstanding this negative statistic, according to Stillerman Jones & Co., shoppers spent an average of $48 per hour at the malls in 1995, a 17% increase from 1991; see "Tempting the Jaded Shopper," Forbes, May 20, 1996.

[4] For example, DeBartolo Realty Corporation's comparable mall store sales increased on a sales per square foot basis from $248 in 1990 to $267 in 1995, an average compounded annual gain during that time of only 1.5%.

[5] "Tempting the Jaded Shopper," Forbes, May 20, 1996.

[6] Value Retail News (May 1996), p. 14.

[7] Value Retail News (May 1996), p. 14.

[8] Montgomery Securities, "The REIT Review," December 1995, p. 60.

[9] Green Street Advisors, Inc. Research Report on The Factory Outlet REITs, August 1995, p. 7-8.

[10] Ibid., p. 7.

[11] Barron's, "The Ground Floor," by Barry Vinocur, p.36.

[12] "Industrial REIT Peer Group Analysis," dated June 26, 1996, by Apogee Associates, LLC.

[13] Self-Storage Almanac, 1995-1996.

[14] Self-Storage Almanac, 1995-1996.

[15] Green Street Advisors, Inc. issued an excellent report covering the dynamics of this industry. See "The Self-Storage Industry," February 9, 1995.

[16] A REIT must derive at least 75% of its gross income from rents, mortgage interest, gains on the sale of property and other real-estate related items. Income derived from managing a hotel is considered as income from an operating business, and is thus outside these categories. However, leasing the hotel to an outside management company "transforms" the business income into rental income.

[17] "No Laughingstock," by Harlan S. Byrne, Barron's, January 6, 1997, p. 15.

Part II

History and Mythology

Chapter Four

Of Ugly Ducklings and REIT Myths

"I don't get no respect!"
— **Rodney Dangerfield**

All right, you've got the REIT basics now. You know what they are, where they invest their funds, and what kinds of returns they produce. You may even, by this time, be mulling a call to your broker for an overhaul of your portfolio. Or you may not (at least not yet!). If you're one of those cautious types, you might be raising an eyebrow while thoughts of "too-good-to-be-true" run through your head.

And that brings us to our next question.

If REITs are so good, how come so few investors own them, and why do people look at you funny when you advocate their purchase?

The reason is twofold: First, they're neither fish nor fowl (and still yet to be seen as swans!) in the investment world, and, second, there are certain myths and misconceptions surrounding REITs that they haven't been able to shake off.

Outcasts in the Investment Community

Despite their long history, REITs have never been able to shed their status as investment orphans. They have always been regarded as somehow "different" from traditional investments. Even their name — "REIT" — implies that the standard criteria applicable to most investments don't apply to them ("that's not a regular company, Mr. Jones, that's a REIT — forget about it"). Standard & Poors still will not admit even the largest REIT into their S&P500 Index. Bruce Andrews, the very astute C.E.O. of Nationwide Health Properties, noted that even the term "Trust," as in Real Estate Investment *Trust*, implies that REITs are not like normal companies. One of the main reasons for their being outcasts is that most investors in real estate have been uncomfortable with the concept of a publicly traded real estate security, while most investors in common stocks have rarely taken the time to understand REITs.

Fish: Traditional Real Estate Investors

Traditionally, most real estate investors have invested in property directly, whether it be apartment complexes, shopping centers, malls, office buildings or industrial properties, and not in real estate securities. That's bricks and mortar, not pieces of paper. Direct ownership historically has provided the opportunity to use substantial leverage, as for many years lenders would loan 60-80% of the purchase price of a building. Leverage is a wonderful thing when prices are going up, and for decades (since the Great Depression) real estate values pursued a relentless upward path, albeit not without some major blips along the road. Appreciation of 10% on a building bought with 25% cash down would generate 40% in capital gains. Further, being able to take depreciation expense on a building owned directly would provide the investor with operating income that could be largely tax-sheltered. As a result, when real estate continues to appreciate and provide easy profits, most real estate investors will focus on direct ownership.

Psychology may also hurt REITs' cause. Many real estate investors distrust public markets, which are often regarded as gigantic commodity pits where one's assets are at the mercy not only of faceless managers but also feckless investors. A large number of such investors will be entirely uninterested in owning REITs which, after all, share as many characteristics with common stocks as they do with real estate. I recently visited our local Barnes & Noble bookstore and checked out the "Real Estate" section; there were hundreds of books on how to buy, finance, manage and make profits on real estate but not one on investing in publicly traded real estate securities.

Then there's institutional investment in real estate. For many years institutional and pension funds "earmarked" for real estate have been invested in properties either directly (where their own property and investment managers were retained) or through "commingled funds" sponsored by the huge insurance companies where funds provided by various institutional investors are "commingled," or added together, and used to buy portfolios of properties. Who managed these properties, supervised their performance and answered for their results? Real estate people, of course. And these guys have always classified REITs as common stocks, with the result that any decision to invest in REITs could be made only by the *"equities* investment officer" rather than the *"real estate* investment officer" of the institution or pension fund. The institutions' common stock investment funds were placed and monitored elsewhere. Furthermore, various "investment guidelines" have often precluded the equities investment officers from investing in REITs even if they knew about them and wanted to pursue this sector of the market. So why should they even bother?

A further discouragement has been volatility. Real estate investors have complained that REITs, even though less volatile than the broader stock market, nevertheless fluctuate in price. With non-traded assets (and by relying upon occasional appraisals), the private fund managers could maintain the illusion that the values

78

of their assets were "steady as a rock" despite the real ebbs and flows of the real estate markets.

Finally, institutions buy and sell stocks in large blocks, and it's been only recently that REIT shares have had sufficient liquidity to attract institutional types. In fact, one of the most oft-quoted reasons why pension funds have been reluctant to invest in REITs is their "lack of liquidity." The REIT market was pretty thinly traded prior to 1993-1994, when its size expanded geometrically, and it would have been quite difficult for an institution to accumulate even a modest position in a REIT without disrupting its trading market.

As a result of these dynamics, real estate people, both individual and institutional, historically have had little interest in acquiring interests in real estate indirectly through common stock investments in REITs. In fact, ever since REITs were "invented," they have been discussed in the financial press as a suitable way for real estate to be owned by "the little guy," who presumably has neither the time, the resources, nor the expertise to invest in real estate on his own. But what self-respecting real estate investor wants to be regarded as "the little guy"? REITs, therefore, have never been taken seriously by individual or institutional *real estate* investors, on the grounds that "REITs aren't real estate."

Fowl: Common Stock Investors

REITs, then, are not "fish" to the real estate anglers. But neither are they the "fowl" that common stock investors are gunning for. As a result, REITs have not been taken any more seriously by common stock investors than they've been taken by real estate investors. There are many reasons for this.

First and foremost, REITs' only business is real estate, and stock investors focus primarily on companies who manufacture products or provide services; real estate is perceived, with substantial justification, as a different "asset class." This problem is particularly acute in the institutional world where, as we have seen, the decision to invest in REITs rests with officers who are generally not familiar with real estate investments and are thus not inclined to pursue the investment opportunities in REITs. Second, the public perception of REITs is that they are "high-risk" but low-return investments. Even though way off the mark, this perception has caused most common stock investors to shy away from REITs. Third, those investors who bought construction-lending REITs in the late '60s and early '70s got badly burned, as did many others via real estate limited partnerships bought in the '80s. These investors have not taken the trouble to distinguish between these ill-fated real estate-related investments and well-managed Equity REITs; they have long memories and, like generals, they are always fighting the last war.

Fourth, investors have long been told that companies which pay out a high percentage of their income in dividends do not retain much of their earnings and cannot grow rapidly. And, to most common stock investors, growth is the hallmark of successful investing; who wants to invest in a company that cannot grow? Finally, the lack of individual investors' interest in REITs is typified by the fact that, until the last few years, most major brokerage firms did not even employ a REIT analyst. Stock brokers were never educated as to REITs' investment characteristics or total return potential and, as a result, generally have not recommended REITs for their clients. When was the last time your stock broker suggested that you buy a REIT (aside from the occasional underwritten offering where the commissions to the brokers are unusually generous)?

Other than recommendations by one's local stockbroker, most folks who desire to invest in common stocks buy mutual funds. While a handful of mutual funds are devoted to REIT investments, they do not advertise widely, and finding them takes a good deal of initiative. The amount of investment funds being put into individual common stocks today by the individual investor, apart from brokers' recommendations and mutual funds, is but a very small segment of the available investment capital. Further, such do-it-yourself investors quite likely feel that they need a significant background in the peculiarities of the REIT world to venture into this area, and it's a simple fact that most of them don't take the trouble to pursue it. Instead, they prefer to invest in growth stocks (whether high-tech, small caps or whatever), while those who are income-oriented have, for many years, invested primarily in bonds and electric utilities, with a few convertible preferreds thrown in for diversification.

Neither Fish Nor Fowl

The bottom line is that traditional real estate investors, both individual and institutional, have not followed nor been interested in REITs, on the basis that they are common stocks, not real estate. And traditional common stock investors, both individual and institutional, have not followed nor been interested in REITs, on the basis that they are really just real estate, and have little to do with common stock investing. *Neither fish nor fowl* — the ugly ducklings of the investment world. Will REITs' outcast status continue, or will they be adopted by either real estate investors or common stock investors? It's likely that *both* groups of investors will come to know and love REITs. Although it's too early to claim victory, REITs are steadily gaining interest in the investment community and will not remain castoffs forever. Indeed, if the widespread buying of REIT shares in 1996 is any indication, REITs' long period of neglect may already be a relic of the past.

"Neither Fish"...real estate investors	"Nor Fowl"...common stock investors
Direct ownership preferred	Focus on manufacturers & service cos.
Distrust of public markets	Perception of high risk
Lack of interest by real estate investment officers	Confusion with limited partnerships
Price volatility	Perception as slow-growth companies
Lack of liquidity	Lack of interest by stockbrokers
	Mutual funds have ignored REITs

The Myths about REITs

As if being neither fish nor fowl weren't a sufficient obstacle to garnering investors' affections, REITs have had to contend with a number of myths that have scared off all but the bravest investors. Although these myths are based upon misunderstandings of the investment characteristics of REITs, they have discouraged many would-be investors and have caused them to view these investment swans in a much less favorable light. Let's review them.

Myth: REITs Are Packages of Real Properties

This myth, which is probably based upon many investors' experience with the ill-fated real estate limited partnerships of the late '80s and some of the sleepy REITs of yesteryear, may be the single most important reason for REITs' past failure to attract a substantial investment following. Whatever REITs may have been a number of years ago (and some of them were indeed collections of properties), such is certainly not the case for most today.

Companies that merely own and manage a basket of properties — whether they be limited partnerships, REITs or any other type — face several specific investment concerns. First, experienced and imaginative management is apt to be in short supply, and mediocre management is unlikely to react quickly to the problems that inevitably arise in real estate markets from time to time. Second, management of such passive companies is unlikely to be given the compensation incentives necessary for a successful real estate business in today's highly competitive environment. Third, long-term planning and the development of effective growth strategies are unlikely to be found in such entities, as they are lacking the motivation and resources. Finally, access to attractively priced capital is unlikely to be available, which makes it unlikely that the REIT will be able to take advantage of the opportunities presented by "buyers' markets." An investment in such a company, although perhaps providing an attractive dividend yield, offers little or no opportunity for growth or expansion beyond the original portfolio.

Conversely, a very large number of today's REITs are vibrant, dynamic real estate organizations first and "investment trusts"

81

second.   They can boast of entrepreneurial and incentivized management that has many years of real estate operating and development experience and that owns significant equity stakes in the company.   They plan intelligently and carefully for property acquisitions and developments in either areas they know well or areas in which they perceive they can become dominant players. And they have easy access to the necessary capital with which to carry out their growth plans. To think of a Beacon, Federal, Kimco, Post Properties, Simon DeBartolo, Security Capital Industrial, United Dominion or Weingarten, for example, as merely a collection of properties is ludicrous. Yet this myth still persists.

Myth: Real Estate Is a High-Risk Investment

Another major reason for REITs' lack of investment popularity is the concept that real estate (other than one's own home, of course), is a "high-risk" investment. The idea is that investors can be wiped out by tenant defaults, declines in property values, sudden increases in vacancies, a downturn in the quality of the neighborhood, earthquakes, locusts, acts of God, whatever, and thus the risks in owning real estate must be exceedingly high. Likewise, investing in REITs (which, after all, do own property) must also be very risky. The problem with this thinking is that it doesn't take into account three essential determinants of risk: leverage, diversification and management quality.

Leverage. Leverage is no different in real estate than in any other investment endeavor: The more of it you use, the greater your potential gain or loss. *Any* asset carried on high margin, whether an office building, a blue-chip stock or even T-notes, will involve substantial risk, as a small decline in the asset's value will cause a much larger decline in one's investment in it. However, because real estate historically has been bought and financed with lots of debt, many investors have confused the risk of debt leverage with that of owning real estate.   In other words, simply because real estate investors have been able to borrow a high percentage of a property's value from a willing bank or other lender doesn't, by itself, mean that real estate, as an investment asset, carries with it high risk.   In fact, there's a better argument the other way, *i.e.*, that if lenders will loan a higher percentage of a real estate asset's value than the Federal Reserve will allow banks and brokers to loan on a stock investment, the former should be less risky than the latter.

Diversification. As with any investment, diversification is a critical concern when buying into real estate.   Highly intelligent persons, who would never dream of owning a portfolio consisting of only a single stock, go out and buy, individually or with friends or business associates, a single apartment building. Things happen — an earthquake, neighborhood deterioration, a recession — and all of a sudden the building becomes a money-losing venture. Never mind

82

that a similar apartment building thousands of miles away (or even in another part of town) is doing great, or that an office building upstate is hauling it in. Investors who own real estate directly often forget that cardinal rule of investing: diversification. So when the going gets tough, many investors rashly conclude that real estate as a whole is an extraordinarily risky asset class. The investor similarly might just as well label the stock market as being an extremely high-risk endeavor following his investment in a single stock that heads south.

Management Quality. Then, of course, there is the issue of management. As Chapter Seven will explain, the quality of management is as crucial in real estate as it is in any other commercial endeavor. Just as incompetent management can ruin what would otherwise be a profitable business, neglect, poor execution and mismanagement can ruin a promising real estate investment. Real estate, like virtually all other types of investments, cannot simply be bought and forgotten about; it requires active and highly capable management. Yet many intelligent investors have bought apartment buildings, small offices or local shopping centers and tried to manage them themselves in their part time or have hired local "managers" who are given no incentives to manage the property intelligently. What happens? The building does poorly, the investor loses a bundle, and he then concludes that real estate is a high-risk investment. Obviously, it can be, but no more so than a business that's neglected, or managed by stumblebums.

Owning real estate is an investment much like any other. In many ways, running it properly and profitably is a business, just like any other. The intelligence, foresight and imagination with which real estate is managed will usually determine its long-term success as an investment; in this way, it's no different from any other business investment, whether traded on the New York Stock Exchange or run by Mom and Pop. And taking on debt leverage will add to the risks and rewards in both endeavors. But the assertion that real estate is "high-risk" and that owning it, directly or through a REIT, is dangerous to one's financial health, is merely a misconception that discourages investors from examining the significant opportunities presented to them every trading day in the REIT world.

Myth: Real Estate Is a Good Investment Primarily During Times of High Inflation

This myth assumes that real estate (and, indirectly, REITs) are good investments during periods of high inflation, but mediocre or even poor performers when inflation is well under control. Real estate is really nothing more than just buildings and land and, like all assets (whether scrap metal, oil or used cars), its value will ebb and flow with local, national and even global supply and demand

83

conditions, as well as conditions in the capital markets. Inflation is only one factor that affects these market conditions; others are interest rates, recessions, unemployment, consumer spending, levels of new personal and business investment, government policies and even wars. The ownership and operation of commercial real estate is a business, much like any other, and its success will depend upon many factors besides inflation.

Part of the reason for the real estate-as-inflation-hedge myth may come from the fact that real estate happened to do well during the inflationary 1970s, while stock ownership was not as productive. This, quite likely, was a simple coincidence. According to data compiled by Ibbotson Associates,[1] equities have been very good inflation hedges over many decades. So has real estate. But the reality is that neither real estate nor equities are substantially better or worse in this regard.

Yes, there are times when inflation appears to help the real estate investor by boosting the replacement cost of real estate; but such inflation can also significantly hammer a property's net operating income and thus negatively affect its market value. The value of a commercial building is determined essentially by two factors: the amount of rental and net operating income the owner can earn from the property (now and in the future) and the multiple of that income that the typical prospective buyer will pay for it. Both of these factors change over time in response to various market forces, and inflation is only one of many.

High inflation rates can positively or negatively affect rental rates and net operating income. The positive influence, at least in the retail sector, can come from the higher tenant sales that normally result from increased inflation and higher prices on goods sold to consumers. These higher sales can translate into higher rents for the property owner, but this benefit will be transitory in nature if the retailer is unable to maintain its profit margins; otherwise, this "profitless prosperity" will not justify higher rental rates when the lease comes up for renewal (percentage rent clauses will help the property owner for a time, but there's only so much blood one can squeeze out of a turnip). Similarly, higher inflation can help apartment owners by increasing tenants' wages and thus their ability to afford higher rental rates, but only if wages are rising at least as rapidly as the prices for goods and services.

When supply and demand are in balance for a particular property type in a particular location, inflation may enable the owner to raise rents for the use of his property. This is because development and construction costs to build new competing properties will rise in inflationary environments, and developers will need higher rents in order to make new developments profitable. If the demand is sufficient to absorb the new units coming into the market, owners of pre-existing properties will often be able to take advantage of the new property's "price umbrella" to charge higher rents to their own tenants. However, real estate is not an effective "hedge against inflation" when there is a large oversupply of property in the relevant market.[2]

Higher inflation rates can also negatively affect the value of real estate. As the Federal Reserve's "Public Enemy No. 1" is high inflation, short-term interest rates normally rise when the inflation ogre rears its ugly head. Rising interest rates generally will slow the economy and can sometimes choke it into recession. A slow or recessionary economy is not conducive to a property owner's ability to raise rents and increase net operating income at the property level.

Now to the second part of the property value equation: the multiple a buyer of property will place upon the property's net operating income (or its reciprocal, the cap rate). There is an argument that buyers will sometimes be willing to pay more for, or accept a lower cap rate on, real property during inflationary periods. Investors often view real estate as a "hard asset," such as gold and other commodities, and may be willing to pay a higher multiple for every dollar of operating income if they think that inflation will enable them to increase future rental income at a healthy pace, or that another buyer will offer them an even higher multiple in the near future.

Nevertheless, cap rates are determined essentially by supply and demand forces, which in turn (in the absence of the occasional real estate mania) are influenced primarily by both interest rates and expectations with respect to the pace of future rental and net operating income growth, as well as the perceived security of the anticipated rental stream. Cap rates may indeed be influenced by inflation, but in reverse. Higher inflation may drive up interest rates, which in turn will increase the "hurdle rate of return" demanded by investors in a property; this will have the effect of increasing the required cap rate and *decreasing* the price at which the property can be sold.

As an example, if the demand for apartments in, say, San Francisco exceeds the available supply of such units, rental rates will increase and the apartment building owner's net operating income will increase. Furthermore, assuming that interest rates remain stable and that investors believe that such apartments' operating income will continue to increase for an extended period, the cap rate for similarly situated buildings is likely to drop. In other words, buyers will accept a lower yield on their investment in a property and be willing to pay a higher purchase price for each dollar of operating income expected to be received from the operation of such "hot" properties. In such a situation, the owner of the San Francisco apartment building will do very well despite the lack of inflationary conditions. On the other hand, if the supply of existing apartment units in San Francisco exceeds the demand by renters, rents will not rise nor will the apartment building's value appreciate even during inflationary periods. In such a case the apartment owner's efforts to boost rental rates merely will be answered by his tenants moving down the street, and it would be very unlikely that the value of the apartment building would rise notwithstanding a high rate of inflation.

Thus market factors such as supply and demand are almost always much more important than prevailing inflationary conditions in determining a property's value at any particular time. If that is so, investors in real estate, including REITs, should focus much more on existing and prospective market conditions and management's ability to respond to such conditions than whether or not higher inflation is just around the corner.

Myth: Investors Must be Bullish on Real Estate to be Bullish on REITs

Real estate, throughout many periods of U.S. history, has been a great investment. At other times, it's been a lousy investment, to which owners of downtown office buildings (until quite recently), apartment buildings in the late '80s, and single-family residences in the '90s will readily attest. While most real estate markets today are not suffering from an oversupply of properties, there appears to be no clear consensus as to whether "real estate," as an asset class, will be a particularly good investment through the rest of the decade and into the 21st century.

After the stock market has risen quickly and forcefully following a long bear market, observers have an apt expression: "The easy money has already been made." In the real estate markets, most sectors have rebounded very well from the depression-like years of the late 1980s and the early 1990s, and the easy money has been made there, too. Thus as the twentieth century draws to a close it is likely that in many sectors of the real estate industry it will be difficult for property owners to generate investment returns significantly in excess of existing property cash flows.

The rapid industrialization and intense competition occurring today in North America, Europe, Asia and Latin America seem to be major and perhaps long-lasting phenomena. Today, we are all capitalists, even in the former Soviet Union and in China. The good news is that we've won the Cold War; the bad news is that we've got to compete on a global basis. U.S. companies must now go toe-to-toe with foreign competitors virtually everywhere in the world. This, in turn, requires our businesses to be very cost-efficient, which has forced downsizings, restructurings and lay-offs. Companies find it very difficult to raise prices, and employees find it equally as difficult to get higher wages. As a result, business tenants resist significant rental increases from owners of offices and industrial properties.

Likewise, consumers are exceedingly stingy with their spending money, which in turn causes retailers to resist substantial rent hikes from retail property owners. For their part, renters, trying to make do with stagnant wages, will pick up and move rather than pay a hefty apartment rent increase.

No end to these trends is in sight; they are keeping the rate of inflation well under control, which continues to surprise economists. Although same-property net operating income has been strong in many real estate sectors during the last three to four years as real estate has rebounded from its depressed conditions of the late '80s and early '90s, this trend may not continue in the face of highly competitive conditions everywhere. The bottom line for real estate owners is that, as long as these competitive trends continue, it will be difficult for rents and "same-store" net operating income to rise at rates much beyond inflation.[3]

Yet it doesn't necessarily follow that those who are cautious (or even negative) on real estate generally should shun all REITs. It is true that those REITs that are little more than portfolios of individual properties will not be particularly attractive to the real estate bears. But today, as noted above, a significant number of REITs are much more than just bundles of properties supervised by mediocre management; these high-quality REITs are real estate organizations run by savvy, imaginative and experienced entrepreneurs who can cause their REIT to do well and even thrive under hostile real estate environments.[4]

How can this be? It's an ill wind that blows no one good, to which Joseph Kennedy could attest as he bought up much of New York City at rock-bottom prices during the Great Depression. Great managements take advantage of difficult conditions and turn them into opportunities. United Dominion and Merry Land went on buying sprees during the apartment depression of the late '80s and early '90s. Nationwide Health, Health Care Properties and LTC Properties bought defaulted nursing home loans from the RTC at 16-18% yields. Kimco has bought poorly performing shopping malls and turned them into open-air shopping complexes occupied by vibrant tenants.

Reckson Associates, in 1995, bought back the same suburban office building at $78 per square foot that it sold to John Hancock Insurance in 1981 for $100 per square foot, which in turn sold the same property to an investment group in 1987 for $165 per square foot. Vornado bought a controlling interest in Alexander's out of bankruptcy and will take full advantage of its great retail locations. Several years ago, Weingarten actually *increased* its occupancy rates during the Texas oil bust, as quality tenants vacated half-empty locations and migrated to Weingarten's attractive shopping centers. These are but a few examples of how lemons can be turned into lemonade by imaginative and capable real estate organizations with access to capital.

Conversely, it often happens that good real estate markets are *bad* for REITs. For example, many REITs encountered significant difficulties in the mid-'80s, when real estate prices were skyrocketing. Most REITs during that time period couldn't find properties to buy at prices that would provide acceptable returns for their shareholders. In addition, their properties experienced difficulties competing against newly constructed properties in what rapidly were becoming overbuilt markets. As a result, the FFO growth of most REITs slowed markedly during such period.

To illustrate the point further, take a quick look at the apartment sector. What would happen to apartment markets if a severe recession hit? The picture would not be pretty for apartment owners. Markets previously in equilibrium could weaken considerably. Occupancy rates would decline and rents would stay flat, at best. Market values of apartment buildings would likely fall. Most apartment REITs would report flat to declining FFO, and their stock prices could fall; dividends could be stagnant until recovery arrived. But Equity Residential, Merry Land, Security Capital Pacific, United Dominion and a significant number of other quality apartment REITs would be out there buying apartments at exceedingly attractive entry yields, taking full advantage of these difficult conditions. While FFO growth could slow temporarily in response to difficult rental markets, these REITs' ability to buy sound properties at cheap prices would allow FFO to grow quickly when market conditions stabilize.

It is worth noting that during the very difficult apartment market climate of 1989-1991, United Dominion's FFO grew very slowly, due to declining occupancies and slow rental growth. Yet that period was one of the best for apartment buyers, and United Dominion bought its full share of available properties. Further, there were few competing buyers. Not only was this REIT able to buy at very cheap prices, but it also took full advantage of rising occupancies and rental rates when the market stabilized starting in 1992. As a result, United Dominion's FFO grew sharply from 1992 through 1995, more than making up for the slow growth of two years earlier.

One final caveat is in order here. The extent to which a well-managed REIT is able to take advantage of acquisition opportunities in order to offset temporarily declining internal growth due to weakness in its markets depends, in large part, upon several factors. These include the amount (and cost) of financing available to the REIT, the depth of the market weakness and the extent to which it encounters competition for great deals. Nevertheless, the above example of United Dominion shows that poor markets need not be all bad for high-quality REITs which happen to own and manage

88

properties in poorly performing sectors, and can often provide a springboard for a period of future highly rapid growth.

Some of the best investment opportunities arise when a company or even an entire industry is overlooked or misunderstood by the great mass of investors. Legendary investors Warren Buffett and Peter Lynch have made their reputations not by buying the growth stocks that everyone else owns but rather by taking advantage of investors' misperceptions. Buffett's investment in Wells Fargo Bank is a good example. While most investors and cocky short-sellers were predicting disaster for this California bank several years ago, he knew that investors were caught up in the "impending collapse of the major banks" and completely blind to Wells Fargo's strengths and staying power. He took full advantage of the situation.

The same principle applies to REITs. Investors' fears and hesitations have, until very recently, left these lucrative investments largely undiscovered. Like our good friend Mr. Dangerfield and the little unloved duckling, REITs have been unjustly shunned. However, at least in regard to investor perceptions, much respect and admiration is in store. The change in perception has already begun, and astute investors are now beginning to see REITs as beautiful, feather-preening swans.

---

[1] Ibbotson Associates, "Stocks, Bonds, Bills and Inflation 1995 Yearbook."

[2] See "Why Should Anyone Invest in Commercial Real Estate Under Today's Market Conditions?", a paper written and presented by Anthony Downs, Senior Fellow at The Brookings Institution, dated May 1996. Mr. Downs concludes that there is a very good case that can be made for investing in commercial real estate as a diversification to common stock investments. The same point has been made by numerous others, including Burton Malkiel, Professor of Economics at Princeton University and author of "A Random Walk Down Wall Street." However, neither of these scholars cited inflation as a reason to own real estate.

[3] Judicious use of the leverage provided by debt financing, particularly if fixed-rate in nature, may enable property owners to increase investment returns by an extra one or two percent. Of course, risk is also increased.

[4] A study was recently done by Messrs. Mahoney, McCarron, Miles and Sirmans and the results published in an article appearing in Real Estate Finance, entitled "Location Differences in Public and Private Investment", which compared the performance of the NAREIT Equity Index (without Health Care REITs) to the NCREIF Property Index (a proxy for institutionally-owned properties) for the period 1986 through 1995. Although there are many factors which make a comparison between the two indices a bit like comparing apples and oranges, the study found that the correlation between the two "series" was actually *negative*, meaning that there was no apparent relationship in performance between REITs and institutionally-held real estate. Others, however, have disagreed, attributing the differences in performance to different methods of analysis.

For example, Michael Giliberto, in a speech given at the NAREIT Institutional Investors' Forum in Chicago on November 13, 1996, stated that much of the apparent differences in performance between the NAREIT Equity REIT Index and the NCREIF Index can be attributed to the very different nature of these indices and the failure to make necessary adjustments.

Chapter Five

A Short History of REITs and REIT Prices

"Those who do not know history are condemned to relive it."
— **George Santayana**

As investors, we want to be equipped with as many useful tools as possible. Those of you who believe that a good understanding of history is helpful to the investment process will want to know how REITs and their stocks have behaved over the last 35 years. The answer is: Like a child, like a teen-ager and like an adult, depending upon which time period you examine. Like any new creation, REITs have undergone a lifetime of development and experienced their share of growing pains. Here, we'll take a look at those developments — specifically, how REITs performed in their infancy, how they created havoc in their wild adolescent years and how they've matured into solid citizens of the investment world.

Infancy: The 1960s

The first REITs were born a few years after the REIT format was officially sanctioned by Congress and signed into law in 1960; REITs were authorized for the purpose of allowing individuals to "pool their investments" in real estate in order to get the same benefits as might be obtained by direct ownership. However, they were not pretty babies by today's standards. There were very few REITs in existence during the 1960s and they were all small in size. Most of them were managed by outside advisors, and all property management functions were handled by outside management companies (many of which were affiliated with the advisor — which created significant conflicts of interest). Their market caps were miniscule, and their portfolios were very small at the beginning. For example, in the early 1960s Washington REIT (one of the few survivors) had a portfolio of just over $10 million; one of the larger REITs, REIT of America, owned less than $50 million in properties. Their total real estate investments in the early years amounted to just $200 million. For comparison purposes, at the end of 1995, according to NAREIT, REITs owned assets of more than $88 *billion*.[1] In addition to the REITs' use of outside advisors, lack of internal property management and small size, REIT insiders owned very few shares — typically less than 1%. Despite these weaknesses, a Goldman Sachs report[2] shows that these early-era REITs turned in a pretty respectable performance, aided by generally healthy real estate markets in the 1960s. "Cash flow" (an early version of today's

91

funds from operations) grew 5.8% annually, on average, and the average dividend yield was 6.1%. Assuming that the multiples of cash flow which investors were willing to pay for these early REITs remained steady, investors would have enjoyed an average annual total return of approximately 11.5%. Not a bad performance, considering that from 1963 to 1970 the S&P500's annual total return averaged only 6.7%. Thus, despite their numerous initial weaknesses, the performance of these new babes of the investment world embarrassed their more well-established common stock siblings.

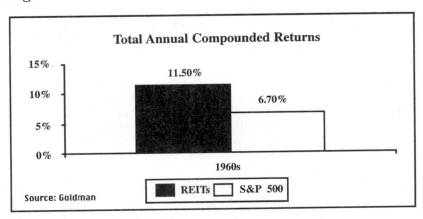

Adolescence and Turbulence: The 1970s

The 1970s were tumultuous times for the economy and the stock market, and REITs were similarly affected. Inflation, driven by the OPEC-led explosion in oil prices, roared out of control, as evidenced by the Consumer Price Index, which increased 6.3% in 1973, 11% in 1974 and 9.1% in 1975. This menace continued to soar throughout the rest of the decade, ending with an 11.3% increase in 1979.

Not content with such external hardships, the REIT industry was busy creating problems of its own. Between 1968 and 1970, with the willing connivance of many investment bankers, the industry hatched 58 new Mortgage REITs. Most of these used a modest amount of shareholders' equity and huge amounts of borrowed funds to provide short-term loans to the construction industry, which in turn built hundreds of office buildings throughout the United States (many of which would later be referred to as "see-throughs" — they had so few tenants you could see right through 'em). Such stalwart banks as Bank of America, Chase, Wachovia and Wells Fargo got into the act, and it seemed no self-respecting major bank wanted to be left out in sponsoring its own REIT. Largely as a result of these new Mortgage REITs, the REIT industry's total assets mushroomed from $1 billion in 1968 to $20 billion by the mid-1970s.

When the office building market — hammered by high interest rates driven up by the onslaught of inflation — began weakening in 1973, the new Mortgage REITs found that leverage works both ways. Helped along by some pretty sloppy underwriting standards, non-performing assets got way out of control, rising to close to 75% of invested assets by the end of 1974 — needless to say, share prices for these Mortgage REITs virtually collapsed. Investors tend to have long memories, and their investment experience with the Mortgage REITs caused them to become disenchanted with the entire REIT industry for many years thereafter. For the first time, "REIT" became a four-letter word.

Ironically, outside of these Mortgage REITs (the ungainly behemoths of the REIT world at that time), non-lending *Equity* REITs didn't do badly during the decade of the '70s, as most real estate markets remained strong. Federal Realty and New Plan, among others, made their first appearances, and these retail property REITs have done quite well for investors in the years that followed. While asset growth slowed, operating performance was reasonably good, as a group of Equity REITs charted by the Goldman Sachs report referred to earlier turned in a 6.1% compounded annual growth rate in cash flow during this decade, and growth was negative in only one of such years. These Equity REITs also enjoyed an average annual compounded growth rate of 4.2% in their stock prices, which, when added to their dividend yields, produced a compounded total annual return of 12.9% during the '70s. Compared with the total compounded annual rate of return of 5.8% for the S&P500 index, the Equity REITs did very well indeed in the unsettled '70s.

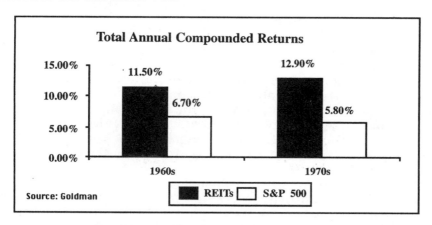

Nevertheless, as the decade drew to a close, REITs were still unloved outcasts in much of the investment community, as investor sentiment during that decade focused upon the spectacular crash and burn of the Mortgage REITs. By then, most investors had come to disdain REITs and didn't distinguish between the solid, if slowly growing, Equity REITs and their villainous siblings, the construction loan-oriented Mortgage REITs. Furthermore, virtually no pension money was allocated to the Equity REITs during this time; not only were they unproved and their stocks too illiquid for the institutions, but also most of them still lacked independent management. Further, very few of them focused upon specific property types in specific geographical regions. The term "local sharpshooter" was virtually unheard of in the REIT world at that time. Yes, there were a few exceptions such as Washington REIT, Federal Realty and New Plan, but by and large the REITs were still suffering growing pains and were not widely respected. That their stocks did as well as they did in the '60s and '70s was largely a result of stable and growing markets in most real estate sectors throughout much of that period and, in a few cases, very good management, but certainly not as a result of general interest and knowledge by investors.

The 'Overbuilding Ogre' Rears Its Head: The 1980s

As we've just seen, despite the wild inflation and the Mortgage REIT fiasco of the 1970s, real estate in general and REITs in particular didn't fare too badly during those years, notwithstanding the problems with office buildings. As the '70s drew to a close, investors of all types were feeling "asset-minded" and, like generals who continue to fight the last war, they looked for "hard assets" such as gold, silver and other commodities in which to invest so as to protect themselves from the high inflation they were certain would continue. During the early 1980s, real estate and its cousins, the Equity REITs, benefited from this investment environment.

The inflation of the '70s caused construction costs to mushroom, which made new building uneconomical unless rents rose enough to provide a reasonable return on new investment capital. As occupancy rates rose, real estate owners (including, of course, the REITs) were able to substantially increase their rental rates; for several years, there was little new building, as it would take some time before rents rose to the point where new construction could be justified. Building was also significantly inhibited by the extraordinarily high mortgage rates of the early '80s, which ranged from 10-15%. This favorable supply/demand imbalance favored property owners, which led to most REITs reporting healthy increases in funds from operations during the early 1980s. During this period the Equity REITs' annual total rates of return to shareholders were truly awe-inspiring; for the six years from 1980 through 1985, such total returns, respectively, were (as reported by NAREIT) 24.4%, 6.0%, 21.6%, 30.6%, 20.9% and 19.1%.

But, as Ecclesiastes once said, "For all things there is a season, ..." and the good times went out of season in the last half of the decade. The outstanding returns achieved by real estate owners in the early '80s did not go unnoticed by investors, public and private, who just *had* to own real estate, and lots of it. Congress, with its usual acumen and foresight, stoked the fires further by passing the Economic Recovery Act of 1981, which provided major tax benefits for real estate owners, in particular authorizing property owners to depreciate assets much quicker than had been allowed previously. All of this set off a real estate feeding frenzy.

Almost immediately, major brokerage firms and other syndicators formed real estate limited partnerships and sold interests in them to the public. The brokers touted these soon-to-be-turkeys as "can't miss" investments, offering (they said) both generous tax benefits and large capital gains that would result from the continuing appreciation of real estate. Never mind that the fees payable to the brokers, to "finders" and to the real estate managers were so high that earning profits on such investments would be all but impossible. Never mind that the assets put into the partnerships were frequently inflated in price to begin with. Never mind that the partnerships' asset managers were mediocre at best, and that they had little incentive to maximize operating performance. This occurred because in many cases the project could be a total flop but the tax benefits would still give the investor a handsome return (until the tax laws changed — they always do). Investors ignored these major issues, and bought partnership interests with wild abandon. Michael Dowd, a REIT and real estate analyst at Equity Research Collaborative, has estimated that so much investment capital flowed into real estate limited partnerships, public and private, during the latter part of the 1980s that they were able to buy well over $300 million in properties. REITs, offering greater stability but insignificant tax write-offs, were largely ignored by investors.

As the limited partnerships, real-estate-hungry institutions and foreign investors poured mega-billions into real estate, several unfortunate events occurred. First, REITs could not raise capital, competing as they were against the limited partnerships and other private investors who could factor substantial tax savings into their equations when figuring out how much they could economically pay for a building. Second, lo and behold, real estate prices escalated quickly in response to the increased demand resulting from the flood of new funds; even if REITs could raise the capital, properties were being priced at levels that precluded the REITs from earning an adequate return on them. And third, worst of all, the torrid real estate markets, when combined with an excessive amount of capital made available to developers, created that bane of real estate owners from time immemorial: *overbuilding*. Virtually every developer who had ever built anything (and many who hadn't) visited his friendly banker, laid his projections and budgets on the table, shouted "construction loan time!" and walked away with 90%-plus financing.

Years of overbuilding followed. To make matters worse, Congress again entered the act. Whereas in 1981 it passed the Economic Recovery Act which had the effect of stoking the fires of already-hot real estate markets, this time it passed the Tax Reform Act of 1986, which chilled already-cooling property markets. Investors lost the tax benefits they'd gained only a few years earlier, and, to make matters worse, their properties were performing poorly. Most sectors of the real estate market were in a heap of trouble by the late '80s.

As early as 1985, year-to-year growth rates in funds from operations (FFO) for most REITs were peaking, to be followed by a slow decline (the growth rate for Goldman Sachs' representative REITs, according to its report, dropped from 13% in the first half of the '80s to only 2.5% in the second half of the decade). Dividends continued to rise through the end of the decade, in most cases faster than FFO increases. So, dividend payout ratios got way out of whack, rising into the mid-90% range in the latter half of the 1980s. Ironically, despite the problems encountered by the REITs in the later years of the '80s (overbuilding, difficulty in raising capital and lack of attractive investment opportunities), their stocks didn't do all that badly. Total annual returns for the Equity REITs (based on NAREIT data) were 19.2%, -3.6%, 13.5% and 8.8% in 1986 through 1989, respectively. Nevertheless, these negative factors would catch up with and take their toll on REIT stock prices in 1990.

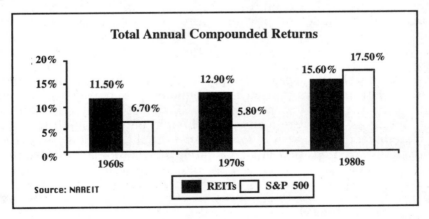

The REIT Industry Comes of Age: The 1990s

Emerging from the '80s' excesses, the decade of the '90s got off to a miserable start. REIT shareholders suffered through a horrible bear market in 1990, which cut their share prices down to bargain levels not seen since the '70s. NAREIT statistics show that Equity REITs' total return for 1990 was a *negative* 14.8%, which was the worst year for Equity REITs since 1974, when their total annual return was a negative 21.4%. This was quite a shock to us REIT investors, as we had become quite spoiled: From 1975 until 1990, Equity REITs had experienced only one year of negative total return, which was in 1987 when the figures were "in the red" by just 3.6%.

1990's Bear Market

The big negative numbers in 1990 most likely resulted from investors' discovery of rising vacancies and stagnating (and sometimes reduced) market rents in the apartment and office markets, as well as continued inroads made by Wal-Mart and other discounters onto the turf of the traditional neighborhood shopping center retailers. Investors may also have been "discounting," on Wall Street, a general decline in property values in many sectors which would surface on Main Street over the next few years due, in large part, to these problems, as well as to overbuilding. Dividend cuts by several REITs, who found that their high payout ratios were too aggressive during tough economic times, didn't exactly help. While a general markdown in real estate securities was warranted, investors overreacted, as they are wont to do, and share prices fell below reasonable levels. Excellent bargains thus sprouted up in the REIT world by the end of 1990, and these bear-market lows set the stage for a major REIT bull market that thrived from 1991 through 1993 and ushered in the Great IPO Boom of 1993-1994.

Though the opening of the decade proved a tough time for REITs, the investment vehicle itself, by this time, had nearly completed its metamorphosis. REITs of the late '80s and into 1990 had made great strides in quality over their 1960s ancestors. First, insider ownership increased and, thanks to the Tax Reform Act of 1986 which liberalized the rules pertaining to REITs, many REITs terminated their outside investment advisory relationships (and the major conflicts of interest that accompanied them) and brought in-house most or all of the functions normally expected of a fully operating real estate company, such as leasing, maintenance services, redevelopment, new construction and similar functions. Nevertheless, by the end of 1990's bear market, still only a very few REITs with strong management and good track records could be found; some of these included Federal Realty, Health Care Properties, MediTrust, Nationwide Health, New Plan Realty, United Dominion, Washington REIT and Weingarten Realty. It would not

97

be until 1993-1994 that a large number of new high-quality REITs would blossom.

1991 to 1993:   The Bull Returns

A combination of factors caused the prices of Equity REITs to do exceedingly well from 1991 through 1993. According to NAREIT data, total annual returns for Equity REITs in 1991, 1992 and 1993 were 35.7%, 14.6% and 19.6%, respectively.   This outstanding performance amply rewarded patient REIT investors who stuck with them through the weak markets of the late 1980s and especially the demoralizing bear market of 1990. Why REIT stocks did so well following the tough years is pretty easy to explain in hindsight. For one thing, investors overreacted terribly when they dumped REIT stocks in 1990, so some of the gain came merely from getting prices back to reasonable levels.

Perhaps a more important reason, however, was the incredible property bargains available to REITs in the early '90s in the aftermath of the depression-like real estate conditions and overbuilt markets of the late '80s and early '90s. Beginning in 1991, many REITs were able to again raise capital, and they bought properties at fire-sale prices from banks that had foreclosed on mega-billions of defaulted real estate loans, from insurance companies that wanted to reduce their exposure to real estate, from real estate limited partnerships that crashed and burned following the real estate investment frenzy of the '80s and, last but certainly not least, from the Resolution Trust Corporation, which was organized by Congress to acquire and re-sell real estate and real estate loans from bankrupt (and near-bankrupt) lenders. REITs were able to pursue "positive-spread investing" (PSI), which refers to the ability to raise funds (both equity and debt) at a cost far less than the initial returns that can be obtained on real estate acquisitions.

Both the rebound from the ridiculously low bear-market prices and the new availability of PSI were major factors in driving the REIT bull market onward from 1991 to 1993, but lower interest rates also played a significant role. Between January 1991 and the end of 1993, the Federal Reserve Board slashed interest rates in order to get the economy out of a shallow but long recession. For example, the yield on three-month Treasury bills fell from 6.2% in January 1991 to 3.1% by the end of 1993. As REITs are high-yielding investments, investors continued their romance with REIT shares during this time as they were seen as an "antidote" to the puny short-term yields available on CDs and T-bills. These investors may not have known much about REITs, but that didn't stop them from buying in with wild abandon.   Individual investors and institutions alike flocked to REIT investing, not only for the hefty yields but also for the prospects of rich capital gains.

The Great 1993-1994 REIT IPO Boom

According to Robert A. Frank, who for many years was head REIT analyst at Alex. Brown & Sons,[8] 1993 saw 93 REIT share offerings raise $12.6 billion, including $8.7 billion by 43 new REITs and $3.9 billion by 50 existing REITs. An additional $10.3 billion was raised in 1994, which included 30 new REIT IPOs raising $6.4 billion and 53 follow-on offerings by existing REITs raising $3.9 billion. The offerings in 1993 alone "surpassed the total amount of equity that REITs had raised during the previous 13 years," according to a Merrill Lynch report, titled "Sizing Up the Equity REIT Industry."[9] At the end of 1990, the estimated market capitalization (shares outstanding times the market price) of all publicly traded Equity REITs was $5.6 billion; by the end of 1994 it exceeded $38.8 billion, thanks primarily to the REIT offering boom of 1993 and 1994. (For contrast, while 71 REIT offerings were completed in the following year (1995), only $6.2 billion was raised, including only five REIT IPOs garnering just $800 million).

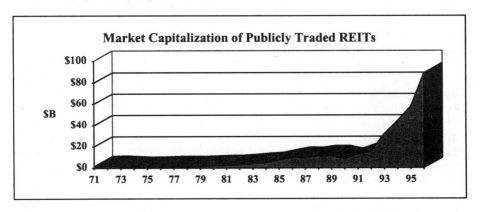

Market Capitalization of Publicly Traded REITs

While the major bull trend in REITs' stock prices would slow in 1994, bringing with it a sub-par year for REIT investors, the REIT IPO boom of the '90s had a revolutionary effect on the REIT world: It was largely responsible for a huge increase in the number of REITs and property types in which investors could participate. Unlike many small stock IPO frenzies which occur from time to time in U.S. stock market history, the REIT IPO boom brought public some of the most solid and well-respected real estate operating companies in the United States. These included, to name just a few, Cali Realty, DeBartolo Realty, Developers' Diversified, Kimco Realty, Post Properties, Simon Property Group, Taubman Centers and Weeks Corp. Furthermore, the types of properties owned by REITs expanded widely. As a result of the IPO boom, these new sectors now include regional malls, factory outlet centers, industrial properties, manufactured home communities, self-storage facilities and hotels. Another significant side effect of the IPO boom was to enhance the likelihood that the major institutions would become important investors in REITs; indeed, this is already happening, as we'll see in a later chapter.

Why many of these companies went public has been the subject of much discussion. The cynics claim that insiders at some companies were partially cashing out their ownership at the expense of their new public shareholders, and that others were merely taking advantage of a hot IPO market. While some of these shenanigans undoubtedly occurred, other more-legitimate reasons may explain the IPO boom. In the early 1990s, the banks and savings and loans were so badly burned by non-performing loans as a result of the real estate depression that they refused to provide the types of real estate financing that had been available for many years prior. Gaining the ability to access public capital was a good (and oft-stated) reason for many of these companies to go public. Another major reason was the perception in the minds of many managements that the "securitization" of real estate through REITs was becoming a major new trend, and that a company needed to go public in order to tap both public as well as private sources of capital. A third reason could have been managements' desire to transform highly illiquid partnership ownership interests into publicly traded shares that could be easily sold from time to time, transferred to other family members or used for estate planning purposes. In this respect, these new REITs were not any different from other thriving enterprises that have decided to go public as a way of solving financing, liquidity and estate tax issues. (Chapter Eleven goes into these issues in more depth).

The bottom line to the REIT IPO boom is that approximately 90 Equity REITs went public from 1992 through 1994, including some of the best real estate organizations in the country. Some have been merged or otherwise acquired and, yes, like any other industry, a significant number of them have been and will continue to be mediocre performers, both in their own right and in the stock market. However, a large number of this new generation of REITs can legitimately claim to be outstanding real estate companies that should provide investors with excellent returns for many years into the future.

1994-1995: The REIT Market Takes a Breather

Even before the end of the IPO boom of 1993-1994, the prices of many REIT stocks cooled off considerably, particularly in the apartment and retail sectors. The stocks of such outstanding REITs as Post Properties, United Dominion and Weingarten, at the end of 1995, were trading at prices well below their 1993 highs. And this was despite the continuing impressive FFO growth turned in for both 1994 and 1995. Post reported FFOs of $2.07, $2.25 and $2.53 in 1993, 1994 and 1995, respectively. FFO thus increased by 22.2% from 1993 to 1995, yet Post's stock traded at $31 in October 1993 and had risen to only $31-7/8 by the time 1995 drew to a close. Another way of looking at this disappointing performance is to compare P/FFO ratios, which consist simply of the stock price (P) at any given time divided by the most recently reported (or estimated) FFO figures, on a per share basis (FFO). In October 1993, the P/FFO ratio for Post was 15.0; at the end of 1995 it was 12.6. Investors were therefore not willing to pay anywhere near as much for a dollar of FFO in 1995 as they were in 1993. Post's experience was not unique; the same story applied to most of the apartment and retail REITs.

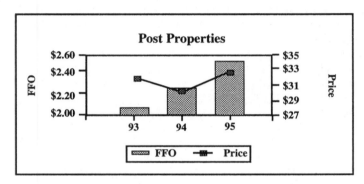

Other sectors did better, particularly in 1995. The prices, as well as the P/FFO ratios, of the industrial, office and hotel REITs rose in response to investors' convictions that the overbuilt conditions plaguing these sectors from the late 1980s had dissipated, and that positive-spread investing was alive and well for those REITs with access to capital.

In all, the average total return of the Equity REITs was a disappointing 3.2% in 1994 but recovered nicely in 1995, up 15.3% (according to NAREIT data). While the Equity REITs' 1994 performance was similar to that of the S&P500 index in 1994 (+3.2%), they were clearly clobbered by their ordinary common stock brethren in 1995, when the S&P500 index rose by a whopping 37%.

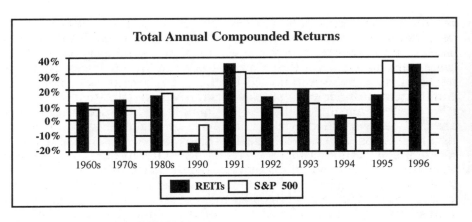

Total Annual Compounded Returns

Reasons for the REIT Lull

Why did many REITs fall out of favor in 1994-1995, and why did the P/FFO ratios in the apartment and retail sectors decline so markedly? One of the benefits in documenting history is that the causes of prior events often become clearer with the passage of time. A problem arises, however, when the history is so recent that sufficient time hasn't passed for these causes to make themselves apparent. Still, several factors can be linked to the disappointing performance of some REIT shares in 1994 and their relative under-performance in 1995.

First, lots of "hot money" was invested in REITs by non-real estate and non-REIT investors (such as individuals and mutual funds) in 1993 and early 1994, much of which was invested in the REIT IPOs of those years. Some of these investors were "momentum traders," riding the up-trend in REIT prices. Such investors tend to be fickle, and they exited "stage left" when REIT stocks' appreciation began to slow. Others simply were seeking higher yields than were available on short-term T-bills, and as a result sold their REITs when interest rates rose in 1994.

Second, the REIT IPO boom overstayed its welcome, with supply eventually overwhelming the still limited demand for REIT shares by yield-oriented investors. This was particularly true in the apartment sector, as the number of widely-followed apartment REITs exploded from only five (before the IPO boom) to more than 28 three years later.

Third, common stock investors became very excited by the major equity bull market that unfolded in 1995, led (until late in the year) by the high-tech stocks. Many investors, I suspect, turned a cold shoulder to the steady 12-14% total returns historically provided by REITs in favor of stocks that would skyrocket if the bull market continued to charge ahead.[10]

Fourth, many new REIT investors were misled by the unusually high FFO growth exhibited by REITs during the early '90s, resulting from unusually strong internal growth (as occupancies and rental rates both rose briskly) as well as strong external growth due to ample positive-spread investing opportunities. They thus were unprepared when the growth rates of many REITs returned, in 1995, to their more normal levels of 5-8% annually. Their selling tended to retard the REIT stocks' continuing advance.

A final reason, at least with respect to the apartment and retail REITs, was that investors had become increasingly concerned about the prospect of supply-demand imbalances. In the apartment sector, new permits had been rising for quite some time, as the economics of apartment ownership continued to improve. Some major cities (*e.g.*, Tucson) were seeing supply catch up with (and even exceed) demand, which was to lead to lower occupancy rates and very small rental increases. On the retail side, news stories appeared almost daily of consumers suffering from stagnant wages and refusing to spend at the malls and shopping centers, and many retailers were filing for bankruptcy. Although these problems were temporary, investors have always hated uncertainty. Their concerns quite likely contributed to the contraction of P/FFO ratios in 1994 and 1995.

A final note on the REITs' 1994-1995 performance: The stock market seems to have done a pretty good job of looking ahead and "discounting" future events. The P/FFO ratio contraction might be explained by investors' realization that the incredibly powerful forces favoring the REIT industry in the early '90s (cheap property prices providing for great acquisitions, rising rents and occupancy rates and a shortage of competing properties) were cooling down a bit and the markets were returning to more normal conditions. In view of this "normalization" of the REIT market, it's a tribute to the REIT stocks that they performed as well as they did in those years. Outstanding FFO and dividend growth offset the declines in P/FFO ratios to produce good, if not outstanding, total returns.

1996: New REIT Bull Market?

1996 was an exciting year for REIT investors. NAREIT's Equity REIT Index logged in a total return of 35.3%, which compared favorably with a 23.0% total return for the S&P500 Index. Why were REITs able to tack on a 35.3% total return on top of the 15.3% total return posted in 1995? Again, insufficient time has passed, as this book went to press, to enable me to write intelligent history, but here are some likely possibilities:

Faster Growth. REIT investors may have decided that REITs' future FFO growth will be significantly higher than previously anticipated. This increased optimism may have been based on a steadily growing economy, stable interest rates and low inflation, together with REITs' growth opportunities through new property acquisitions. Whereas in 1995 folks might have thought that

103

Beacon, for example, would be able to grow FFO at 8% for the next few years, they might have concluded, as 1996 progressed, that 10% growth would be a "slam dunk." An upward revision in expected growth rates can cause a stock's price/earnings ratio (or, in REITs' case, the P/FFO or P/AFFO ratio) to leap upwards, which will have a major positive effect upon its price. When the projected growth rates for Bristol-Myers were being revised upwards by analysts in 1996, its "appropriate" price/earnings ratio rose from 14 to 18. Similarly, if investors are willing to pay a higher FFO or AFFO ratio for Beacon, its price will levitate. In October 1995, BCN was priced at $21.75, as investors were willing to pay only 10 times its estimated 1995 FFO of $2.17. In November 1996, its FFO was estimated at $2.42, but investors were willing to pay a 12.4 multiple of such FFO, pushing its price to over $30. Thus the mere expectation of higher growth rates could have been a major force driving REIT share prices higher.

Higher NAVs. Those REIT investors who focus on net asset values (NAVs) when evaluating REIT stocks (on the belief that, in the final analysis, REIT values are based upon the values of their properties) may have been a bit chagrined by investors' enthusiasm for REITs in 1996. Why were investors willing to pay 35-40% premiums over NAVs for many REITs as 1996 drew to a close? The answer might be that cap rates for real estate on "Main Street" will be declining and, as it did in 1991-1993, the REIT market may have been "discounting" these lower cap rates. Investors of this school may note that as cap rates come down, the value of real estate goes up, and the hot market for REIT stocks in 1996 may have been discounting higher property values ahead. Lower cap rates may, indeed, be justified by three possible scenarios. First, milder real estate cycles than we've had in the past (this will be discussed in more detail in a later chapter). Second, a very strong bond market (and lower interest rates and inflation) as President Clinton and Congress are perceived as working towards reducing the budget deficits. And third, with the continuing securitization of real estate and the increasingly deep pockets of REITs as buyers of commercial properties, both institutions and individuals alike may find it easier to sell or exchange their properties, in many cases without tax effect.[11] Thus milder cycles, lower interest rates and greater liquidity of real estate may, together, have the effect of significantly reducing cap rates and increasing the values of commercial real estate — all of which the strong market for REIT stocks may have been anticipating in 1996.

Money Flows. Another possible reason for 1996's enthusiasm for REIT stocks is based upon the fact that REITs are liquid securities and thus compete with stocks and bonds for investors' attentions. If REITs are a viable asset class with sufficient liquidity to enable them to compete with these other investments, they are a legitimate alternative to them. And as the Dow Jones

Industrial Average rose well above the 6,000 mark and the "long bond's" yield fell to 6.5%, investors may have decided that these investments were too pricey to provide further double digit returns following their excellent performance throughout the prior two years. So perhaps they headed for another liquid asset class — REITS. As a truly competitive investment, REITs may have been viewed as less expensive than the others, while providing the prospects of reasonably good dividend yields and healthy FFO growth.

Institutional Demand. Another possible explanation for the "Great REIT Bull Market of 1996" is that the *institutional demand* for REIT stocks drove prices relentlessly higher. Institutions are slowly but inexorably coming to the conclusion that the way to maximize the performance of their real estate investments is to invest in outstanding real estate companies rather than to own real estate directly or through "commingled funds." While it's exceedingly difficult to compare the performance of directly-owned real estate with the REIT market over the past five, 10 or 20 years (and may not be terribly relevant even if you could), a significant number of institutional investors are becoming very comfortable with REITs — and those folks whose business it was to provide and manage direct investments for these heavy hitters are now setting up new businesses devoted to the management of REIT portfolios. Just take a look at the trading volumes and volatility of such stocks as Starwoods, Crescent, Beacon, Patriot American, Avalon and the like, and it's pretty clear that the institutions are leaving their footprints all over REITland.

Other Recent Developments

As 1996 drew to a close, several newer trends were becoming apparent to REIT investors. These included an acceleration in merger and acquisition activity among REITs, a significant rise in follow-on (or "secondary") stock offerings (including an increasingly popular form of equity financing often referred to as a "spot offering") and larger market caps (market values of the outstanding shares) for many REIT stocks.

We'll discuss the issue of consolidation within the REIT industry in Chapter Eleven, but it's important to note here that the pace of merger and acquisition activity in the REIT world has accelerated in 1996. Such activity was infrequent prior to 1995, but that year saw the acquisition of Holly Residential by Wellsford Residential, the merger of McArthur/Glen into HGI Realty and BRE Properties' acquisition of REIT of California. These were significant transactions, but not earth-shaking events.

1996 was a different story, as several major merger and acquisition transactions were announced or completed. The most significant, of course, was the merger of mall REITs DeBartolo Realty and Simon Property Group, which was to create the largest company, by far, within the REIT industry. Yet other major transactions were also announced. Bradley Real Estate acquired the troubled Tucker Properties in early 1996, Highwoods Properties bought Crocker Realty later in the year in a $540 million transaction and South West Property merged into United Dominion at the end of the year, creating yet another $1 billion market cap apartment REIT (the others being Equity Residential, Security Capital Pacific and Post Properties). Early in 1997, Equity Residential announced a proposed acquisition of Wellsford Residential. But perhaps the most interesting was the near-war that was waged over Chateau Properties, a manufactured home community REIT which was betrothed to ROC Communities. Sam Zell's Manufactured Home Communities tried to break up the marriage by offering a sweeter deal to some of Chateau's shareholders, which was followed by yet another offer, this from Sun Communities. As this book went to press, Chateau and ROC had just completed their merger. Whether this heavy "M&A" activity was a flash in the pan or a portent of things to come will be discussed in Chapter Eleven.

Another important event for REITs in 1996 was the significant amount of funds raised in the equity capital markets, which enabled the securitization of real estate to continue its accelerated pace. There were 139 secondary equity offerings completed by existing REITs in 1996, which raised a record $11.5 billion (according to NAREIT data). This was a significant increase from the $7.3 billion raised in 93 secondary offerings in 1995 and only $3.9 billion raised in just 52 secondaries in 1994. These funds are being used primarily for the continuing acquisition of commercial real estate from both individuals and institutions. Data concerning the amount of commercial real estate acquired by REITs in 1996 was not available as this book went to press, but is believed to have been a record for the industry. A total of $12.3 billion was bought in 1995 and only $8.1 billion in 1994. Chris Lucas, NAREIT's research director, has estimated that REITs now own approximately 30% of all equity in institutional-grade commercial U.S. real estate, compared with just 10% at the end of 1993.

All of this financing activity, aided a bit by the merger and acquisition activity discussed earlier and the strong market for REIT stocks in 1996, has had the effect of significantly increasing the market caps of a large number of REITs. At December 31, 1995 and 1994, there were only nine and four REITs, respectively, which had market caps of at least $1 billion. At the end of 1996, there were 21 of them. Perhaps even more impressive, the number of REITs with market caps of over $2 billion grew from zero at the end of 1995 to four by the end of 1996.

A significant portion of the funds raised in 1996 was completed via "spot offerings," which is a new concept in the REIT industry. As REITs must pay out, in dividends, at least 95% of their net income, it is difficult for them to retain capital with which to grow, develop and acquire additional properties. They must, therefore, continually raise additional equity capital. The spot offering allows a REIT to file and maintain a "shelf" registration statement with the Securities and Exchange Commission and to sell shares "off the shelf" repeatedly and in small offerings. Thus rather than offer $200-300 million in common shares in a major underwriting (which is time-consuming, expensive and often disruptive to the REIT's trading markets), the REIT will offer more frequently, on a "spot" basis, a relatively small number of shares and raise, for example, $35-40 million each time. These offerings, along with related (but more traditional) "private placement" type offerings, are sold to a limited number of buyers (usually institutions), are closed generally within a few days or a week and are commenced and concluded almost before anyone finds out about them. This type of financing mechanism should prove very helpful in REITs' continuing capital-raising activities.

Where do REIT stocks go from here? Well, that would take us away from history and into foretelling the future. While I assure you I'm no better at this than anyone else, I'll offer a few thoughts in a later chapter (Chapter Eleven) titled "Tea Leaves." Meanwhile, the lessons learned from this brief history will now be applied in Part III: What We Need to Succeed, beginning with the following chapter.

---

[1] "The REIT Investment Summary," dated January 1996.

[2] "REIT Redux," August 12, 1992.

[3] "REIT Redux," August 12, 1992.

[4] American Realty Trust, Denver R.E. Inv. Ass'n, First Union Realty, Franklin Realty, Greenfield REIT, National Realty Investors, Pennsylvania REIT, REIT of America, U.S. Realty Investors and Washington REIT.

[5] "The REIT Investment Summary", dated January 1996.

[6] Federal Investment Realty Trust, First Union Real Estate, General Growth Properties, Greenfield REIT, Hubbard Real Estate Investments, New Plan Realty, Pennsylvania REIT, Property Capital Trust, REIT of America and Washington REIT.

[7] These REITs included BankAmerica Realty Investors, Federal Realty Investment Trust, First Union Real Estate Investments, IRT Properties, New Plan Realty, Pennsylvania REIT, Property Capital Trust, Property Trust of America, Washington REIT and Western Investment Real Estate Trust.

[8] Interview with Mr. Frank, appearing in Barron's, December 18, 1995.

[9] Merrill Lynch, "Sizing Up the Equity REIT Industry," p.12 (August 8, 1994).

[10] Approximately one-half of REITs' total returns come from dividend payments; this provides for strong stability in total returns from year to year. However, the individual investor may not notice the importance of such dividends because they are paid quarterly and not added to REITs' stock prices. Thus such an investor may look at his or her REIT stocks and become disappointed. For example, an investor who owned XYZ REIT might notice that XYZ stock closed at $15 at the end of the current month and closed at $14 at

the end of the same month of the prior year, for a "gain" of only $1, or 7.1%. However, XYZ might have paid out, in dividends, another 6.5% in dividends during that time period. The investor's total return would have been 13.6% but he or she might have noticed only the 7.1% capital appreciation portion.

[11] In Chapter Two we discussed UPREITs and DownREITs, which in many cases enable sellers of real estate to receive "operating units" in a partnership organized by a REIT, and thus defer the payment of taxes.

Part III

What We Need to Succeed

Chapter Six

The Dynamics of FFO Growth

"Mary, Mary, quite contrary, how do your REIT shares grow?
"With upgraded tenants, and percentage rents,
and acquisitions all in a row"
— **With apologies to Mother Goose**

What makes REIT shares so attractive compared with other high-yielding investments such as bonds and utility stocks is their significant capital appreciation potential and steadily increasing dividends. The engine that drives both rising stock prices and dividend growth is ever-increasing funds from operations (FFO) (as we've seen in Chapter Two, FFO is the REITs' equivalent of net income). If our ugly-duckling REIT never grew its FFO, it would walk like a bond, swim like a bond and quack like a bond, and it would be bought only for its yield. The yield would always be higher than that of a U.S. Treasury bond (due to the stock's higher risk), and would fluctuate in price according to prevailing long-term interest rates and investors' perceptions of the REIT's ability to continue paying its dividend.

A fair number of REITs — today and throughout the REIT industry's history — have traded in the stock market as bond-surrogates. These REITs are perceived by investors, rightly or wrongly, as not having the ability to grow their FFO to any meaningful extent. In some cases, they are viewed as being subject to the risk of declining FFO, which would put their dividend in jeopardy of being cut or even, in rare cases, eliminated entirely. Some such REITs may trade at yields above 11%[1]; in view of the 6.7% yield on 30-year Treasury bonds at the time this book went to press, 11% indicates quite clearly investors' belief that not only will such REITs not grow their FFOs, but that funds from operations may actually shrink, which could necessitate a dividend cut.

While bottom-fishers and value investors often can do well investing (or speculating?) in such REITs, chasing yields is a dangerous game that often leaves the shareholder something the worse for wear. The dividend cuts and related share price declines experienced by Burnham Pacific, Crown American and FAC Realty (formerly Factory Stores of America) shareholders are good examples. Accordingly, most long-term investors should seek to invest in REITs whose dividends are not only safe but, even more importantly, have good prospects for growth. Not only will such investments allow us to sleep better at night, but also they offer the prospects of truly

111

long-term dividend and share price growth with a minimum of account churning and unpleasant surprises. As if that weren't enough, the numbers prove the point: We'd rather own a REIT that pays 6% currently and can grow at 7% year after year as opposed to its sick cousin that pays 11% with no growth prospects. Can we get the best of both worlds — an 11% yield and 7% growth over time? Well, maybe occasionally, if we are able to discover a REIT whose prospects have been completely misunderstood by investors, but such serendipitous occasions are rare. In REIT investing, as is true almost everywhere, there's no such thing as a free lunch.

OK, then, how does a REIT generate growth in FFO, and what should we look for? First of all, we must be careful to look at FFO growth on a *per share* basis. It does the shareholder no good if a REIT grows FFO rapidly but, due to the issuance of huge amounts of new shares, the shareholder receives no benefit from such "profitless prosperity." Also, we need to remind ourselves that REITs, to remain as such, must pay to their shareholders at least 95% of their net income each year. As a practical matter, most REITs pay out considerably more than this. In Chapter Two we noted that FFO is a more appropriate measure of a REIT's operating performance than net income, and is almost always higher than net income due to the add-back of depreciation expense. REITs normally base their dividend rates on FFO, and most REITs distribute about 80-85% of their FFOs to shareholders in the form of dividend payments. Therefore, REITs have limited ability to retain much of their earnings from year to year. That fact makes growth much more difficult, and usually requires periodic visits to the capital markets. That being said, REITs *can* grow their FFOs, and they do it in two basic ways: internal growth and external growth.

REIT investors and analysts believe it important to understand exactly how much growth is being achieved both "internally" and "externally." External growth, such as through new developments and property acquisitions, may not always be available to a REIT; this could be due to a lack of available opportunities, inability to raise the necessary capital, the high cost of such capital or other reasons. In contrast, internal growth is generated through a REIT's existing resources, and as such is more easily achieved and reliable. Still, both are readily viable methods by which a REIT can expand.

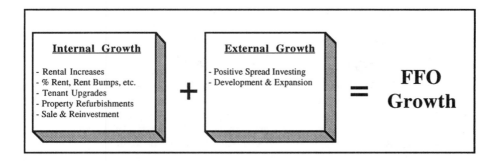

One caveat: We must keep in mind that when we're talking about real estate and REITs, we are dealing with a wide-ranging subject. Growth in real estate FFO is clearly no exception. As we covered in Chapter Three, REITs own quite a few different property types, and the methods of internal and external growth available to apartment owners, for example, are in many ways different from those available to owners of nursing homes. Furthermore, the growth prospects for owners of the various property types will change over time. As a result, while I'll provide some thoughts concerning the rental growth prospects for various property types, the following discussion should be used merely as a starting point when analyzing the growth prospects for a particular REIT.

Internal Growth

Internal growth, as mentioned above, is growth via an improvement in profits at the *property* level; this is achieved through increased rentals or reduced expenses at one or more of the specific properties owned by the REIT. It is the most stable and reliable source of FFO growth, as it depends upon neither acquisitions or development opportunities nor the REIT's ability to obtain substantial additional capital.

Before we examine the specific sources of REITs' internal growth, however, we should review the concept of "same-store" sales. To help determine how much of a REIT's growth in any fiscal period has come from internal sources, REIT analysts have borrowed from their retail analyst colleagues a concept called "same-store" sales, which generally refers to sales from stores open for at least one year and excludes sales from stores that have been closed and from new stores (which often have unusually high sales growth). The caution flag might be raised if a retailer's "same-store" sales have been flat, while most of its revenue growth has come from building or acquiring new stores — at some point, markets will become saturated and sources of new growth will become problematic.

113

Similarly, REIT managements are often asked how much of their increase in FFO has been derived from "same-store" rent increases (and net operating income on a "same-store basis) and how much from new stores, *i.e.*, recent property developments and acquisitions. The answer provides a good picture of how well the REIT is doing with its existing properties and how much growth is being generated internally rather than externally. The "same-store" concept is so popular and useful that we not only use it in the context of retail stores but also apply it to apartment buildings, offices, industrial buildings, nursing homes and self-storage facilities — in short, to almost *all* individual properties. Therefore, when we talk about a REIT's internal growth, we should keep in mind that internal growth is often measured by "same-store" rental revenues, operating expenses and operating income.[2]

There are several important tools that property owners, including REITs, frequently use to generate growth on a "same-store" basis. These range from the simplest and most common, such as rent increases, to more imaginative strategies, such as upgrading the tenant roll or making the property more attractive to the consumer. As we'll see in this chapter, those REITs that are more aggressive and creative in their use of these tools are the most likely to sustain the highest internal growth rates.

Rental Increases

The most obvious and frequently used type of internal growth is the ability to raise rents to the lessee of the property, whether it be an apartment building, mall, or virtually any other property type. The ability to raise rents over time is probably the most important determinant of internal growth for a REIT. Yet it's not always easy to do, and there are certain periods in the cycles of most real estate when effective rents (quoted rental rates adjusted by rent concessions) actually fall rather than rise. Owners of office buildings in the 1980s and early 1990s know full well there's no guarantee the tenant will pay the same rate when the lease comes up for renewal, and that the tenant may demand so much in the way of tenant improvements that the lease becomes marginally profitable at best. Apartment owners faced such problems in the late '80s, as half-empty apartment buildings allowed tenants to practically name their own rent. Even today, rent concessions made in order to fill vacant apartment units in some areas are not uncommon. Some investors have worried that the owners of many regional malls may not be able to continue to charge higher rental rates on lease renewals in view of the fact that same-store sales have been sluggish for several years.

Clearly, then, the ability of property owners to increase rental rates year after year is no sure thing. Furthermore, unit rental increases can be wiped out by declining occupancy rates. Many factors can limit rent increases to very small percentages, such as the supply/demand for the particular property and property type, the current economic climate, the condition and reputation of the particular property, and other factors.

At the present time, the apartment sector is well along in its recovery cycle (see Chapter Three), and the recent pace of new construction has brought the level of available units into equilibrium with demand in most areas throughout the U.S. Overbuilding does not seem to be a problem in most regions and localities, and thus rental growth for apartments should continue, although more slowly than the torrid pace of the last few years. Growth will come from mildly increasing rental rates, rather than from occupancy gains. In the event of a recession, however, projected absorption rates may prove to be too optimistic, and apartment owners could see some occupancy slippage and have difficulty raising rates to any meaningful extent until the economy recovers.

In retail, both malls and factory outlet centers have been able to raise rental rates steadily despite the punk retailing environment of recent years; for malls, this has been accomplished by the signing of new leases in replacement of those signed years earlier when sales volumes were much lower. In the long run, however, it will be difficult for retail store owners to increase rents at a pace faster than sales at the individual store.

Self-storage facilities have shown similar steady success, thanks in large part to their recent growth in popularity. That popularity, coupled with only moderate building over the past few years, has enabled owners of these facilities to increase rental rates frequently since 1991, and this situation looks like it will continue (albeit at a slower rate). Hotels likewise have enjoyed increased room rates in recent years, and investors in hotel REITs expect this to continue (particularly with respect to the full service and extended-stay sub-sectors).

In contrast, owners of neighborhood shopping centers have had a very difficult time raising rental rates, as the existing supply of stores in such centers has exceeded the demand for them in much of the U.S. This is probably due to the large number of stores developed during the "shop-till-you-drop" era of the 1980s and the consumers' preference for such "value retailers" as Wal-Mart, Target and other so-called "category killers."

Office rental rates also have endured many years of softness but have bottomed out in most areas of the country, and office owners are now getting significant rental increases on many expiring leases. The same situation applies to industrial property, where steady rent increases are being obtained.

Unlike other sectors, health care facility owners generally enter into fairly long-term leases with their operators; while the base rent

115

may thus remain in effect for several years, the leases provide for "rent bumps" and "percentage rent," as will be discussed in the next section. Base rents for these facilities should remain stable.

At the risk of major oversimplification, most real estate observers seem to think that owners of reasonably well-maintained properties in markets where supply and demand are in balance can continue to get rental increases which, at the least, approximate inflation. Keep in mind that we are talking here only about broad-based industry trends; as we'll see in the next chapter, some REITs — and their managements — are much more adept than others at getting lease renewals, and leasing property to new tenants, at higher rates than the typical owner of a property of a similar type. Trying to determine *which* REITs have better than average potential rental growth is the challenge — and the fun — of REIT investing.

Percentage Rent, Rent Bumps and Expense Sharing

Some property owners have been able to increase their rental income at the property level by using methods that focus on the tenant's needs and their financial ability to pay higher effective rental rates. These include percentage rent, rent bumps and expense sharing.

Percentage Rent. "Percentage rent" clauses are traditional in retail store leases, where the property owner is entitled to receive, in addition to the base rental rate, additional rents if store revenues exceed certain pre-set levels. For example, the lease might be structured so that if the store's sales exceed $5 million for any calendar year, the lessee must pay the landlord 3% of the excess, in the form of additional rent. This allows the property owner to share in some of the "gravy" if the store does well. The extent to which lessees will agree to this type of revenue sharing will depend upon the property location, the market demand for the space, the base rent and the property owner's reputation for upgrading shopping centers to make them more attractive to shoppers. Health care REITs for many years have been able to structure their leases (and even their mortgages, when the REIT provides mortgage financing) so that the owner shares in "same-store" revenue growth above certain minimum levels. In some cases, however, the rental increases are "capped" at predetermined levels.

Rent Bumps. Some property owners, such as Vornado Realty, like to structure their leases so that the base rent "bumps up" every several years. This is also typical for industrial properties. Such leases provide a built-in rent increase, and make more likely a steady improvement in same-store net operating income. Some owners of nursing homes and similar facilities likewise are writing leases with their health care operators in this manner. This approach is popular with many retailers (including lessees in today's "power

116

centers"), who can use it to match their leasing costs with their projected longer-term revenues derived from the store's operations.

Expense Sharing. A third similar type of mechanism owners often use to increase rental revenues from the property is the "cost-sharing" clause. Office building owners have been able to get their lessees to pay a portion of the increased operating expenses of the building, such as insurance, property taxes, management expenses and the like. Similarly, malls and factory outlet center owners have, over the last several years, been able to obtain reimbursement from their lessees for certain "common area" operating expenses, such as janitorial services, security, advertising and promotion. On the apartment front, many savvy owners have put separate electricity and water usage meters into their units, thus getting their tenants to pay for these types of expenses in addition to rental payments.

All of these methods have been successfully used by property owners (including, of course, the REITs) to increase "same-store" rental revenues and net operating income, which contributes to increased funds from operations. The degree to which such features can be successfully included within a given lease is largely dependent upon both the supply-demand situation for a particular property and property type, including its location, and the ability of the property owner to convince the lessee that it can provide the kind of operating environment that would justify these additional costs to the lessee. For example, Simon DeBartolo Group may be able, on the basis of its size and reputation for creative marketing, to get provisions in its leases which may not be available to a weaker mall owner.

Tenant Upgrades

Creative owners of retail properties have been able to significantly augment rental growth at the property level by replacing mediocre or poorly performing tenants with attractive new ones. Retailers that offer new and innovative products have always been able to generate much higher customer traffic, which boosts sales at the both the store and the shopping center; these successful tenants can afford higher rental rates. Furthermore, every retailer wants to locate its newest store in a center with high traffic count; therefore, attracting the "best" tenants is crucial to success.

This ability to upgrade the tenant mix is one of the factors that distinguishes a truly innovative property owner from all others. Kimco Realty, which boasts one of the most respected managements in the retail REIT sector, maintains a huge database of potential tenants that could be brought into a shopping center in order to improve its profitability for the benefit of both the owner and the other retailers located there. This asset, together with the strong relationship Kimco has built over the years with high-quality national and regional retailers, allows it to continually upgrade its

117

tenant base within an existing retail center. In the factory outlet center niche, Chelsea/GCA has been a leader in replacing poorly performing tenants with those who can draw big crowds. Such a process both enhances the value of the property and provides higher rent to the property owner.

Tenant upgrades become even more important during weak retailing periods. Late in 1995 and into 1996, many retailers had been squeezed by sluggish retail demand from customers and the inroads made upon them by Wal-Mart and other discount stores; as a result, several major retailers filed for bankruptcy. During such periods, it is crucial for retail property owners, particularly mall owners, to replace poorly performing tenants with those who have the merchandising and marketing savvy to do well in weak retail environments or who offer merchandise that is in demand by consumers. For example, those mall owners who can close out poorly performing apparel stores and replace them with theaters, restaurants and other unique retailing concepts will prosper; those who cannot will encounter flat-to-declining mall revenues, as vacancies increase and lease rates stagnate or even decline upon renewal.

Property Refurbishments

Another skill that often separates the innovative from the passive property owner involves property refurbishment and restructuring. This ability can turn a tired mall, neighborhood shopping center or office building into a vibrant, upscale center likely to be very attractive to lessees and customers. This could be accomplished by adding amenities such as clubhouses, security gates and tennis courts to apartment complexes, or repaving parking lots and adding new attractive signage and landscaping to retail facilities. In the self-storage sector, Storage U.S.A. and others have been adding computer-controlled security gates and climate control to many of their facilities. These types of improvements are often made by well-managed REITs following the purchase at a bargain price of an under-performing property.

Successfully refurbishing a property has several benefits. The upgraded and beautified property is more likely to attract desirable tenants, is able to command higher rents and, for retail properties, attracts more shoppers. The returns to the REIT property owner on such investments can often be almost embarrassingly high.

Federal Realty, in particular, has had a long track record of completing successful property refurbishing/retenanting programs in the retail sphere, often with excellent investment returns. Likewise, Kimco Realty's very imaginative management has successfully acquired and "de-malled" older, poorly performing malls and turned them into more exciting, easily accessible open-air shopping complexes. In the apartment sector, United Dominion

118

has, for many years, successfully upgraded and refurbished apartment buildings following their purchase at very cheap prices. Reckson Associates has bought several poorly-performing office buildings in New York and, more recently in New Jersey, and intends to refurbish them substantially. The lesson here for us REIT investors is that excellent and imaginative REITs create value for their shareholders through refurbishing, retenanting and similar programs, and can earn investment returns substantially higher than those of other real estate owners.

Sale and Reinvestment

Truly entrepreneurial management is always looking to improve investment returns. Sometimes this can be accomplished by selling properties in which further rental growth prospects have dimmed and then reinvesting the proceeds elsewhere. This is a conservative and highly effective strategy. For example, a property might be sold at an 8% cap rate (roughly equivalent to the cash flow available to the purchaser as a percentage of the purchase price, based on existing rental and occupancy rates), and the net proceeds could be invested in another (perhaps under-performing) property which, with a modest investment of capital and perhaps upgraded services, might provide a return of 11% or more to the REIT within a year or two. This approach to value creation does not require significant use of a REIT's capital resources, as all or most of the necessary capital to acquire the new property is created through the sale of the old.

Here again, as in the case of retenanting and refurbishing, we tend to see this happen at the better REITs. Managements of such companies are always alert for new opportunities, and they have no emotional attachments to a property just because it's been in the portfolio and performed well in the past. Post Properties, one of the premier apartment REITs, has sold off some apartment properties with less than exciting future growth prospects and reinvested the proceeds elsewhere. Another excellent apartment REIT, Security Capital Pacific, has been selling a large number of apartment buildings in order to raise cash for its new apartment development program and for acquisitions in higher-growth areas. Yet another outstanding apartment REIT, United Dominion Realty, has been selling off its shopping center properties and redeploying the proceeds into additional apartment buildings.

As we've seen here, REITs' internal growth opportunities are as numerous as their property types. In the hands of shrewd management, these options can be maximized with lucrative results for both the REIT and its investors. However, internal growth isn't the only way REITs can expand revenues and funds from operations. There is another.

119

External Growth

Let's assume, for purposes of discussion, that the typical REIT can get average annual rental increases equal to the rate of inflation, say 3%, and that expenses and overhead also grow by 3% annually. Let's assume further that modest fixed-rate debt leverage is used, which would enable the typical REIT to grow funds from operations by 4%. Finally, let's assume that the well-managed REIT can achieve another 1% annual growth through tenant upgrades, refurbishments and property sales and reinvestments. How do we get from this 5% FFO growth to the 6-10% pace some REITs have achieved for a number of years? The answer is through *external growth*, a process by which a real estate organization such as a REIT acquires (and in many cases also develops) *additional properties* that generate further profits for the organization's owners. Let's look at the ways in which this can occur.

Positive-Spread Investing

The term "positive-spread investing," or "PSI," was coined only a few years ago at the beginning of the major REIT bull market that began late in 1990. However, this concept has been applied successfully for many years previously by long-established and successful REITs such as Federal, New Plan, United Dominion, Washington and Weingarten. PSI refers to a REIT's ability to obtain capital, through equity and debt offerings (and temporary bank borrowings) at inexpensive rates and to use the funds to buy properties yielding substantially higher returns than its cost of capital. For example, Storage U.S.A. might sell additional shares at a cost of capital (we'll discuss this often-misunderstood term below) of 8%, raising $75 million, and using the proceeds to buy storage facilities from others that yield 10% on their acquisition cost. The net result of such transactions would be incremental FFO equal to 2% of $75 million, or $1.5 million on "day one" (additional returns are generated later as operating income from the acquired properties increases). For REITs, as well as other property investors with access to low-cost capital, PSI is the next-best thing to printing money.

PSI is available to almost all REITs at certain times, and to only a few of them at other times. The variables depend upon a REIT's access to the capital markets, the cost of such capital, the strength of its balance sheet (*e.g.*, how much debt it already has) and the prevailing cap rates on the type of property which it desires to acquire. For example, PSI is simply not available to a REIT that cannot raise either equity capital (perhaps due to its poor prior performance, unproven management or limited growth prospects) or debt capital (when its balance sheet is already heavily leveraged). And it's also unavailable if the REIT's cost of capital, whether equity or debt, is higher than the yields that can be obtained from new acquisitions.

The early '90s were a golden era of PSI for apartment REITs, which may be a reason why so many of them went public during that time period. The best of them, like United Dominion, could raise equity capital at a nominal cost of 7% or debt capital at 8% and acquire apartment properties in the aftermath of the real estate depression of the late '80s that provided them with entry yields of 11% or more (the sellers were troubled partnerships, over-leveraged owners, banks owning repossessed properties, or the RTC). This ideal situation helped United Dominion boost its per-share FFO from $.66 at the end of 1989 to $1.18 at the end of 1995, a total increase of 79%, which was a key factor in its share price rising from $9 on December 31, 1989, to $15 on December 31, 1995.

At first glance it may seem odd that properties could become available at such substantial entry yields (i.e., high cap rates). The explanation is that property yields are nothing more than cash flow available from the ownership and operation of a property, before depreciation and interest expense, divided by its purchase price, and such purchase price is determined by prevailing supply and demand factors. If there are few willing buyers for a type of property in a particular location but lots of anxious sellers, the purchase price will be low in relationship to the anticipated cash flow from the property, and entry yields to the property buyer will be substantial. At the bottom of property cycles we often see such supply/demand imbalances, as foreclosures are prevalent, owners are anxious to cut their losses, property refinancings are unavailable and confidence levels are low.

PSI opportunities had waned for most apartment REITs by 1995 (as entry yields on potential acquisitions declined to a rate just a bit above the REITs' nominal cost of capital) but are alive and well in other sectors. The largest health care REITs have enjoyed PSI for many years, and continue to do so today. Stubbornly high cap rates on office buildings, industrial properties, self-storage facilities, hotels and neighborhood shopping centers are driving excellent PSI growth for REITs specializing in those sectors, and most observers expect this to continue for another 12-24 months, at the least. Mall REITs, on the other hand, have not been able to pursue PSI until recently, as mall cap rates have generally been equal to (or in many cases even lower than) the mall REITs' cost of capital, due to a lack of willing sellers in this sector (most malls have traditionally been owned by major institutions and pension plans, often financed without leverage) and the stable yields provided by high-quality malls.

The importance of PSI to a REIT, its FFO growth rate and its stock price cannot be overemphasized and is a key variable that all REIT investors need to acknowledge. The substantial decline in the price/FFO ratios of the apartment REITs from 1993 to 1995 can be explained in substantial part by their declining PSI prospects from the latter part of 1994 through 1996, brought on by the stagnant stock market prices of these REITs until late in 1996 (making equity capital more expensive) and a decline in the cap rates on apartment buildings available for acquisition.

The true value of property acquisitions to a well-managed REIT goes far beyond the initial yield spread from PSI. Professional real estate organizations, as typified by many REITs today, are often able to operate and manage acquired properties more efficiently and profitably than had been the case under the prior owner. United Dominion and Equity Residential are prime examples. Thus, not only can such a REIT earn additional income on the PSI "spread," but it can also obtain excellent *internal* growth from acquired properties by controlling expenses and spreading them over more units, even assuming no change in rental rates.

A final point on PSI: When we talk about positive-spread investing, we are talking about the difference, or *spread,* between what the REIT can earn on its invested capital (for example, the cash flow that a newly acquired apartment will provide to the REIT buyer) and the REIT's cost of capital. But just what *is* the REIT's "cost of capital?" The cost of *debt* capital is fairly straightforward — it is simply the interest that the REIT pays for borrowed funds. However, we should be careful not to use *short-term* interest rates, as drawdowns under a credit line must be repaid relatively quickly, and REITs generally hold their property assets for long periods of time. Instead, we should use actual or implied interest rates on debt having a maturity of at least seven and preferably 10 years, which will usually be higher than short-term interest rates. Using this more conservative calculation will eliminate the fictitious PSI that results from borrowing short-term at 7% to buy 9% cap rate properties at times when the cost of long-term debt is 9%.

The cost of *equity* capital, however, is a more difficult concept. What does it really cost a REIT and its shareholders to issue more shares? The REIT must pay dividends on its new shares, so that's a cash outflow (if not a "cost" under generally accepted accounting principles). But because there will be more shares outstanding following the issuance, the value of the REIT (including its net assets and its stream of income well into the future) must be shared with more investors. There are several ways to calculate such cost of equity capital. "Nominal" cost of equity capital refers to the fact that a REIT's current earnings (FFO or AFFO) and its net assets must be allocated over a larger number of common shares, while "true" or "full" cost of equity capital considers such dilution over longer time periods and gives credence to shareholders' total return expectations.

The foregoing subject, though quite important, is rather arcane, and I believe it best not to get into this here. Readers interested in this issue may want to refer to Appendix C, "Cost of Equity Capital," for a more detailed discussion. Suffice it to say that (a) investors will want a REIT to acquire or develop properties of sufficient quality and which will offer such prospects for internal growth that investors' total return expectations (e.g., 12-13%) will be met, and (b) a REIT whose shares trade in the market at a relatively high price in relation to its current and projected FFO and its current net asset value will generally have a lower nominal cost of equity capital (though not necessarily a lower true cost of equity capital) than its less fortunate siblings. This lower nominal cost of capital enhances the REIT's ability to exploit PSI — in the REIT world, as elsewhere, it thus often happens that "the rich get richer," and higher stock prices may translate into faster FFO growth rates.

Development and Expansion

Some REITs can also grow FFO externally by developing entirely new properties, whether they be apartments, malls, outlet centers, neighborhood shopping centers, or any other property type. Until the REIT IPO boom of 1993-1994, very few public REITs even had the capability to develop new properties from the ground up; doing so takes specialized expertise. Today, many REITs can boast of such expertise; most of these are concentrated in the apartment, retail, office and industrial sectors.

A well-conceived development program requires capital as well as know-how. New properties require financing during the 12-24 months required to build them out and bring in the new tenants. Some REITs (many apartment-owning REITs, for example) have the expertise but lack the capital. Nevertheless, having development capabilities is a key advantage, for they allow such REITs to grow externally when markets are hot, which often occurs when cap rates are low and PSI is therefore simply not available, e.g., the apartment market in Northern California in early 1997. Successful developments can provide 10-11% returns on the REIT's investment in them, which is almost always higher than can be obtained through the acquisition of existing properties. Furthermore, the REIT's net asset value will be significantly enhanced; when lower cap rates are applied to newly developed and fully leased properties, extra property value is created which, over time, may enhance the price of the REIT's stock.

Such capability also allows a REIT to capitalize on unique opportunities. For example, Weingarten was able to obtain a parcel of property directly across the boulevard from Houston's Galleria, one of the premier shopping complexes in America, and build an attractive new center in that location. Although a REIT can contract with an outside builder to complete a development, the profitability will not be as good, and the REIT will be subject to the decisions and actions of others beyond its control. Thus, all else being equal (although it rarely is), we want to own those REITs with successful track records of property development, as such REITs have yet another avenue for growing FFO per share.

Of course, property developments do have a down side — they have certain inherent risks. What can go wrong? Plenty. Cost overruns can significantly reduce expected returns. So can failure to attract the anticipated tenant base or projected rental rates. These latter events can occur if the development takes place at a time when a favorable property cycle has abruptly ended. Overbuilding can also decimate rental and occupancy estimates; some analysts fear that this may soon happen in certain apartment markets, perhaps made worse if the national, regional or local economy goes into recession. There is, again, no free lunch, as doing development projects is more risky than buying established properties. Investors and REIT managements alike *should* expect higher returns from development in order to be compensated for taking more risks.

A companion method of external growth that is closely related to new development is the expansion of existing successful properties. Some development capability is required here, but the risks are significantly smaller due to (a) the proven nature of the *existing* property and (b) the lower cost necessary to successfully complete "add-on" space. Further, while the total profit potential from an expansion may be less than that from an entirely new project, the *percentage* return from the expansion is often higher. Nothing beats seeing a REIT announce it's adding "Phase 2" or "Phase 3" to an existing successful property. This generally indicates the existing property is doing well, that management has had the foresight to acquire adjacent land and that a high rate of return is likely with a relatively small degree of risk. Many well-regarded REITs in various property sectors have the ability to add expansion properties, sometimes even when they don't have full development capabilities.

To briefly summarize the above discussion, REITs, like all property owners, can grow their FFO from two sources: *internal* and *external*. *Internal* sources include rental increases, percentage rent, rent bumps, expense reimbursement, retenanting, refurbishment and the sale and reinvestment of properties, all of which often provide attractive growth in FFO and dividend payments. Well-run and widely-respected REITs can also add significantly to FFO growth through *external* means, including property acquisitions (through PSI) and developments. The combination of both internal and external growth can provide the recipe for very rewarding long-term investment returns.

Hypothetical Internal and External Growth: A Case Study of Post Properties

Let's conclude this chapter by taking a quick look at what we might reasonably expect from a well-managed REIT in terms of both internal and external FFO growth. We'll take Post Properties, a very well-run apartment REIT, as our study.

Post reported rental revenues for the first nine months of 1995 of $98.6 million, property operating and maintenance expense of $37.4 million, corporate general and administrative expense of $4.4 million and $17.3 million in interest expense. If we ignore other income, expenses and charges which do not directly relate to the ownership and operation of rental properties, such as Post's property management and landscape services business, non-property interest (or other) income, depreciation and amortization, minority interest and other extraneous items, Post would have generated FFO of $39.5 million for such period. Now, let's also assume that, due to excellent management, the quality and location of its apartment properties and the skill of its on-site apartment managers, Post can increase rents for existing units by one percentage point above inflation — say 4% — while its operating expenses rise at only the rate of inflation — 3%. This would result, 12 months later, in revenues of $102.5 million, property operating and maintenance expense of $38.5 million, and corporate general and administrative expense of $4.5 million; we will assume that interest rates are stable (or that the debt is fixed-rate in nature), so that interest expense will remain unchanged at $17.3 million. Thus Post's FFO would be $42.2 million for the same fiscal period one year later. Based upon these assumptions, the increase in 1996 over 1995 would amount to 6.8%, all generated internally.[4]

Growth via Internal Means	Year 1	Year 2	Growth Rate
Revenues	$98.6	$102.5	4.0%
Operating Expenses	37.4	38.5	3.0%
G&A Expense	4.4	4.5	3.0%
Interest Expense	17.3	17.3	0.0%
Funds from Operations	39.5	42.2	6.8%

But what about *external* growth? Can we squeeze some additional percentage points of FFO growth out of this source? Post had a "market cap" (shares outstanding multiplied by market price) of approximately $683 million on September 30, 1995. Post sold 3.7 million shares of new common stock in a secondary offering in the fall of 1995, raising $105.7 million; this was about 15% of its market cap prior to the offering. Let's assume that, on the strength of its reputation in the investment community, it can do this every 12 months (it raised $82.7 million in a 1994 offering), supplemented by additional debt or even preferred stock[5] (of course, debt leverage will increase risks as well as returns). Next, we need to determine Post's cost of capital to see how additional financings can boost external FFO growth.

(Note that the following discussion will be based upon the concept of *nominal* equity capital costs, as discussed in Appendix C). Post netted $105.7 million from the 1995 offering, after expenses and underwriting discounts, and was expected to earn $65.7 million in FFO over the next 12 months (prior to its expected returns from new properties acquired or developed from the use of the new equity capital). Assuming a 10% return on the new equity capital gets us to $76.3 million in FFO which, divided by all the shares outstanding (including the new shares) results in per-share FFO of $2.69. Dividing the net sale price of $28.50 per share by the pro-forma per-share FFO figure of $2.69 results in a nominal cost of equity capital of 9.4%. Let's also assume that, when it raises debt capital, its cost of such capital will be 150 basis points (1.5%) over the yield on the 10-year U.S. Treasury note; this would have amounted to approximately 8% at the time this book went to press but the cost of debt capital will, of course, fluctuate with prevailing long-term interest rates. Assuming an equal amount of debt and equity, Post's "blended" nominal cost of capital would be 8.7%.

Post has historically been able to generate at least 10% initial returns on its new developments. If it can maintain such returns, it will be able to generate a spread over its cost of capital of 1.3% (10% less the 8.7% blended cost of capital). (We should note here that a spread of 1.3% is a bit below what we would normally expect from a REIT of Post's quality, due to the relatively low price/FFO ratio at which the shares traded during much of 1995.) Having raised $105.7 million in additional equity capital in 1995, it's safe to assume that Post can borrow an additional $40 million due to the additional equity on its balance sheet and its continuing growth prospects. Assuming a 1.3% net return from this additional $145.7M in new financing, we get additional incremental FFO of $1.89 million (($105.7M + $40M) x 1.3%). Divided by the shares previously outstanding and the newly issued shares (28.4 million), the additional $1.89 million results in additional FFO per share of $.067 per share, or a 2.5% increase in FFO just from external growth.

External Growth - Post Properties	(all figures in millions except per share)
Return on investment	10.0%
Blended cost of capital	8.7%
Spread	1.3%
Shares outstanding	24.7
Funds from operations (FFO)	$65.7

126

Equity: funds raised (# of shares)	$106 (3.7)
Debt: funds raised	$40
Additional FFO created	$1.89 [($106+$40) x 1.3%]
New shares outstanding	28.4
Additional FFO per share	$0.067
% increase in FFO	2.5%

Summing up, in our hypothetical example we have Post growing FFO internally by 6.8% and by 2.5% externally, for a total projected growth rate of 9.3% each year. Of course, we cannot be assured that such growth is "in the bag," as it rests on many assumptions that may not prove true. For example, vacancy rates may rise in certain years, cutting into rental growth. Or Post may not be able to increase rents by one percentage point over expenses every year. Interest rates may rise, thus decreasing (or even eliminating) the extra internal growth provided by debt leverage. The costs of debt or equity capital may increase, or the yields available on new developments may decrease, thus eliminating the prospects of external growth. Any or all of these things could happen in a given year; nevertheless, these assumptions could be unduly conservative in some years, such as when the apartment markets are very favorable for owners, as has occurred during the last several years, or when the "spread" of operating income over the cost of capital is higher than the 1.3% assumed above. On balance, Post's hypothetical total internal and external growth potential isn't too far afield; no less an authority than Post's well-respected management has included 10% increases in FFO as part of its business plan.[6] If Post can achieve such growth, on top of its regular dividend yield, the total returns that would be enjoyed by Post's shareholders would be well over 15% — truly an impressive (but realistic) performance.[7]

---

[1] Kranzco Realty, Malan Realty, Mark Centers, Paragon Group and Town & Country, for example, all traded at prices which yielded shareholders close to or exceeding 11% as of December 13, 1996, based upon dividends payment rates then in effect.

[2] Some analysts use the term "EBITDA" to describe this type of income. EBITDA is an acronym for "earnings before interest, taxes, depreciation and amortization," and thus ignores a REIT's "corporate level" expenses such as interest charges, depreciation and amortization expenses.

[3] Some investors have looked simply at a REIT's dividend yield, which is patently absurd; FFO or AFFO is far more important than dividend payments in the context of

determining a REIT's warranted valuation and thus in determining the dilution from issuing additional shares.

[4] If you do the actual math, when an apartment owner is able to increase rents by 4% and limit expense growth to 3%, operating income (before depreciation, amortization, and interest expense), or EBITDA, will rise 4.7%. However, by keeping interest costs constant (as any apartment owner would be able to do by obtaining fixed-rate debt), the leverage from the debt (assuming that the interest rate is less than the percentage return from the property) will increase funds from operations beyond the unleveraged 4.7%. That is why, in Post's case, the projected return twelve months later is 6.8% rather than 4.7%. In fact, virtually all REITs use modest leverage; and like all leverage, it works quite well when the returns from real estate exceed (as they normally do) the interest expense on the borrowed funds. Of course, debt leverage will magnify the risks as well as the rewards.

[5] In October 1996, Post sold 1 million shares of non-convertible preferred stock, raising net proceeds of $48.7 million.

[6] The following statement appears in Post Properties' 1994 Annual Report to Shareholders: "Our goal of achieving annual 10% increases in our per share FFO, the primary goal of our annual business plan, remains unchanged..." (p. 8).

[7] Merrill Lynch's widely-respected REIT analyst Eric Hemel issued a research report on Security Capital Pacific Trust, a fast-growing apartment REIT, in November 1996, in which he went through a similar exercise. He included forecasts of both internal growth and growth via acquisitions and new developments, and concluded that this REIT could be expected to enjoy a long-term FFO growth rate of 10.5%.

Chapter Seven

Analyzing a REIT's Quality:
The Good, The Bad and the Ugly

"Today REITs are operating businesses in which some of the outstanding entrepreneurs in the U.S. are managers and substantial shareholders."
— **Milton Cooper**

Now let's fine tune our analytical skills so that we can make some serious money investing in REITs. As with any type of investing, we can apply a number of different techniques to pursue our goal. We can find companies of the highest quality and own them long-term, allowing us to sit back and be patient, or we can go for the quick payoff. We can try to pick up REITs that are down on their luck and look for the turnaround, or we can stress hidden value and search for those little-known gems. It's a question of blue chips, black sheep and everything in between. It's my own personal view that most REIT investors will do best by concentrating on the largest and most stable companies, the so-called "blue chips." These REITs have a proven record of success, and their methods of long-term growth are worth examining. Here, we'll take a look at what makes a "blue-chip" REIT, and how these high-quality organizations differ from their lesser competitors.

Investment Styles

There are many ways to make money investing in common stocks, and many profitable investment styles. Some investors do well by buying and owning the large, steadily growing companies with excellent long-term track records, such as Coca-Cola, General Electric or Merck. Peter Lynch calls these stocks "stalwarts." Other investors look for companies growing at very rapid rates, such as Intel or Microsoft. Other "contrarian" or "value" investors buy shares in companies that, due to unfavorable industry or company-specific conditions, a problem product or other adverse publicity, are shunned by much of the investing public. Still others buy shares in small but growing companies none of us have ever heard of. All these approaches can work well if the investor is disciplined, patient and exercises good judgment. While the same diversity of styles can be applied to REIT investing, there is no consensus as to which style works best. Few famous REIT investors have emerged about whom numerous articles can be written; there is not yet a Warren Buffett of the REIT world.

129

While *most* investors will want to own blue-chip REITs, they may not appeal to *all* REIT investors. Those seeking quality and safety, above all else, certainly will. Those looking for extraordinary growth, however, will pay less attention to long-term quality and will seek the fastest-growing sectors and the REITs occupying that niche, only to rotate when they perceive a change in future trends. Those investors seeking value will look for REITs that have fallen on hard times or whose future prospects are deemed to be misunderstood by the market. Nevertheless, it is vital for *all* REIT investors to know what makes a blue-chip REIT and how such REITs differ from their cousins. These REITs truly set the standards by which all others should be measured, even if the growth- or value-oriented REIT investor would prefer to buy others. But, first, let's take a brief look at a few investment approaches that do *not* emphasize blue-chip REIT investing.

Virtues of a Blue-Chip REIT
Management
Positive Spread Investing
Balance Sheet Strength
Focus
Insider Stock Ownership
Low Payout
Absence of Conflicts

Growth REITs

Growth REITs are those viewed by investors as having the ability to grow FFO at rates much faster than those of the typical REIT. This may be due to their ownership of properties which are enjoying the best part of their property cycle, such as when rental rates and occupancies are rising rapidly, or due to their management's "game plan," which emphasizes a major acquisition or development program. These "gazelle" REITs usually require lots of new equity and debt capital to expand their business and property portfolio and will often assume the substantial risk that their markets will not quickly become overbuilt in response to favorable market conditions. For example, hotel REITs were, at the time of publication, in a high-growth phase; they were enjoying above-average internal growth, and were busy acquiring lots of hotels. Their FFOs were increasing rapidly. Those REIT investors

130

who bought them in 1995 and 1996 have done very well, as their stock prices have increased substantially, and may continue to appreciate. Growth-oriented REIT investors will seek out such opportunities and may, with good market timing, "beat the market." The key is being quick to exit before market conditions deteriorate or the anticipated rapid rate of growth commences to slow.

Value or "Turnaround" REITs

Always available are a large number of REITs that may be run by management which has not impressed REIT investors for one reason or another, own marginal properties or have gotten into trouble but which may be excellent short- or even long-term investments if bought cheaply enough or just prior to a turnaround in such REIT's business prospects. For example, investors who bought shares in CarrAmerica early in 1995 have done very well indeed. Carr has been operating in a property sector (offices) that has experienced difficult market conditions for many years. However, this sector has bottomed out, and the savvy folks at Security Capital Group, a $2.75 billion real estate investment organization, agreed to acquire a controlling interest in Carr in November 1995. Carr now is definitely different from what it was, and investors who bought into this "value" REIT early have done quite well.[1]

While investors can do very well with these types of REITs, they should be aware of the above-average risk. The dividend is often not adequately covered by the REIT's FFO (meaning that the dividend may be cut), and debt leverage is often very high; such REITs may be compared to junk bonds, which can be very rewarding to investors but which involve more than modest risk. Furthermore, these REITs will not usually have access to capital, which is the fuel necessary for strong external growth in the years ahead; even if they can scrounge up equity or debt capital, such financing is likely to be very expensive (which puts the REIT at a disadvantage to its competitors). Although many REIT investors have done well with some of these downtrodden "REITdogs," most investors would do well to remember that some dogs bite.

Bond Proxies

Another type of REIT that may appeal to some investors is one I like to call the "bond proxy." These REITs may be expected to generate slow FFO and dividend growth, but have relatively secure dividends (due to lack of significant debt leverage and the stable nature of their properties). Such slow but steady performers — perhaps we might call them "oxen" — might include certain health care, retail and apartment REITs that don't have attractive investment opportunities (or the resources necessary to take advantage of them). For example, Tanger Factory Outlet Centers is a well-respected REIT whose very substantial dividend is well covered by its FFO, and its debt levels are not out of line; however, due to the unpopularity of its sector with investors (outlet centers), it currently lacks access to reasonably priced capital. Another type might be "triple-net" REITs that enter into leases with credit-worthy tenants for long periods of time but which provide little opportunity for meaningful rental increases.

Bond proxy REITs do provide high dividend yields (*e.g.*, 7-9%), due to their perceived limited growth prospects, and may be suitable for those investors where stable high income is of paramount importance and capital appreciation is of lesser consideration. However, most investors will achieve a higher total return, over time, with blue-chip REITs that have more meaningful growth opportunities.

The Virtues of Blue-Chip REITs

We've talked about gazelles, REITdogs and oxen. Continuing with our menagerie, blue-chip REITs may be compared to the strong, proud and stately "king of the jungle" — the lion. These REITs are likely to provide steady and predictable FFO growth over several property cycles, can deliver consistent (and rising) long-term FFO and dividend growth, and generally subject investors to less risk of major internal problems that could devastate the REIT's stock price. These financially strong and widely respected REITs will always have access to additional equity and debt capital with which to grow their businesses in a consistent manner. They will not provide the highest dividend yields or even the best total returns to shareholders during certain time periods and they are not likely to be found on the bargain counter — but they should provide years of double-digit returns with a high degree of safety. These "lions" may intimidate their competitors but rarely turn on their owners.

The qualities that make a blue-chip REIT are many, each of which plays a critical role. Of the utmost importance is management quality, together with access to capital, a strong balance sheet, geographical and property type focus, high "insider" stock ownership and other vital attributes. We don't necessarily need to see *all* of them to label a REIT a "blue-chip" lion, but we'd like to find as many as we can. Let's now take a closer look at these all-important factors.

The Supreme Importance of Management

Management is the single most important factor in identifying a blue-chip REIT, and it is management that can make the crucial difference in determining whether a REIT is merely a collection of properties or a growth company whose stock-in-trade just happens to be real estate. Most REITs can do relatively well when their property market is healthy — the rising tide will lift all boats. Even if

132

management is mediocre and has no ability to develop or acquire properties during a boom phase in its property cycle, rapidly rising rents and occupancy rates will generate strong internal growth. Virtually all REITs in that sector will perform well through the "sweet spot" of the cycle; thus almost all the apartment REITs that came public from 1993 through 1994 have reported significant FFO increases into 1996. When difficult property markets return, however, *external* growth opportunities become more important than ever. For example, in today's difficult market for retail properties, quality management will often have the reputation and ability to access the capital markets so that troubled properties can be acquired cheaply, refurbished and retenanted and cash flows greatly improved. In the apartment sector, attractive development opportunities may be necessary to augment slowing internal growth — for example, in some Southeast markets in 1997.

To ascertain overall quality, we want to focus on those REITs whose managements have been able to build a sound portfolio with modest amounts of debt and who have the ability to raise additional capital with which to exploit the opportunities that invariably become available, whether they be property acquisitions or new developments. These managements will have the ability to increase their REIT's FFO externally by making very attractive acquisition deals and, where appropriate, developing new properties. Internal growth is also achieved by, among other things, improving property management and upgrading properties and tenant rolls. Meanwhile, management and administrative costs are strictly controlled. Let's proceed, then, by reviewing the ways in which we can determine the best REIT managements.

FFO Growth in All Types of Climates. Superior management knows how to grow FFO and dividends for a REIT's shareholders in almost all types of real estate climates. Growth is easy to attain when markets are favorable, *e.g.*, when demand exceeds supply in a given geographical area or for a particular type of property. An apartment REIT's management would have to verge on total incompetence if it couldn't generate significant FFO growth between 1993 and 1995, when occupancy rates were rising steadily and landlords were getting major rental increases in most areas of the United States. But only outstanding management can sustain FFO growth at 6-8% when markets are in equilibrium, occupancy rates are static and significant rental increases are difficult to achieve.

Truly outstanding managements can also take advantage of problem markets. Their REITs will acquire properties during difficult times at cheap prices, thus generating additional FFO growth from positive-spread investing. They will attract quality tenants who desire to leave poorly performing shopping centers. They will have structured their lease terms to coincide with underlying real estate values; this approach enables a REIT to find replacement tenants

133

willing to pay the same or even higher rental rates if the original tenants go out of business or file for bankruptcy. Their tenant rosters will be of high quality, thus reducing the risk of tenant defaults (which, even assuming replacement tenants can be readily found, will be disruptive to cash flow and may require significant tenant improvements). And they will pursue innovative ways of taking advantage of the problems that have been encountered by others.

An example is Kimco Realty, a neighborhood shopping center REIT. Shopping center owners have been facing a challenging real estate environment, as the U.S. has been "over-stored" for several years and changing consumer spending patterns have taken their toll on many retailers. Capitalizing on these difficulties, Kimco bought a package of retail stores in early 1996 from a retailer, Venture Stores, that was trying to restructure its business. They were bought at prices believed to be well below market, and leased to Venture at a yield estimated at almost 13%. If Venture cannot continue to make the lease payments, Kimco should be able to lease the sites to one or more other retailers at yields substantially higher. Kimco has been growing its FFO at close to 9% annually, and these kinds of transactions should help it grow FFO at near the same rate in future years. Investors will want to own REITs like Kimco that have the ability to do well even in difficult environments by making favorable acquisitions, upgrading tenant quality, continuing to generate good rental growth and pursuing new business opportunities.

Extra Growth Internally. Positive spread investing isn't always available to a REIT (*e.g.*, when the cost of capital exceeds the entry yields available on new acquisitions), and often there just aren't any development opportunities to be had. Furthermore, when supply and demand are in balance, internal growth rates may be low, as it will be difficult to generate rental increases which exceed the rate of inflation. We therefore would like to ferret out those REITs that have the ability to grow FFO *internally* at a rate not limited by the economic conditions of the geographical areas in which the properties are located. To accomplish this requires some type of competitive edge or innovative business approach. Post Properties creates this through its "Post" brand-name, signifying a high quality living experience in its apartment units. The brand-name recognition, the quality of the units, the extraordinary landscaping and the service-oriented nature of on-site management have historically allowed Post to charge higher rental rates and enabled it to suffer less tenant turnover. This, together with firm cost controls, has provided for extra internal growth that has not been available to all apartment owners.

Another good example of this ability to generate extra growth internally is Kimco's extensive database of tenants' space

134

requirements. As a result of Kimco's deep and long-standing relationships with hundreds of national, regional and local retailers, it has been able to build this database over many years and is able to use it to quickly fill vacant space in its own properties or in properties recently acquired.

We talked earlier about the ways a REIT is sometimes able to charge higher rentals for properties it has enhanced — whether through new signage and paving for a retail shopping center, tennis courts and business centers in apartment complexes, or climate control in self-storage facilities. Innovative management will continually seek to develop ways to implement higher rental rates and new profit centers at the property level in order to increase FFO growth at a rate faster than would be dictated by the economics of the local market.

"The Art of the Deal". One unique characteristic of a high-quality management is its ability to make, from time to time, unusual but very profitable real estate deals. Many REITs merely acquire properties at reasonable prices and manage them well; some of them develop new properties at attractive rates of return. Only a few are able to pull off the unusual transaction that significantly enhances FFO growth.

A prime example of this is Vornado's Alexanders coup. Alexanders was a department store chain operating in New York City that filed for bankruptcy in 1992. It owned seven department store sites and a 50% interest in an adjacent regional mall. These sites, according to a Green Street Advisors, Inc. research report,[2] were very valuable, including a full square block in mid-town Manhattan. In March 1995, Vornado bought a 27% stock interest in Alexanders from Citicorp for $55 million, a purchase price 20% below the prevailing market price. Vornado also loaned $45 million to Alexanders, at a weighted average interest rate of 16.4%. Alexanders has since become a REIT, and Vornado is entitled to include, in its earnings reports, its proportional share of Alexanders' funds from operations. Furthermore, Vornado structured the deal to earn fees for managing, leasing and developing Alexanders' real estate. Green Street has estimated that not only will Vornado be able to significantly increase its FFO in future years as a result of the Alexanders transaction, but that it has caused the per share net asset value of Vornado to increase substantially as a result of its concluding the transaction. Investors may expect additional such sweet deals from Vornado in future years. Kimco's Venture Stores transaction, discussed earlier, is another example of the type of deal that excellent managements are able to accomplish. More recently, Crescent Real Estate has been impressing REIT investors with highly attractive and innovative acquisitions.

Other instances of "the art of the deal" include purchases of nursing home mortgage loans from the RTC by Health Care

Properties and Nationwide Health in 1992 at interest rates exceeding 14%. LTC Properties, another well-run health care REIT, has been purchasing and securitizing certain of its own nursing home mortgage loans as a means of obtaining additional leverage on an "off-balance sheet" basis (while increasing LTC's risk level, this program is highly profitable to the shareholders so long as LTC's management continues to do an excellent job in its loan underwriting). More recently, Reckson Associates bought, for $20 million, a 70% interest in a $50 million non-performing first mortgage loan. The company's objective was to acquire title to the property for a total cost of approximately $35 million, which would be about two-thirds of replacement cost, and which would provide Reckson with a 13.5% return on its investment, not to mention increasing returns in later years. As REIT investors, we want to look for REIT managements that can find and consummate these kinds of "value-added" transactions.

Attracting the Best Tenants. A well-managed REIT will not be entirely dependent upon the quality and creditworthiness of its tenants; such a REIT should, even in difficult environments, be able to re-lease space vacated by a financially troubled tenant at rates comparable to what it had been earning previously, if not more. Most of the retail REITs boasting quality management were not hurt in the last retail contraction of the late '80s, nor have they been significantly affected by the 1995-1996 wave of retail bankruptcies.

Nevertheless, a REIT's ability to attract a roster of high-quality tenants is very important, particularly in retail sectors such as malls, neighborhood shopping centers and factory outlet centers. Outstanding tenants can afford to pay higher rents in future years through rent bumps and sales overages built into the lease, attract more shoppers to the shopping center (thereby boosting the sales of the other stores located there), and reduce the risk of periods of lost rent and higher leasing costs that result from frequent tenant turnover. Just as important, quality tenants, whether users of retail space, industrial properties or office buildings, will usually be looking to expand, and enjoying good relationships with these tenants gives the REIT an inside track on filling their additional space requirements. For example, Security Capital Industrial Trust's business plan is to develop long-term relationships with America's major corporations, which will lead to acquiring and developing additional properties for these companies.

In the health care sector, tenant credit quality may be even more important than it is in traditional real estate, as the real estate value of a health care facility is of lesser importance. When investing in health care REITs, investors might want to concentrate on those who lease their properties to the most profitable and financially stable health care providers. Health Care Properties, MediTrust and Nationwide Health have been leaders in this area.

The best management teams perform well even when their tenants do not. In the mid-1980s, when the downward spiral in oil prices sent Texas and its neighboring states into a virtual depression, retail sales in Houston weakened considerably and retail store occupancy rates fell to below 90% in the "oil patch." However, Weingarten Realty, a blue-chip REIT, came out of the downturn completely unscathed, retaining occupancy rates of 93-95%. This company was able to continue to do well, despite the horrendous economic conditions, by retaining excellent relationships with its tenants, owning centers in strong locations and anchoring its centers with stores that cater to consumer necessities, such as drug stores and supermarkets. In fact, many retailers relocated to Weingarten's centers, which continued to draw a steady clientele.

Cost Control . It has always been axiomatic in business that the "low-cost provider" has an edge on the competition, and that maxim was never more true than in today's highly competitive business environment. Outstanding REIT managements are likely to build a very cost-efficient internal property management team, while also keeping overhead costs (such as administration, legal, accounting and other expenses of operating as a public company) under tight control.

A highly cost-effective property management team enables the REIT to acquire properties at prices that might be unprofitable to competing bidders, and to earn greater profits after the properties are acquired. For example, let's assume that an attractive apartment building is available for $7 million. Let's assume further that the property provides total rental income of $1 million annually and would cost most property owners $500,000 in property management expenses, leaving the owner with an unleveraged return of $500,000, which represents a return of only 7.1% ($500,000 divided by $7 million) on the asking price. Assuming that the prevailing cost of capital is 8%, this is not a property that will attract many offers. But suppose that, due to a REIT's cost-effective management team, the apartment building could be managed for a cost of only $400,000 annually, providing $600,000 in operating income; at the same asking price of $7 million, the return would be 8.6%, somewhat greater than the REIT's assumed 8% cost of capital.

Aside from keeping property management expenses under control, it's important to shareholders to keep other overhead costs low as well. A low-overhead REIT can significantly increase the company's net return to its shareholders. Let's assume that a REIT owns $10 million of properties that generate an unleveraged 9% yield, or $900,000 per year. Assume further that overhead costs amount to 1% of assets, or $100,000 per year. This REIT's net return on its investments will be $800,000, or 8%. Compare this with a REIT whose overhead costs amount to only 0.5% of assets, or $50,000; this REIT will generate $850,000 in net operating income, providing an 8.5% return to its shareholders. To look at this another way, assume that there are 1 million shares outstanding, and that both REITs trade at 12 times FFO. In the first instance, FFO will be $.80 per share, and the share price will be 12 times $.80, or $9.60. In the second case, FFO will be $.85 per share, and that REIT's stock price will trade for $10.20, or 6% higher. The first company's total market cap will be $9.6 million, compared with $10.2 million for the second company. Thus an overhead savings of only $50,000 per year translates into an increased total company market valuation of $600,000.

	Higher Costs	Lower Costs
FFO Before Overhead	$900	$900
Overhead	$100	$50
FFO After Overhead	$800	$850
Return to Shareholders	8.0%	8.5%
FFO per Share	$0.80	$0.85
FFO Multiple	12	12
Share Price	$9.60	$10.20

Track Record of FFO Growth. Wasn't it one of our founding fathers, speaking of the dubious conduct of King George and the English parliament, who said something to the effect that "I know of no lamp by which to light my feet other than the lamp of experience?" One of the most obvious (but oft-neglected) methods of determining quality management is to review the REIT's historical operating performance. Has the REIT had a long and successful track record of increasing FFO on a per-share basis and increasing dividends to its shareholders (supported by the underlying FFO growth)? How long has the REIT been a public company? Does it find a way to turn in a satisfactory performance even when its property markets are experiencing difficult economic conditions or have been exposed to significant competition from new developments? Does it acquire properties just to expand its portfolio, or does it find properties with significant upside potential?

As we've discussed, REITs have been around for more than 30 years, but we can count on just two hands the number of REITs that have established impressive track records of consistent and substantial growth of at least seven or eight years' duration and lasting through a complete property cycle. These include Merry Land and United Dominion in the apartment sector, Washington REIT (which owns several different property types), Health Care Properties, Nationwide Health and MediTrust, serving the health care segment, and Federal, New Plan and Weingarten, which own neighborhood shopping centers. REITs that have performed extremely well for investors over long periods of time are REITs we will frequently want to own if we can buy them at reasonably attractive prices (Chapter Eight discusses how we can determine value in REIT shares).

138

Fortunately, we are not limited to the above-named old-timers even if we want to go with the highest quality. As we discussed earlier, the large crop of new REITs that came public from 1991 through 1994 contains some of the most outstanding names in the real estate industry, most of which have operated very successfully for many years as private companies. Additional companies with very capable managements and well-conceived growth strategies have also gone public since then. These companies have built solid (albeit moderately short) track records since they've been public. If we can satisfy ourselves that they did well for many years previously as private companies, we should feel confident that we are buying REITs with strong and experienced management teams. These REITs would include, to name just a few, Bay Apartment Communities, Evans Withycombe, Post Properties and Summit Properties (apartments), Developers Diversified and Kimco (neighborhood shopping centers), Macerich, Simon DeBartolo Group and Taubman Realty (shopping malls), Chelsea/GCA and Tanger (outlet stores), Reckson Associates, Spieker Properties and Weeks Corp. (office/industrial), and Shurgard Storage and Storage USA (self-storage).

Nevertheless, these newer REITs should bear the "burden of proof" that they can develop the kind of long-term successful track record as public companies in the same manner as their more-established cousins have done over the last several years through good cycles and bad. Many REITs that have come public in recent years have been highly touted by their underwriters but have failed to show that they can "deliver the goods" as public companies. Some of them now languish in the backwaters of the REIT world.

One final note on this subject: Investors should be very wary of any new REIT that has been put together specifically for the purpose of going public. Many of these, labeled "make-a-REITs" by Green Street Advisors, have been cobbled together by opportunistic promoters and underwriters during those infrequent times that REITs have enjoyed very enthusiastic receptions from the investing public but have no track record of successful real estate ownership and management. Many things can go wrong with such REITs (and, in fact, they have); enough REITs with established managements who have done well over many years are available today at attractive prices that investors need not chase these unproved commodities.

Quality	Critical Ability
FFO Growth	How will management grow FFO in static markets?
Internal Growth	Does management have an innovative business approach to grow its existing business and property income?
Deal Making Ability	Can management find and structure deals at unusually attractive prices and with significant upside potential?
Attracting Best Tenants	What quality of tenant can management attract?
Cost Control	Can management leverage the return on acquisitions by keeping

Access to Capital and PSI Availability

Once we've established the quality of management, we should consider the next key factor in determining, at least on a short- to medium-term basis, which REITs deserve the "blue-chip" label: access to capital. We have already discussed the legal requirement for REITs to pay out to their shareholders 95% of net income each year, which prevents REITs from building up substantial retained earnings. Accordingly, if a REIT is to grow FFO at a substantial pace, it must have access to capital; furthermore, the cost of such capital, in the form of interest rates (on borrowed funds) or dilution (on new shares sold), is often a key factor in determining whether the REIT will grow merely for growth's sake or on a basis that will be rewarding to its shareholders. It's therefore imperative that, in considering a REIT's quality and its ability to grow its FFO and dividends at a rate significantly above inflation, we study the REIT's access to capital and the likely cost of such.

A typical commercial property — whether an apartment building, retail shopping center or office building — if not situated in a highly favorable location where the demand for space is consistently strong and where it's difficult to develop competing properties, is unlikely to provide its owner with income growth that substantially and consistently exceeds the rate of inflation. Even if leveraged with long-term debt at a fixed interest rate, growth in net operating income still will normally not exceed 4-5% annually, at best. A REIT that owns such assets, especially when it distributes most of its FFO to shareholders (which prevents it from retaining much equity capital), will not grow at a very rapid rate unless it can make new investments from which additional FFO can be generated. And in order to get the funds with which to make such new investments, a REIT will normally need to be able to tap the capital markets regularly.

Which REITs can do so? The answer, of course, is only those REITs that are well-respected in the investment community, have developed excellent track records with REIT investors, have solid balance sheets, and have the apparent ability to earn a satisfactory return on the capital they hope to raise. According to the November 29, 1996, issue of Realty Stock Review, an excellent REIT newsletter published by Dow Jones Financial Publishing Corp., there were 111 publicly traded REITs having market caps of at least $100 million and which were followed by at least three analysts.[3] Of those 111, probably less than half have the ability to raise additional capital through the issuance of additional shares (although this percentage may increase in years in which REITs are particularly popular with investors). These will be the "have" REITs, those that will be able to grow at a rate significantly faster than the modest internal growth rates expected by most commercial property owners.

To state the point perhaps more simply, an owner of a typical commercial real property might expect it to generate increased annual cash flows, during periods when supply and demand are in equilibrium, in an amount equal only to the rate of inflation, say 2-3%, without leveraging the returns by taking on debt. If such an owner cannot raise additional capital with which to buy additional properties, his or her business venture will not be able to grow, over a long time period, at anything other than a very slow rate. However, if such a property owner can get access to additional equity capital, and leverage it by taking on additional debt, he or she will be able to buy additional properties that, assuming they provide a return exceeding the cost of capital, will allow the venture to grow at a rate significantly faster than 3% annually. This, simply put, is one of the principal reasons why many outstanding REITs will be able to report FFO growth, over long time periods, of at least 6-8% per year. Access to capital is thus a key factor in separating the blue-chip REITs from their ordinary cousins.

The flip side of the "access to capital" coin is the availability and profitability of new investments, either through acquisition or new development. To determine the value to a REIT of positive-spread investing ("PSI"), we need to take a good look at the *spread* between the cost of capital and the likely profits that will accrue to the REIT from deploying it. The same situation is present with regard to new developments; if the anticipated return is less than the cost of the capital needed to build the new project, the REIT will not be doing any favors to its shareholders, at least over the short term, by taking on the risk of building. A REIT may be able to raise all the capital it will ever need and at reasonable prices, but if it is not able to engage in PSI or to develop new properties at attractive rates of return, such capital will be of dubious value to the REIT's shareholders. Conversely, capital can be seemingly expensive in absolute terms, but if a REIT is able to buy properties at high cap rates or create new developments that yield substantially more than the cost of the capital, the REIT can still do well.

A couple of examples should be helpful. Mall REITs have not had, until very recently, many PSI opportunities; from the moment they went public their properties have been valued, based upon their share prices, at a discount to what similar properties have sold for in the private market. Simon DeBartolo Group is one of the most well-regarded mall REITs, but its FFO yield (estimated 12-month forward-looking funds from operations divided by the stock price) has been in the 8-9% range during much of the last few years. Thus Simon's "nominal" cost of equity capital (ignoring certain capitalized costs such as routine (but capitalized) property maintenance, tenant improvements and leasing commissions) has likewise been in the 8-9% range; borrowed funds would probably have been somewhat less expensive, but Simon, like most mall REITs, has carried substantial debt, so additional borrowed capital has not been a major opportunity. On the other hand, mall cap rates have been in the 7-8% range until recently. PSI has therefore not been available to mall REITs since they went public in 1993-1994 (although this situation was beginning to change late in 1996, as mall cap rates were rising while the mall REITs' cost of capital was declining). Furthermore, mall REITs have had few opportunities to develop new facilities; not only has much of America been "malled over," but it has been questionable as to whether a REIT (or, indeed, any builder) could consistently earn a return on its investment in a new mall in excess of its cost of capital. This lack of both PSI and new development opportunities may be a key reason why mall REITs have been mediocre performers during much of the time that they've been public companies.

Now, let's look at a more pleasant example. LTC Properties, a health care REIT specializing in the ownership and financing of nursing homes and other health care facilities, went public in August 1992 and has issued additional shares and convertible debentures from time to time thereafter. Due to the reputation and credibility of its management, it has always had access to capital with which to finance its growth. However, being a new REIT and specializing in an area (nursing homes and assisted-living facilities) that has not stirred investors' enthusiasm, LTC has been paying a fairly high price for its capital. At the time of its IPO, LTC sold convertible debentures, which carried an interest rate of 9.75%. Shares were issued in March 1994 at an FFO yield of almost 10%. In addition to periodic share offerings, follow-on convertible debenture offerings were completed in September 1994, September 1995, February 1996 and August 1996, at interest rates of 8.5%, 8.5%, 7.75% and 8.25%, respectively. One would have to admit that this is not particularly cheap capital on an absolute basis.

Yet due to the very attractive acquisition opportunities available to LTC since it went public, which have provided LTC with entry yields in the 10-11% area, this REIT has been able to take full advantage of PSI despite the relatively high cost of its capital. As a result, investors who bought LTC at its August 1992 $10 IPO price have enjoyed a 80% increase in its share price to $18 as of December 1996 (a compounded annual growth rate of approximately 15%), and have enjoyed dividend yields of between 7.5% and 10% per year, providing total annual returns of 22.5% to 25%. This, despite LTC's nominally high cost of capital, is PSI at its finest!

142

Balance Sheet Strength.

A third factor that is extremely important in determining whether a REIT deserves the blue-chip label is its balance sheet. Property owners, probably commencing from biblical days, have often financed their assets with some amount of debt. At times the amount of debt has dwarfed the amount of equity put into the property, such as the purchase of a single-family residence by an individual (particularly when using government-assistance programs) or during certain times in the not-too-distant past when developers were able to obtain 90-100% financing. As we've discussed earlier, debt leverage increases both the risks and rewards of owning real estate.

Property owners (including REITs), due to the stable cash flows normally available on well-located and well-tenanted properties, can justify a moderate amount of leverage by using a reasonable amount of debt when financing property acquisitions. Several years ago Washington REIT made a big issue of the fact that it had reduced its debt to almost zero; that's not terribly impressive to most knowledgeable real estate (and REIT) investors, as such low debt levels will normally result in sub-par FFO growth rates. What *is* impressive to investors is a REIT that carefully manages a modest amount of debt in order to increase the rate of return on its properties and the rate of growth of FFO while, at the same time, keeping the balance sheet strong enough to take advantage of new opportunities.

A strong balance sheet enables a REIT to raise new equity capital (investors are loathe to buy shares in an over-leveraged company) for ongoing business expansions and new developments and acquisitions, through PSI, as well as to take on additional debt in order to leverage such growth. Conversely, a REIT with an excellent management and track record of growth and which is in the midst of a very favorable development or acquisition climate could nevertheless be shut out from these ample opportunities if its balance sheet is so weak that it cannot obtain the necessary capital.

Debt Ratios and Interest Coverage Ratios. What constitutes a "strong" balance sheet? First, the total amount of debt should not be excessive in relation to total assets; we don't want to see a REIT owe $200 million when its total assets are valued at only $300 million. Furthermore, the interest payments on that debt should be well-covered by operating cash flows. Let's talk about debt levels first.

Debt Ratios. Most REIT analysts use a ratio known as "debt to total market cap" to determine the extent to which a REIT is leveraged with debt. This term is simply the total amount of debt divided by the total market capitalization of the REIT as determined by combining (a) equity (the number of shares outstanding

143

(including any operating partnership units convertible into common shares) multiplied by the share price), (b) outstanding preferred stock and (c) indebtedness. For example, on September 30, 1995, Highwoods Properties, an office/industrial REIT, had total indebtedness of $181.7 million, 23.0 million total shares (and partnership units convertible into shares) outstanding when the market price was $26.375 per share and no preferred stock outstanding. The debt-to-market cap ratio can thus be determined by dividing debt ($181.7M) by the sum of the equity cap (23.0M x $26.375 = $606.6M) and debt ($181.7M), resulting in a ratio of 23%.

A few analysts (including Green Street Advisors), rather than using debt to total market cap, prefer to use a similar formula, but which is based on the asset values of a REIT. For example, if a REIT had $100 million in debt and total asset values (based upon an estimation of the fair market values of its properties) of $300 million, its debt to asset value ratio would be $100 million divided by $300 million, or 33%. This method thus focuses on the asset value of a REIT rather than the valuation of its shares in the stock market. It has the advantage of being more conservative (as most REITs trade at market valuations in excess of their net asset values) while avoiding fluctuation as a REIT's share price bounces around from day to day. Advocates of this approach wonder why a REIT's leverage ratio should increase just because its stock price happens to decline temporarily for reasons having nothing to do with operations or property values. Nevertheless, the debt to asset value ratio is less frequently utilized than the debt to total market cap ratio.

Just what is the "right" amount of debt leverage for a REIT? First, let's look at some averages. At the end of 1995 Robert Frank, who at the time was chief REIT analyst with Alex Brown & Sons, estimated that REITs' median debt to total market cap ratio was 30% and the average was 34%.[4] The typical ratio did not change significantly in 1996. Some sectors use more debt than others; the mall REITs, for example, have been using much more leverage than office and industrial REITs. The table in the following sub-section (see "Interest Coverage Ratios"), based upon information provided by Realty Stock Review, shows the average debt to total market cap ratios for various sectors of the REIT world as of November 29, 1996.

Should we therefore conclude that mall REITs are over-leveraged and office and industrial REITs are under-leveraged? No; unfortunately, there is no "appropriate" debt ratio that, if exceeded, would make a REIT "over-leveraged." Much depends upon the nature of the real estate in which the REIT invests, the geographical area in which the properties are located, existing and prospective business conditions and the supply-demand situation for the REIT's real estate. Taking on leverage is really nothing more than putting one's invested assets into a position of being able to generate higher

144

rewards if business turns out to be favorable and exacerbating the difficulties if business is disappointing. Under adverse economic or real estate conditions, a high debt level can be a time bomb waiting to explode. Mall owners have been able to use substantial leverage because their business has generally been very steady and predictable; retailers have always needed to be in their malls, and their rental rates moved steadily upwards. If this situation should change, what may have been reasonable leverage for a mall REIT in the past might be too aggressive in the future. The reverse may be true in the office and industrial sectors, where conditions have been improving substantially; several years ago a 35% debt to total market cap ratio may have been too high for such property owners, whereas today and for the next few years they may be able to safely take on a higher amount of debt.

As we can therefore see, it's very difficult to say what debt to total market cap ratio (or debt to asset value ratio) is "about right," as everything depends upon the stability of the expected future income streams to the REIT, whether the threat of overbuilding is on the horizon, whether rental rates are moving up, down or sideways and many other similar factors. Nevertheless, a few rules-of-thumb should be followed. First, a debt to total market cap ratio exceeding 50% substantially exposes a REIT to negative surprises, and may be regarded as dangerous; investors should take a very hard look at whether such a REIT may be uncomfortably overleveraged. Second, a ratio under 25% is generally quite conservative, as such a ratio normally gives a REIT significant flexibility in obtaining additional debt and/or equity capital. Third, if competition is becoming intense or overbuilding is likely to cause downward pressure on rents, a ratio above even 35% could become problematical.

Interest Coverage Ratios. Another method by which we should address the issue of whether debt levels are reasonable or excessive is to look not at the aggregate amount of debt but rather at the amount by which total interest payments on that debt is *covered* by the REIT's net operating income (prior to interest payments, taxes, depreciation and amortization). This measurement is often expressed as the *ratio* of net operating income, or "EBITDA,"[5] to total interest expense. For example, if "AggressiveOffice REIT" has annual net operating income (before taking interest charges, depreciation and other non-operating income and expenses into account) of $14 million and carries debt of $100 million, which costs it $9 million in annual interest expense, its "coverage ratio" would be $14 million divided by $9 million, or 1.55.

Many analysts prefer this measure of debt to simply looking at the ratio of debt to either total market cap or asset value, as it tells us how burdensome the debt is in relationship to its current operating income. In other words, if the REIT is doing very well with its properties at a particular time (perhaps due to very favorable conditions within a sector or geographical area) and can obtain fixed-rate financing at reasonable rates, it may be able to very comfortably afford a higher level of debt. It will also avoid one obvious problem with the debt to total market cap ratio (but which is not present in the debt to asset value ratio), which is that as a REIT's stock price declines, the debt to total market cap ratio becomes higher. For example, let's assume that TimidOffice REIT has debt of $100 million and 10 million shares outstanding which are trading at $20. Its debt to total market cap ratio would be 33% ($100 million in debt divided by the sum of $100 million (debt cap) and $200 million (equity cap)). Now, 33% is a very comfortable ratio. But suppose that the price of TimidOffice's stock declines, due to a general market decline, from $20 to $15 per share. Now its debt to total market cap ratio has shot up to 40% ($100 million divided by the sum of $100 million and $150 million). Does TimidOffice now need to go out and raise additional equity capital in order to get its debt to total market cap down to a more comfortable level? To do so would require this REIT to sell additional shares at a time when its stock price is down substantially, which is clearly a strange (and undesirable) result.

Advocates of interest coverage ratios seem to ignore, however, the fact that real estate markets do change over time, and managements don't always make perfect decisions. To use the interest coverage ratio method to the exclusion of either debt to total market cap or debt to asset value is to ignore the fact that a REIT's net operating income may be *temporarily* high due to favorable economic conditions. If rental income declines (perhaps due to a major recession or overbuilding), net operating income will be reduced and will cause what might have been a comfortable coverage ratio to become rather skimpy. This, in turn, may require the REIT to raise equity capital at a time when investors are already nervous about future prospects — again, a very bad time for capital-raising activities. The careful REIT analyst will therefore look at *both* debt to total market cap (or debt to asset value) and interest coverage ratios in order to determine whether a REIT might be over-leveraged (which will mean that it must raise additional equity capital shortly) or under-leveraged (and can thus take on additional debt with which to acquire or develop additional properties).

Like debt to total market cap or debt to asset value ratios, there is no "magic number" by which we can determine whether a REIT has taken on so much debt that interest expenses become "too high" in relation to current operating income. Generally speaking, an interest coverage ratio of below 2.5 will often be cause for some concern, and blue-chip REITs will rarely have ratios that low. Realty Trust Review provides these ratios, and the following table sets forth, at November 29, 1996, the average interest coverage ratios and the average debt to total market cap percentages for the various REIT sectors (based upon the REITs in their "universe"):

REIT Sector	Interest Coverage Ratio	Debt to Market Cap.
Apartments	3.5	40.6%
Neighborhood Shopping Centers	3.7	40.1%
Regional Malls	2.8	45.6%
Factory Outlet Centers	3.7	50.0%
Manufactured Home	3.9	29.0%
Health Care	7.9	29.2%
Hotels	8.4	13.8%
Industrial	3.9	30.2%
Office	3.6	23.7%
Self Storage	10.7	14.3%

Variable-Rate Debt. Almost as important as the ratios of debt to total market cap (or net asset value) or interest rate coverage is the amount of debt that is *variable-rate* in nature. Variable-rate debt, of course, subjects the REIT and its shareholders to significantly increased interest costs in the event that interest rates rise. Mike Kirby at Green Street Advisors has made the point that REIT investors normally like or dislike a REIT for its business and real property prospects, and don't want to see what would otherwise be a good REIT investment spoiled because a REIT's management guessed wrong on the direction of interest rates. The enlightened investor's attitude toward a REIT's management is normally "take my equity capital and invest it wisely in real estate; I, not you, will accept the responsibility for interest rates." Mr. Kirby is absolutely correct; it's clearly a negative for a REIT investor when the REIT has loaded up on variable-rate debt that exposes the REIT's FFO to the risk of rising interest rates. Given the large portion of a REIT's expenses that is comprised of interest expense, substantially higher interest costs could cause a significant reduction in FFO, and even result in a dividend cut. Conversely, fixed-rate debt is a positive, as it allows REIT investors to be able to predict future FFO growth without having to guess whether rising interest rates will throw all forecasts askew.[6]

As variable-rate debt is normally priced lower than fixed-rate debt, a REIT's management can "subsidize" FFO growth by opting for a heavy dose of the former. Thus the *quality* of a REIT's FFO and its growth rate are suspect when the REIT relies heavily upon variable-rate debt. All else being equal, investors should not pay as much for a dollar of FFO generated with substantial variable-rate debt. For example, let's take two REITs, each in the same industry, identical in almost all respects, and each is expected to generate FFO of $1 per share. However, REIT "A" has variable-rate debt on its books equal to 15% of its asset value and REIT "B" has no variable-rate debt at all. Investors might be willing to pay 12 times FFO for the shares of REIT "B," or $12 per share, whereas they might want to

147

pay only 11 times FFO ($11 per share) for REIT "A," due to its much greater use of variable-rate debt.

Some variable-rate debt is inevitable for entities such as REITs that are constantly looking for additional capital. The typical pattern is for a REIT to establish a line of credit that can be used on a short-term basis and then paid off through either a stock offering or the placement or sale of longer-term fixed-rate debt. Borrowings under such credit lines are almost always at variable rates. The key is the *amount* of such variable-rate debt in relation to the REIT's net asset value or its market cap. A Green Street Advisors report[7] noted that, in their universe of REITs, the amount of variable-rate debt as a percentage of net asset value averaged 6.8%. This appears to be a reasonable ratio, and a ratio of this size would not expose a REIT to significant negative earnings surprises should interest rates start to rise. However, 19 REITs in their universe at the time of the report had ratios exceeding 10%, and five of them had ratios in excess of 18%. Needless to say, a REIT carrying such a high ratio of variable-rate debt would have difficulty qualifying as a blue-chip REIT.

Maturity of Debt. It's often been said that real estate is a "long-term asset" and should be financed with long-term capital, and there is much truth in this. Debt that matures and becomes due in the very near future subjects the borrower to several risks, each of which could cause significant problems. First and foremost, the lender may, for whatever reason, be unwilling to roll the debt over or enter into a new credit agreement with a REIT borrower; if no other source of financing can be found, the REIT will have no choice but to sell off assets (sometimes at fire-sale prices) in order to pay off the debt or, in rare occasions, to file bankruptcy proceedings. Second, if interest rates have risen, the debt will have to be refinanced at significantly higher interest rates. Finally, the mere threat of a failure to obtain adequate replacement financing can cause a severe drop in the REIT's stock price, thus precluding it from raising additional equity capital as an alternative to extending the debt or, at the least, making such equity financing very expensive.

Nationwide Health Properties, today one of the most highly regarded health care REITs, had this type of problem in its early years, when (under prior management) it took on loads of short-term debt that its lender was unwilling to roll over, thus requiring the REIT (then known as "Beverly Investment Properties") to sell off significant amounts of assets and to reduce its dividend.

Accordingly, REIT investors must be mindful of the extent to which a REIT's debt will be coming due within one or two years, and some analysts look at the average debt maturity when examining a REIT's balance sheet. Intelligent investors would prefer that most of a REIT's debt does not mature for several years in the future, and thus applaud a REIT for financing its debt on a long-term basis (at least seven years' duration), and at fixed interest rates. Wise REIT managements will refinance debt well before maturity, and will seek as long a maturity date as is available to them.

The above-cited Green Street report[8] notes that, in their REIT universe, the amount of short-term debt as a percentage of net asset value averaged approximately 4.5%; however, 10 REITs had ratios exceeding 10%, which should raise a yellow flag with investors. Any such REIT not having an excellent relationship with its lender at the time the debt matures could encounter serious and unpleasant problems.

Focus: Beware of the "Jack of All Trades and Master of None"

Ever since the time the first REIT raised its first dollar of capital and until fairly recently, we have heard from certain brokers and investor relations officers that an excellent REIT to own would be one that is well-diversified as to property type and geographical location, as such a REIT diversifies the risks of owning real estate. The only merit to this contention is that diversification in one's real estate holdings is a definite plus. The major fallacy in this premise is that it fails to take into account the fact that, for most property types, real estate ownership and management is essentially a local business, and no two properties or locations are exactly alike. We want to entrust our investment dollars earmarked for REITs with managements who have a wealth of experience owning and managing their particular property type, and who invest and manage their properties in geographical areas that they know exceedingly well. As we'll see in Chapter Nine and as noted below, investors can obtain their own diversification by owning a variety of these well-focused REITs.

A good example of specialized REIT management is that of Evans Withycombe Residential (EWR). EWR went public in August 1994, but has been an active developer and owner of apartments in Phoenix and Tucson, Arizona, since 1977; it does not own other types of properties. The company is the largest developer, owner and operator of apartments in Arizona, and management has survived even the worst of Arizona's periodic overbuilt markets. Until a recent foray into Southern California, this REIT has not owned a single apartment unit outside of the Phoenix or Tucson areas. No one knows the Arizona apartment market like EWR's management. Cali Realty, which acquires, develops and manages suburban office buildings in New Jersey, is another good example of such specialization.

Such local, specialized knowledge gives a REIT several advantages in its markets. It will be more likely to know of a distressed seller who must unload its properties, and thus be able to take advantage of the occasional extraordinary opportunity. If it has development capabilities, it will know who the best and most

149

reliable contractors are, and will know how to get zoning permits and variances. It will be very much aware of local economic conditions, and will know exactly where the city's or region's growth is heading. It will be able to figure out where the competition is building, and who is raising rents. If a retail REIT, it will have good access to the up-and-coming regional retailers. The bottom line is that highly specialized managements have a significant edge in the often very competitive business of buying and managing real estate.

If it's important for a REIT to concentrate on a specific geographical area, it is even *more* important to specialize in one property type. In the late 1990s and into the next century, successful real estate ownership will be no slam-dunk. Each type of commercial real estate has its own peculiar set of economics, and it's not likely that one management will be able to successfully navigate all the potholes that develop in each sector. How likely is it that a REIT's managers can figure out when the local office market has bottomed out, and at the same time snag the best retailers for its shopping centers while refraining from building or buying several new apartment units in an area that is quickly becoming overbuilt?

Most blue-chip REITs will thus be highly specialized as to property type and geographical location. To confuse things, however, there are exceptions, in both the general and individual cases. Health care REITs, for example, should *not* seek geographic concentration; the operators of nursing homes are largely dependent upon state reimbursement policies, and too great a concentration of properties in one state can create problems for the shareholders if tight-fisted and unreasonable regulators are encountered in that jurisdiction. In another area, it will not be terribly important for mall REITs to be concentrated geographically. The economics of developing and operating malls are similar in most areas of the U.S., and a large percentage of mall tenants are nationally known retailers; thus, knowing the peculiarities of local neighborhoods is not as important for mall owners as for the owners of neighborhood shopping centers and other property types, such as apartments, office buildings and industrial properties.

There may be other exceptions to the principle of specialization. As retailing is taking on an increasingly national-retailer orientation, it can be advantageous — even for retail REITs that do not own malls — to have locations in many states. Kimco Realty is a prime example. It operates in many Eastern states and, because of an extensive database of retailer requirements and strong relationships with large numbers of quality tenants, its geographical diversification may not be much of a handicap in relation to the local competition. Another exception is Weingarten Realty. Long known as the dominant neighborhood shopping center owner in Houston, Weingarten recently has been entering new markets such as Las Vegas, Kansas City and Albuquerque. Some veteran REIT investors may decry such wanderlust, but at some point a well-run and growing real estate company like Weingarten is going to exhaust most of the opportunities in its local market. If Weingarten applies the same degree of care and foresight to its new markets as it's done in Houston, investors need not be overly concerned by its geographical forays. Finally, Washington REIT has done very well for many years despite owning several different property types (although each of its properties has been located within the greater Washington, D.C.-Virginia area). Two highly-regarded office REITs, Beacon and CarrAmerica, have recently been buying properties well outside their original territory (Boston and Washington, D.C., respectively). It's too soon to tell how effective this strategy will be, but so far REIT investors are giving these companies the benefit of the doubt.

Notwithstanding such exceptions, REIT investors should be careful about investing in companies that are so spread out, whether by property type or geographical location, that they are unlikely to be market leaders in their areas of concentration. The list of blue-chip REITs is dominated by those that are incredibly knowledgeable as to their particular local property markets; REITs that don't meet this test should have the burden of proving to the investor that they belong in the highest quality echelons of the REIT world.

Before we leave this subject, one earlier issue should be addressed: If we want to own only those REITs that are highly specialized, how do we get adequate diversification? The answer to this question is much easier today than it was before the incredible 1993-1994 REIT IPO explosion: Now we can buy a bundle of high-quality REITs, each specializing in a particular property type and operating in a particular geographical area. If you like apartments in the Southeast, buy Merry, Post, Security Capital Atlantic or Summit; if you like them in the Southwest, buy Camden or Columbus; if you like California and the Northwest, buy Bay, BRE, Essex, Irvine or Security Capital Pacific. On the East Coast, check out Avalon, Home or Charles Smith, among others. Investors can do the same thing in retail properties, office buildings or industrial properties. While it's true that we cannot yet find an apartment REIT operating in, say, Montana, or an office REIT with properties located in Vermont, the range of property types and sectors covered by blue-chip REITs is substantial enough for all but the largest institutional investor that thinks it must own properties in all 50 states. For the smaller investor, a number of mutual funds specializing in REITs are available; buying these shares will provide more than ample diversification (see Chapter Nine for more on diversification and REIT mutual funds).

Insider Stock Ownership

Few investment techniques exist upon which both academics and investors seem to agree whole-heartedly. The former, "ivory tower" types, often come up with conclusions, developed after months or even years of painstaking research, that contradict principles most investors hold dear. There is, at least, one exception: Significant stock ownership in a company by its management usually has a strong bearing on the company's long-term success.

Why this should be true is certainly no puzzle. Believers in the theory (and practice) of capitalism are convinced that there is nothing like the profit motive to cause individuals to exert their greatest efforts toward making an enterprise a success. They point to inefficiencies, inability to compete, mismanagement and waste in government-owned enterprises as proof-positive that the profit motive is essential to the success of any business enterprise. And what better profit motive can there be than owning a significant portion of the enterprise that one manages? Wouldn't you rather own shares in a company in which the CEO and CFO have most of their personal net worths invested than one in which these officers are motivated only by their salaries and bonuses? Further, managements that have a large equity stake in their company tend to align their personal interests with those of the public shareholders, and will be more motivated to manage their companies for long-term appreciation of the overall value of the company than to maximize profits in the short-term.

These principles obviously apply to REITs as well as other publicly traded companies. REIT managements having significant stock ownership in the REIT will be focused on long-term appreciation of the REIT's value as an ongoing successful enterprise, and will sacrifice short-term FFO increases, if necessary, in order to get there. Such managements will avoid "goosing" FFO by taking on too much debt on a short-term basis at variable interest rates, and will tend to avoid buying properties with limited long-term appreciation potential just to increase FFO in the current fiscal year. Furthermore, REITs with high insider ownership will likely be more careful about new development projects. Finally, managements that own large equity stakes will be less inclined to take advantage of the occasional conflicts of interest (as discussed below) at the expense of the shareholders.

Fortunately for us, REITs tend to have a much higher percentage of stock owned by management than most publicly traded companies. A 1996 Green Street survey[9] indicates that the average insider ownership of the REITs in its universe was 17.8% near the end of 1995 (the median was 15.1%), which is very high when compared with other public companies. This is due, in a large part, to the fact that a large number of the REITs that have come

152

public during the last several years were "REIT-izations" of previously large and successful private real estate companies with significant valuations. As these companies became REITs, the insider-owners continued to hold very large stock positions in the public entity. When Post Properties went public in 1993, raising approximately $200 million from public investors, management's property interests in the private entity were translated into a 22% interest in the new REIT.

While the total stock ownership of REITs' management is quite high in general, vast differences exist among individual REITs. Green Street's survey shows that, among the REITs they follow, insider ownership at the time of the survey ranged from 55.3% (Irvine Apartment Communities) to 1.8% (Washington REIT).[10] Needless to say, a high percentage of insider ownership will be a key criteria in determining which of the REITs qualify as "blue-chips" from an investor's point of view. A high percentage ownership will not, by itself, transform a mediocre REIT into one of high quality (or vice-versa), but it should certainly be taken into account. (We should assume, however, that a REIT management's share holdings will, over time, decrease as a percentage of the outstanding shares as the REIT grows through additional subsequent stock offerings and as shares are sold by members of management, over time, in order to diversify their investments).

We should be careful to distinguish between current management's holdings and those of other major shareholders. Sometimes an individual or family will obtain a large percentage of a new REIT's shares as a result of its extensive ownership in the prior private entity, but will not take an active role in managing the new REIT. This was the case in the IPOs of Colonial Properties and DeBartolo, among others. Although a large ownership interest by a non-active shareholder is a positive (suggesting that someone with a large equity stake is continuing to look over the shoulder of management), such a situation is not as meaningful as when active management owns a major portion of the REIT. In these situations, we need to examine whether the *management* owns enough shares to be sufficiently incentivized. We should also look at the total market value of such management's shares in relation to their total salary and bonus compensation from the REIT.

Low Payout Ratios

Another criteria for separating the good from the bad and the ugly relates to the REIT's payout ratio of dividends paid to either FFO or AFFO (the latter, you may recall, is FFO less a reserve for certain capitalized expenditures that do not add to the long-term value of a property, *e.g.*, carpeting, a new roof, tenant allowances and improvements, etc.). A low payout ratio is extremely important in view of REITs' difficulty in retaining earnings, as we've discussed

153

previously. Thus, in order to grow, REITs must continually go back to the capital markets by either selling new shares or borrowing funds, and debt expansion becomes nearly impossible without an expanding equity base. As we've also discussed earlier, new equity capital is very expensive; accordingly, the best-managed REITs will seek to retain as much of their operating income as possible, which is the least expensive form of equity capital. This, in turn, requires a low payout ratio.

Another reason for maintaining a low payout ratio is simply to provide insurance against temporary downturns in FFO or AFFO resulting from unexpected events. While we'd like to think that REITs' earnings climb inevitably higher each year (and many REITs can boast of such a track record), REITs operate in the real world and are subject to unexpected and unpleasant events. These could include higher vacancy rates resulting from major tenant departures or even defaults, lower rental income from apartment units due to overbuilding, or higher-than-anticipated operating expenses due to competitive or other conditions. If a REIT pays out too high a percentage of its AFFO in the form of dividends, it may find itself not "covering" the dividend; this, in turn, will tend to cause investors to worry about a dividend cut, which will depress the stock price. This will not only cause pain to investors, but will make it much more difficult for the REIT to raise additional funds through an equity offering (and any such equity offering will then be much more expensive in terms of dilution to shareholders).

Traditionally, REIT investors have long been attracted to REITs for their high and steady yields. However, with the significant increase in REIT ownership by institutional investors and a greater understanding of REITs (and their dynamics of growth) by individual investors, the importance of retained earnings and low payout ratios is now being recognized and those REITs with low payout ratios will be given higher P/FFO multiples and thus higher stock prices.

Just what should we be looking for in payout ratios? We should start with the premise that FFO is not nearly as reliable as AFFO in determining a REIT's "free" cash flow. If a REIT claims to have earned $1.00 per share in FFO but uses $.05 of that to add new carpeting and drapes to its apartment units each year to maintain the attractiveness of its units, it really doesn't have $1.00 per share to either distribute to its shareholders or to make additional acquisitions; it really has only $.95 available for such purposes. If it pays out the full $.95 in dividends, it will have retained absolutely nothing with which to grow the business. Accordingly, the wise investor will prefer to look at a REIT's ratio of dividends to AFFO. If AFFO is $.95 and the dividend rate is $.85, the payout ratio would be $.85 ÷ $.95, or 89.5%.

Realty Stock Review regularly publishes the payout ratios of the REITs in its universe, using AFFO. Some figures may prove

154

illustrative (the following figures come from the November 29, 1996 issue). The average payout ratios, based upon estimated 1996 AFFOs, were as follows:

REIT Sector	Payout Ratios
Apartments	93.5%
Neighborhood Shopping Centers	96.8%
Regional Malls	94.7%
Factory Outlet Centers	92.6%
Manufactured Home	91.4%
Health Care	90.2%
Hotels	83.8%
Industrial	89.5%
Office	94.2%
Self Storage	81.1%

As you might expect, there were wide differences within these averages. Fifteen REITs had payout ratios of 100% or higher and a large number had ratios exceeding 95%. High ratios do not allow the REIT to retain much earnings, nor do they provide much comfort in the event of a drop-off in AFFO for any of the possible reasons discussed above.

On the other hand, many REITs that are regarded by the investment community as being high on the quality spectrum have low payout ratios. For example, at the date of Realty Trust Review's publication referred to above, six REITs had ratios of under 80%; Bay Apartments and Kimco Realty had ratios of only 76.6% and 78.9%, respectively, while Public Storage won the prize for the lowest ratio, at only 47.8%. (Of course, no REIT may have such a low payout that it distributes less than 95% of its *net income* to its shareholders). I've never seen a study that tried to correlate REITs' growth rates with their payout ratios, but it's reasonable to expect that a low payout ratio (which results in a REIT being able to retain additional capital for growth) will correlate well with high growth rates.

A couple of caveats are in order. There may be times in the economic cycle of the property type owned by a REIT where it just doesn't make sense to expand through acquisition or development; at such times a higher payout ratio might be the best economic decision for the REIT and its shareholders. Also, if a REIT is structured as an UPREIT or a DownREIT and is able to acquire properties through the issuance of its operating partnership units, the necessity to use retained earnings for growth may be lessened (which, in turn, may mean that a low payout ratio will be of lesser importance). Finally, when investing in REITs run by mediocre managements with poorly-defined growth strategies (*e.g.*, "value" REITs or REITs with high dividend yields), we may *want* the REIT to pass through to the shareholders almost all of its AFFO and, in such cases, a low payout ratio isn't necessarily a positive.[11]

Nevertheless, the fact remains that most blue-chip REITs will usually have low payout ratios, and low ratios will generally be rewarded by investors over time in the form of higher stock prices and cheaper equity capital when needed.

Absence of Conflicts

Conflicts of interest between management and the shareholders are inevitable in any public (or even private) company. The shareholders might be interested in selling out to a potential acquirer, which could terminate the lucrative compensation packages of management. Some compensation plans cause managements to emphasize short-term objectives at the expense of building long-term value for the shareholders. Another area of concern occurs when, through stock ownership or special provisions in a company's charter documents, certain favored insiders have the right to block unfriendly merger proposals regardless of whether or not they are favored by the public shareholders. These are but a few of the many ways in which conflicts can arise between management and public investors.

Unfortunately, REITs can have these and other potential conflicts unique to the REIT format. Perhaps the most dangerous occurred with some regularity several years ago, when the charter documents of most REITs did not have prohibitions upon officers or directors selling to the REIT properties in which they had a significant ownership interest. Such sales were made from time to time, occasionally with dire consequences for the REIT when the values of such properties were later determined to be inflated. Today most REITs prohibit such transactions, but there are other types of conflicts, unique to REITs, which must be watched carefully.

One conflict of interest that can arise involves a change in a REIT's management in which *new management* sells a portfolio of properties to the REIT. This occurred in late 1995, when a new chief executive officer was elected at Burnham Pacific Properties. This REIT agreed to buy from the new CEO a portfolio of existing properties, as well as properties under development, for approximately $200 million. Conflicts in this situation relate to the fairness of the purchase price, whether it was prudent to take on the additional debt necessary to finance the acquisition and other issues. While this type of transaction is not exactly identical to earlier types where *existing management* would sell properties to the REIT (and in which clear fiduciary duties to the shareholders are present), it nevertheless should raise a warning flag in the minds of REIT investors.

Another type of conflict can arise when a REIT is "externally administered and advised." Many years ago most REITs did not manage their own business affairs; they entered into agreements with outside companies to handle all administration, property acquisitions and property management. These "outside advisors" were paid a fee based on the amount of assets owned by the REIT, which gave them an incentive to grow the REIT's assets "for growth's sake." Thus the larger the amount of assets, the larger the fee, and the REIT's profitability had no bearing on the fees paid. As a result, the outside advisors were motivated to buy lots of mediocre properties with limited upside potential, and could increase profitability by skimping on management expenses. The conflicts of interest here are obvious. Fortunately the great majority of REITs today are internally administered and managed, while management usually owns a significant equity interest in the REIT (which aligns their interests with those of the shareholders).

Another type of potential conflict can arise from the high-profile or unique reputation of a REIT's founder and the extent to which that person closely monitors the day-to-day affairs of the REIT. Sam Zell, the legendary and highly successful real estate investor, organized Manufactured Home Communities (MHC), a manufactured-housing REIT, several years ago. While his knowledge, expertise and reputation was instrumental in bringing the REIT public, some investors felt that he may not have been as active in day-to-day management as they had been led to believe. When this REIT encountered problems assimilating a major portfolio acquisition, such investors fretted that Mr. Zell may not have personally spent sufficient time monitoring the acquisition. The potential conflict here is the extent to which a widely respected executive spends his or her time closely managing the REIT rather than tending to the myriad of other interests and projects owned outside the REIT.

Another and relatively new area of concern is the potential conflicts created by the "UPREIT" format. As we discussed earlier, an UPREIT is merely a type of REIT corporate structure in which the REIT owns a major (usually a majority) interest in a partnership that owns the REIT's properties, rather than owning them directly. Other partners in the "operating partnership" will often include the senior management. One type of conflict arises when a property has reached its full profit potential and might best be sold in order to redeploy the equity into a more promising property. Such a sale will not cause an adverse tax problem for the shareholders but, because in an UPREIT the partners retain their same (probably low) tax basis in the property prior to the REIT being formed, such a sale may trigger a significant capital gain tax to the partner-officer of the REIT.

In the summer of 1996, the conflict issues inherent in the UPREIT structure surfaced when MHC made an unsolicited offer for Chateau Properties (CPJ), another manufactured home community REIT. At the time of the offer CPJ's shares were trading at $23.25, and the offer was to buy all of CPJ's shares and UPREIT partnership units for either $26 per share in cash or, alternatively, through an exchange of MHC stock. However, the *share exchange* option was worth only about $21.38 per share (based upon the then-prevailing market price of MHC shares). Most of the holders of CPJ's operating partnership units were directors or officers of the REIT, and were believed to have a low cost basis in their units. This low cost basis, due to the tax effects of a cash buy-out, gave them a strong incentive to reject MHC's offer (which, due to the after-tax consequences of the offer, was significantly more generous to the public shareholders than to the insiders). This type of conflict of interest may arise from time to time when a REIT is structured as an UPREIT (due to the different cost bases of the public shareholders and the insider-owners of the partnership units), and shareholders should take greater heed of such potential conflicts when considering an investment in an UPREIT.

Because of the statutory requirements applicable to REITs that generally limit the nature of a REIT's income from non-property ownership sources, hotel REITs can have significant built-in conflicts. With the exception of Starwoods Lodging, whose "paired-shares" structure was "grandfathered" under prior law, hotel REITs must be managed by an outside company in order to avoid receiving income from "non-property sources." Thus the hotels must be leased and operated by an outside entity, which will transform "management income" into "rental income." As hotel ownership is management-intensive and the REIT's shareholders often want the properties managed by the founders or top management of the REIT, we often find that the REIT's hotels are managed or supervised by an entity that is owned or controlled by the REIT's senior management. This type of arrangement gives management a license to pretty much have its way with the shareholders if it's so inclined and, as a result, most hotel REITs are particularly susceptible to significant conflicts of interest.[12]

As with some of the other factors and criteria discussed in this chapter, we shouldn't necessarily shun an otherwise promising REIT if certain significant conflicts are present in the REIT's structure or operating format. This area is, however, one in which REIT shareholders have been badly burned in the past, and merits close scrutiny. The blue-chip REITs will tend to have fewer conflicts between management and the shareholders that could cause unpleasant surprises down the road.

For most investors, owning a portfolio consisting primarily of the blue-chip REITs, having significant, stable and rising dividends and growth prospects and boasting experienced and savvy management teams, will be the best route to financial success. Still, it's not the only route available. Some investors may prefer to buy the gazelle REITs, whose FFOs are expected to grow at a very rapid rate, rotating to others when growth appears to be slowing; others might prospect among the cheap "REITdogs" with high (and hopefully sustainable) dividend yields or where a turnaround in the REIT's fortunes is expected; still others might choose to invest in the oxen, "bond proxies" whose dividends are high and stable but where significant growth is unlikely. But for those investors looking for safe and predictable long-term growth, the blue-chip "lion REITs" clearly are the best option.[13] These REITs will have an abundance of such qualities as excellent managements, access to reasonably priced capital, sound balance sheets, good focus by property type and geography, a high level of insider stock ownership, low dividend payout ratios and the absence of conflicts of interest. Not only will these quality REITs prove highly rewarding, but they also will provide us with one of the most important assets for investors: that famous good night's sleep which can be so easily victimized by poor investment forays.

---

[1] Many investors are searching for the *next* REIT to enjoy a relationship with Security Capital Group.

[2] "Special Update - Vornado Realty Trust," dated March 17, 1995.

[3] Realty Stock Review, November 29, 1996, p. 16-21.

[4] Interview with Mr. Frank, appearing in Barron's, dated December 18, 1995.

[5] As we've discussed earlier, "EBITDA" is normally used to describe earnings before interest, taxes, depreciation and amortization.

[6] The best form of fixed-rate debt is set, by its own terms, at a specified interest rate, and is even better if the borrower is allowed to prepay the debt prior to its maturity; this allows an early pay-off if interest rates fall substantially after the debt is incurred. In recent years, many REITs have taken on variable-rate debt but where the interest rate is "capped" at a certain level somewhat higher than the current rate. As there is no free lunch, these "caps" must be purchased and can be quite expensive, depending upon the length of the cap and "width" of the interest rate band. Capped variable-rate debt is better than the uncapped variety, as it does provide some protection against significantly rising interest rates, but the old-fashioned fixed-rate variety is what investors would normally prefer.

[7] "Reit Pricing - Poised for a Rebound?", January 2, 1996, p. 10 and Appendix 1.

[8] Ibid, p. 10 and Appendix 1.

[9] Ibid, p. 10.

[10] Ibid, Appendix 1.

[11] Many knowledgeable investors like low payout ratios only in REITs which have shown that they can generate above average returns on the new capital invested. In other words, if the investor believes that a REIT is acquiring and developing additional properties just to get larger, such an investor would prefer the payout ratio to be higher so that he or she will have the cash with which to make a more profitable investment (perhaps through buying shares in a faster-growing REIT).

[12] While Starwoods was the only hotel REIT with a "paired shares" organization at the time this book went to press, Patriot American was in the process of acquiring California Jockey Club and Bay Meadows Operating Company (which also have a paired

shares structure), which would give Patriot the ability to manage hotels as well as own them.

[13] My song praising the blue-chip REITs would not be complete without adding an important caveat. Just as investors may pay too much for a great "bandwagon" company that everyone loves and thus fail to earn a reasonable return for many years, REIT investors can make the same mistake with blue-chip REITs. New Plan Realty, for example, is a REIT of the highest quality, but investors who bought it several years ago at sky-high prices have seen very little price appreciation despite New Plan's continuing FFO and dividend growth. Thus valuation of a REIT's shares will always be an important issue for investors, as we'll discuss in Chapter Eight.

Chapter Eight

The Quest for Investment Value

"Genius is one percent inspiration and ninety-nine percent perspiration."
— *Thomas Alva Edison*

And old pro in the investment world once noted that the most speculative company can be a fine investment if its stock is bought cheaply enough and the shares of the finest-quality business can be a rank speculation if bought at a grossly excessive price. Our success in REIT investing will be determined, at least over the short term, by our ability to buy REITs at attractive prices. In this chapter we'll look at some yardsticks which can help us determine whether a REIT's stock provides investment value and, indeed, whether the shares of REITs in general are cheap or dear. Our objective is to avoid overpaying for high quality and growth and to find the best investment values in REIT world.

The Investor's Dilemma

One school of thought says that the key to investment success is to buy a package of stocks representing shares in the largest, most solid companies (or even an indexed mutual fund based upon a major broad-based index such as the S&P 500) and to hold these shares indefinitely. Sure, we can sell off a slice when funds are needed, but it's foolish to sell some and buy others, always trying to find the best performers or to time the market. This group of investors can point to numerous studies suggesting how difficult it is to consistently beat "the market."

The other school believes that with hard work, insight and good judgment, among other skills, one can do better than "the market" or the broad-based averages. This could be achieved by either owning the "right" stocks (the ones that will most increase in value) or by timing the market. Some pupils of this school point to investors such as Peter Lynch and Warren Buffett as examples of what a talented stock picker can accomplish, while others believe that certain "signs" can tell us when the entire market or specific individual stocks will rise and fall, and that we can beat the market by following these signs.

REIT investors are faced with the same dilemma. Should we just buy a package of "large cap" REITs or a REIT mutual fund and add to our investments regularly or whenever we have additional

161

funds, or should we invest a great deal of time and effort seeking to find the "best values" in the REIT world? Should we sell those that become "overpriced" under our valuation models and buy the "bargains?" Should we taper down our entire REIT portfolios when the market looks treacherous or when the REIT sector appears overpriced, buying back in when the market or the REIT sector again looks cheap?

Unfortunately, there is simply no "right" or "wrong" answer to these questions. Most investors, after gaining some experience, generally come to their own conclusions regarding an investment style that's appropriate for them in light of their own temperaments, life styles and financial aspirations. A strategy that works well for some may be entirely uncomfortable for others; in investing, rarely does "one size fit all."

But I'm not to be let off the hook yet, so I'll offer a few thoughts on this difficult issue. Let's take two different REIT investors: One follows the "buy-and-hold" strategy and the other seeks to improve his or her performance by buying and selling from time to time and under-weighting or over-weighting his or her exposure to REITs, based upon certain criteria.

Advice for the "buy-and-hold" investor is simple: Assemble a portfolio of blue-chip REITs that can be bought and held for many years. Alternatively, the "buy-and-hold" investor could simply buy either an actively managed mutual fund devoted to REIT investing or a REIT index fund (see Chapter Nine and Appendix D for more on REIT mutual funds). The owner of such a "carefree" portfolio or mutual fund can go off to Tahiti, collect the steady and rising dividends and not worry about price fluctuations, beating the competition or any other such irrelevancies. If history is any guide, such an investor can expect to average 12-14% in total returns over a long time horizon.

Advice for the more active investor (or perhaps even the trader) is somewhat more complicated. I'll suggest several ways by which REIT stocks can be valued, with a view toward determining when some of them are overpriced or underpriced, given their quality, underlying asset values and growth prospects. I'll also offer several guidelines that may be helpful in determining when the entire universe of REIT stocks is cheap or expensive. How we can best value common stocks is a riddle that investors have pondered for centuries, and the valuation of REIT stocks isn't any easier. Thus, while none of these tools will provide "The Answer" (as there is none), they can help us to make some sound investment decisions — and, after all, that's what successful investing is all about. Most of the rest of this chapter will be devoted to reviewing these valuation tools.

The 'Buy-and-Hold' Strategy

But first, let's take a quick look at the passive "buy-and-hold" approach. The advantages to such a strategy are numerous: One, there's no need to worry about FFOs, payout ratios, occupancy or rental rates, asset values or any of the other information analysts spend their entire lives poring over; two, commission costs and capital gain taxes are minimal; and three, if the "efficient market" folks are correct in their arguments that investment advisors, securities analysts and fund managers rarely, if ever, beat "the market," then the performance of an index-based "buy-and-hold" REIT portfolio will slightly outperform one that is actively managed by the owner or by an outside professional, due to the lower commission and trading costs.

There are disadvantages to this type of strategy. The investor must be very careful to load the portfolio with the highest-quality companies in order to have the best chance of avoiding the occasional disaster; highly attractive new REITs will often be ignored; significant negative changes in the outlook for a portfolio REIT will rarely be spotted beforehand, which could negatively affect total performance; and for those weirdos like me who actually enjoy closely following REITs' portfolios and growth prospects, it's not much fun.

Those of you who like the "buy-and-hold" approach to REIT investing (but who don't want to go with a REIT mutual fund) should be careful to construct a portfolio consisting of a broadly diversified group of REITs, each of very high quality. Owning blue-chip REITs is extremely important, as the success of a "buy-and-hold" strategy depends upon owning those REITs that are likely to grow consistently in all economic climates and whose managements can be counted upon to avoid serious tactical and strategic blunders. Such a strategy would be similar to owning a portfolio consisting of such blue-chip stocks as Johnson & Johnson, Coca-Cola, General Electric, Merck and Procter & Gamble.

The list that follows includes several REITs which, in my opinion, are widely regarded as "blue-chips," based upon many of the criteria that were considered in the last chapter as well as their large equity market caps. Keep in mind that there are also many other excellent REITs, some of which are a bit smaller in size, which aren't included in the following list but which have "blue-chip" credentials — the list below is merely a sampling. These are *not* purchase recommendations, as no consideration has been given to market price or short- (or even medium-) term appreciation prospects. Each of these REITs, however, is currently managed by a knowledgeable and experienced management team with a well-deserved reputation in the investment community and each has a proven track record of FFO growth (although some have been publicly traded companies only for a relatively short period of time).

Each of them has demonstrated a strong ability to develop additional properties or to acquire properties on a basis that should prove profitable to the shareholders, and each is unlikely to commit major blunders. At the time this book was published, each had the ability to raise additional equity and debt capital at reasonable cost with which to develop or acquire additional properties, and each had a relatively strong balance sheet. Here's the list:

REIT Name	Ticker	Type
Equity Residential	EQR	Apartments: Nationwide
Post Properties	PPS	Apartments: Georgia/Florida
Security Capital Pacific	PTR	Apartments: Western U.S.
United Dominion Realty	UDR	Apartments: Southeast/Southwest
Kimco Realty	KIM	Shopping Centers: Eastern U.S.
New Plan Realty	NPR	Shopping Centers/Other: Nationwide
Vornado	VNO	Shopping Centers: East Coast
Weingarten	WRI	Shopping Centers: Texas & Southwest
General Growth Props.	GGP	Malls: Nationwide
Simon DeBartolo	SPG	Malls: Nationwide
Taubman Centers	TCO	Malls: Nationwide
Chelsea/GCA	CCG	Factory outlets: East and West Coast
Highwoods Properties	HIW	Industrial/office: Southeast
Duke Realty	DRE	Industrial: Midwest
Security Capital Industrial	SCN	Industrial: Nationwide
Spieker Properties	SPK	Industrial: West Coast
Beacon Properties	BCN	Office: Nationwide
CarrAmerica	CRE	Office: Nationwide
Crescent Real Estate	CEI	Office (& hotels): Nationwide
Health Care Properties	HCP	Health care (various): Nationwide
MediTrust	MT	Health care (diversified): Nationwide
Nationwide Health Props.	NHP	Health care (nursing homes): Nationwide
Public Storage	PSA	Self-storage: Nationwide
Storage U.S.A.	SUS	Self-storage: Nationwide
Starwoods Lodging	HOT	Hotels: Nationwide
Patriot American Hotels	PAH	Hotels: Nationwide

Of course, owning these stocks is no guarantee of investment success, as individual companies (including REITs) are subject to the mistakes of management, changing economic conditions and a slew of other potentially negative developments, some of which are outlined in Chapter Ten. Further, we are all subject to periodic bear markets that will negatively affect the market values of our investments from time to time.

I will reiterate that the above list is only a sampling of the REITs that might be included in a "buy-and-hold" portfolio; the fact that a REIT isn't on the list certainly doesn't mean that it's of poor or even mediocre quality; indeed, several blue-chip REITs (some of which I own personally) were excluded only due to their relatively smaller market caps. Conversely, it's quite likely that one or more of these blue-chip REITs would not be included on an updated list I might prepare a year or two from now. Long-term investors, like Warren Buffett, would like their holding period to be forever, but in the real world executives retire or lose interest, the economics of a property sector unravel and (to sanitize a quotation from my sons) "stuff happens."

REIT Stock Valuation

What if the REIT investor isn't content with a "buy-and-hold" strategy, and desires to improve his or her performance by selling overvalued REITs and buying undervalued ones? How can we determine what a REIT is worth, independently or in relation to its peers? Further, how can we decide whether REITs, as a type of investment, are cheap or expensive? Virtually all professional REIT investors and analysts have their own methods and models by which to address these issues; there's no consensus as to which works best, and I certainly don't claim to have found the Holy Grail of REIT valuation. But that doesn't mean such analysis is worthless. Far from it. Applying these methods on their own or in conjunction with each other can provide crucial insight into the relative investment strengths and weaknesses among the various REITs, historical and prospective ranges of "fair pricing" and, in particular, whether it's a good time to buy or to sell specific REITs.

Real Estate Asset Values

For many years investment analysts have thought it important to look at a company's "book value," which is simply the net value of a company's assets (after subtracting all its obligations and liabilities), based on the balance sheet. Whatever the merits of such an approach in prior years, today's downsizings, write-offs and restructuring charges have made this a much less popular method of determining a company's present investment merits. Furthermore, for our purposes, "book value" has always been a poor way to value real estate companies due to the arbitrary accounting assumption that offices, apartments and other structures depreciate in value at a fixed rate each year, which reduces "book value," while ignoring the potential appreciation of land values. Although some analysts and investors like to examine "private market" values or "break-up" values rather than book values, today most focus on a company's earning power rather than its value if liquidated or sold.

Nevertheless, while most of today's REITs are operating companies that focus on growing FFO and dividends and will rarely be liquidated, they do own real estate that can be reasonably valued through careful analysis. Furthermore, their assets can be sold much more easily than can, say, the fixed assets of a manufacturing company, a distribution network or a brand name. Thus REITs are much more conducive than other companies to being valued on a net asset value basis, and many experienced REIT investors and analysts believe that a REIT's net asset value is very important in

165

the valuation process, alone or in conjunction with other valuation models.

One of the leading advocates of using net asset value to evaluate the true worth of a REIT's stock price at any particular point in time is Green Street Advisors, an independent REIT research firm that has earned a well-deserved reputation in the REIT industry for its in-depth analysis and evaluation of the larger publicly traded REITs. Green Street's approach is to first determine a REIT's property value by determining and applying an appropriate cap rate to its properties (and then subtracting its obligations and making other adjustments) in order to determine net asset value (NAV). Recognizing that not all REITs are similar in quality, structure and external growth capabilities, it then adjusts NAV upwards or downwards to account for such factors as "franchise value," property and geographical focus, insider stock ownership, strength of the balance sheet, overhead expenses and potential and existing conflicts of interest between the REIT and its management or major shareholders. The net result, under Green Street's methodology, is the price at which the REIT's shares will trade when fairly valued. The firm uses a comparative approach, which weighs the relative attraction of one REIT to another; it doesn't attempt to decide when the entire REIT universe is cheap or expensive.

Let's assume that, under this approach, Montana Apartment Communities, a hypothetical apartment REIT, has an NAV of $20 and, due to good scores on the factors discussed above, the REIT's shares "should" trade for a 30% premium to NAV. Accordingly, Montana's shares would trade, if fairly priced, at $26; if they are trading significantly below such price, they would be deemed undervalued and might be recommended for purchase.

Unfortunately, a REIT's NAV is not an item of information which can be readily obtained. REITs themselves don't appraise the values of their properties nor do they hire outside appraisers to do so, and you won't find them in their financial statements. However, research reports from brokerage firms often include an estimate of NAV, and such information can often be obtained by subscribing to a REIT newsletter such as Realty Stock Review or a buy-side REIT research firm such as Green Street.

This approach to determining value in a REIT has substantial merit. It combines an analysis of underlying real estate value (the "private market" net asset value) with certain subjective and objective factors that, over the long run, are expected to have a significant effect upon the price investors will be willing to pay for a REIT's shares. Because REITs are rarely liquidated (and only occasionally acquired), investors will not be inclined to pay even 100% of NAV for a REIT which, due to poor management, structural problems such as conflicts of interest or a weak balance sheet, presents significant investment risks or is unlikely to grow even at the rate implied by the cap rates at which its properties can be valued. Conversely, investors have, historically, been willing to pay significantly more than NAV for a REIT's shares when the perceived strength of the REIT's organization and its access to cheap capital, among other factors, are expected to enable it to grow FFO and dividends at a rate much greater than what might be expected from a REIT (or, indeed, any real estate company) without such external growth prospects.[1]

At any particular time, the premiums over NAV that investors are willing to pay, as well as the discounts demanded by them, can be very large. Kimco Realty, for example, is widely regarded as one of the highest-quality blue-chip REITs. Due to this reputation, which Kimco has built since going public in late 1991, its shares have always traded at a premium to its estimated NAV, regardless of the then-current strength or weakness of the REIT market. At the end of June 1996, for example, Kimco was trading at a premium of 35% over its estimated NAV of $20.75. Conversely, at the same time, Town & Country, an apartment REIT, was trading at a *discount* of almost 20% from its estimated NAV of $15.50, due to concerns over the coverage of its dividend and a perceived significant slowing of its growth rate. When using this method of valuation, each investor should develop his or her own criteria by which the "appropriate" premium or discount should be determined; these criteria should take into account not only the REIT's ability to grow FFO and dividends at a rapid rate, but such other factors as balance sheet strength and the characteristics of a blue-chip REIT which we covered in Chapter Seven.

Another advantage to using this approach is that it tends to prevent investors from becoming carried away by periods of eye-popping but unsustainable FFO growth that occur from time to time. From 1992 to 1994, apartment REITs enjoyed incredible opportunities for positive-spread investing, as capital was cheap and abundant and good-quality apartments were available for purchase at cap rates above 10%. Furthermore, occupancy rates were rising and rents were increasing, as few new units had been built for many years in most parts of the U.S. Accordingly, FFO was growing at phenomenal rates. Analysts using valuation models based only upon then-existing FFO growth rates might have recommended that investors continue to buy these REITs at sky-high prices. In fact, growth slowed substantially in 1995 and 1996, and investors who bought the stocks of certain apartment REITs at high multiples of estimated FFO for the following year have not seen significant price appreciation in their shares.[2]

Yet another advantage in the use of a net asset value model is that it may help the investor avoid giving too much credit to a REIT that is growing quickly due to excessive debt leverage. If only "P/E-type" models are used (see below), such a REIT might be assigned a

167

premium multiple due to its rapid growth but that doesn't adequately account for the fact that such growth was "purchased" at the cost of an over-leveraged balance sheet.

Essentially, a net asset value approach that focuses primarily upon property values is an excellent REIT valuation method and, if carefully applied, can help the investor to avoid the problems of potential over-valuation resulting from extrapolating recent periods of rapid FFO growth well into the future or from rapid growth due, in large part, to excessive leverage. The trick here is that we must apply an "appropriate" premium or discount to net asset value in order to give sufficient additional value to the REITs with the best organizations, most solid balance sheets and long-term growth prospects, while also recognizing the potential problems and poor long-term prospects for some REITs. These premiums and discounts will change from time to time, depending upon economic conditions then applicable to the particular property type, real estate in general and the unique situation of each REIT.

P/FFO Models

Investors who reject the net asset value approach to valuation argue that "REITs are not real estate" but rather represent equity interests in operating businesses, and that property value is much less a determinant of what REIT investors will be willing to pay for a stock than are expectations of future growth in FFO and dividends. They argue that REITs are rarely liquidated and, even when a REIT is sold, the sale price is not generally based upon liquidation values;[3] further, they argue that if investors wanted to buy properties, they would do so directly. No, they say, REIT investors are becoming more and more like common stock investors — they want to buy growing companies at reasonable prices, and simply need a method by which they can make sure they aren't overpaying for such companies. Just like we don't want to pay 100 times next year's earnings for a great growth company like Coca-Cola, we don't want to pay too much for an outstanding growth REIT. Many of these investors conclude that, just as we often use price/earnings (P/E) ratios to value regular common stocks, we should use price/funds from operations (P/FFO) ratios to value REIT stocks.

This argument has greater merit now than it did several years ago, as more REITs today are truly real estate organizations and operating businesses rather than collections of properties; today most brokerage firms make extensive use of P/FFO ratios when discussing their REIT recommendations. Nevertheless, despite the widespread use of P/FFO ratios, these valuation mechanisms are afflicted by major defects (as we'll see below) which makes it difficult to rely exclusively upon them. Yet they can be helpful tools for the careful REIT investor if used properly, particularly in comparing *relative* valuations among REITs; they are less helpful as a measurement of *absolute* valuations.

The P/FFO ratio approach works something like this: If we think that Beauregard Properties is an outstanding apartment REIT that should trade at a P/FFO ratio of 14 times this year's estimated FFO, and we expect that Beauregard will report FFO of $2.50 for such year, we can conclude that its stock would be fairly valued at 14 times $2.50, or $35; if it trades at a lower or higher price, it's undervalued or overvalued, respectively.

Sounds easy, doesn't it? Well, no. How do we decide that Beauregard's P/FFO ratio should be 14 and not 10 or 18? Do we have a good road map by which we can find our way? History should be our starting point, providing us with the various P/FFO ratios at which the shares of a REIT have traded over various time periods. For example, let's assume that between 1990 and 1996, the average P/FFO ratio for Beauregard REIT, based upon expected FFO for the following year, was 13. We could start with that. Let's assume further that we decide that its management, balance sheet and business prospects have improved modestly from those of most prior periods, and that the prospects for its particular sector are better than they've been previously. That might justify a P/FFO ratio of 14 rather than 13. But we need to do more. If we think that the market for REIT stocks is more attractive today than it was in the earlier periods (perhaps due to changes in the real estate cycle, greater interest in REIT investing or for other reasons), we should move our "appropriate" ratio up by as much as one or two points (or, this factor, if deemed unfavorable, could result in a lower ratio). Thus today's appropriate ratio for Beauregard might be 15 rather than 14. We also need to factor in interest rates, which have historically affected the prices of *all* stocks. We might want to raise or lower the appropriate ratio when the 10-year Treasury note's yield rises above or below a narrow band of, say, 6-7%; perhaps a 1% increase or decrease in interest rates might equate to a reduction or increase, respectively, of one point in the appropriate ratio. But that's not all. We should adjust our appropriate ratio in accordance with prevailing price levels in the broad stock market; if investors are willing to pay higher prices for a dollar of earnings of most public companies, they should be likewise willing to pay a higher price for each dollar of a REIT's earnings.

This process of adjusting the "appropriate" P/FFO ratio for current business, interest rate and market conditions might look like this:

	Historical P/FFO Ratio
+/-	Changes in the REIT's financial condition and business prospects
+/-	Prospects for REITs in general

+/-	Current level of interest rates
+/-	Price levels and P/E ratios in broad stock market
=	Adjusted P/FFO Ratio

We could go through this process with all the REITs we follow, assigning to each its own ratio, based upon historical data, and making appropriate adjustments in which all of the foregoing factors are taken into account. Then, we must compare the P/FFO ratio of each REIT against the P/FFO ratios of other REITs in its sector, as well as against the P/FFO ratios of *all* REITs. These relative ratios must make sense in view of the various qualitative and quantitative differences among them. For example, we would invariably expect a blue-chip REIT to trade at a higher P/FFO ratio than one with poor growth prospects and a weak balance sheet.

Finally, if you recall from Chapter Two, adjusted funds from operations (AFFO) is a better indicator than FFO of a REIT's true earnings, as it does not "pad" FFO with an add-back of depreciation and amortization of capitalized expenses previously incurred that do not prolong the life or enhance the value of a property (such as carpeting, tenant improvement allowances or leasing commissions). Therefore, for greater accuracy, we would like to use AFFO rather than FFO when applying appropriate multiples. AFFOs, however (especially prior to 1996), are not as easily available as FFOs, as many REITs do not report them separately and it usually takes some digging through 10-Q's and other disclosure documents to be able to construct a reasonable approximation of AFFO on a quarterly basis. Alternatively, most brokerage reports on individual REITs and other REIT-oriented publications (such as Realty Stock Review) now set forth their own estimates of AFFO for most REITs (however, historical data on AFFOs will be very difficult to obtain).

After all these adjustments are made to FFO (or AFFO), can we feel confident that our P/FFO or P/AFFO analysis provides us with true investment values for the REITs we follow? P/FFO and P/AFFO models do have a legitimate claim to investors' attentions as a way of valuing a REIT's shares. Such models are widely used by investors (REIT and non-REIT alike) and, for that reason alone, deserve our serious attention. That said, models based upon "appropriate" FFO/AFFO ratios have significant limitations and problems. The principal difficulty, of course, is in determining just what the "right" or "appropriate" ratio should be, even if we could predict future FFO/AFFO to the penny. For example, to what extent are yesterday's ratios truly relevant in today's or tomorrow's investment world? We know that interest rates are important in the valuation of all stocks, but to what extent? Should we factor in long-term or short-term interest rates, and how should we do so? How will the investing public (and the institutions) look upon REITs as an alternative to other common stocks in the future, and will this have a bearing upon the appropriate FFO/AFFO ratio at which REIT prices will sell in the market? Are all the adjustments which we might make in order to "fine-tune" historical ratios shrewd guesses as to what investors are willing to pay for a dollar of FFO in the future, or are they just wild guesses?

And there are other questions. Should we use FFO/AFFO for the last four fiscal quarters? Or the last quarter, annualized? Next year's estimated FFO/AFFO? Or a blend of them? When the average ratio for *all* REITs as a group increases significantly (as it did in the last half of 1996), to what extent should that have a bearing on the appropriate ratio for each REIT? If REIT investors are crazy and decide to pay 30 times FFO or AFFO for the "best situated" and most solid REIT, should a lesser quality REIT sell at a "reasonable" 25 times? In October 1993 the shares of United Dominion Realty, clearly a blue-chip apartment REIT, were trading at $16 (a P/AFFO multiple of over 20 times estimated 1994 AFFO of $.79) in anticipation of the rapid growth that was expected of it. Was that a fair multiple for this outstanding REIT? It certainly seemed fair and reasonable to investors at that time. Yet, although United Dominion came through with outstanding AFFO growth over the next few years, eventually its growth rate slowed, and the P/AFFO ratio on its shares dropped precipitously from October 1993 to the end of 1996. As a result, the shares were trading at just below $16 in December 1996, and investors who bought at that price more than three years ago received nothing more than the steadily growing dividends on their shares. P/FFO ratios at the end of 1996 were much higher than they were at the end of 1995 despite the fact that the business prospects of most REITs didn't change a whole lot between these two years; were REITs undervalued in 1995 or were they overvalued in 1996? Unfortunately, P/FFO and P/AFFO models can't really answer that question (except with hindsight).

These problems and issues involving P/FFO or P/AFFO models shouldn't cause us to discard them entirely as useful tools, but we must understand their limitations. While we don't want to sell too early in REIT bull markets (should REIT prices exceed our "appropriate" target P/FFO or P/AFFO ratios), neither do we want to delude ourselves as to a REIT's inherent value by constantly adjusting our "appropriate" ratio higher as prices rise and thus play the "greater fool" game. These models are, in my opinion, most helpful as *relative* valuation tools. For example, they are more helpful in allowing us to determine whether Apple REIT is a better investment value than Pear REIT at any particular period of time. Thus if we believe that Apple has a stronger balance sheet, better management and more well-defined growth prospects than Pear but the two trade at equal P/FFO or P/AFFO ratios, we might feel confident that Apple has better investment value. But to decide that Apple REIT's stock is overvalued because it sells at 15 times

171

estimated 1997 AFFO when our P/AFFO model says it should sell at only 14 times 1997 estimated AFFO — well, I wouldn't bet my investment funds on that conclusion. We need yet another valuation tool.

Discounted Cash Flow and Dividend Growth Models

Another useful method of valuation is to discount the sum of future FFOs (or, better yet, AFFOs) to arrive at a current value (or "net present value") for the REIT's shares. If we start with current AFFO and then estimate the future AFFO growth of a REIT over a long time period, say 30 years, and discount the value of all future AFFOs back to the present date on the basis of an appropriate interest rate, we can obtain an approximate current value for all future earnings. This method of valuation has the advantage of helping us to determine a REIT's value on the basis of what a private investor might pay for it in its entirety. (We should note, however, that discounting AFFO in this manner probably overstates value a bit, as investors don't receive *all* of the future AFFOs as early as implied by this method; this is because the shareholders receive only the REIT's cash dividend, and the rest of the AFFO is retained — and contributes to higher AFFOs in future years).

Several methods can be used to determine the assumed interest rate by which the aggregate amount of future AFFOs is discounted back to the present date. One way is to use the average cap rate of the properties contained in the REIT's portfolio; if the cap rate on XYZ Apartment REIT's portfolio properties averages 9%, we apply a 9% discount rate. This method has the advantage of applying commercial property market valuation parameters to companies that own commercial properties; a drop in cap rates will translate into a higher current valuation for the REIT under this type of model, and vice-versa. Another approach is to determine one's desired total rate of return on the investment, and to use that; if we feel that a 12% return from a particular REIT is required in order to adequately compensate us for the risk of owning it, we'll use 12% as the discount rate. This second method will produce more consistent valuation numbers, although it will be less sensitive to fluctuations both in interest rates and cap rates.

The difference in results using various discount rates can be dramatic. For example, a REIT with a "first year" estimated AFFO of $1.00 and which we think will grow AFFO by 5% each year over 30 years will have a "net present value" of $17.16 if we use a 9% discount rate. However, using the same set of assumptions but applying a 12% discount rate will give us a "net present value" of only $12.35. Using a discount rate which approximates the expected (or "required") total return for a REIT investment (for example, 12% or 13%) provides a more realistic net present value approximation and is closer to what REIT stocks have generally sold for in the real world.

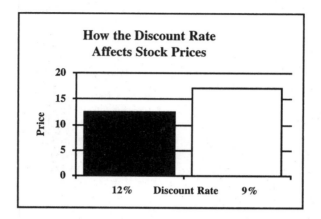

Due to the peculiarities of compound interest, there is little point in trying to estimate growth rates beyond 30 years; the contribution to net present value from incremental future earnings tapers off dramatically after even just five years. Accordingly, accurately forecasting growth rates for the first five years is much more important than doing so for the next 25 years. This is very fortunate, as forecasting growth rates for even short time periods is a significant challenge.

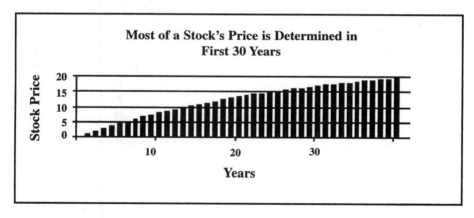

Let's use Nationwide Health Properties (NHP) as an example. If we demand a 12.5% total annual return from a new investment in NHP, we would apply a 12.5% discount rate to our AFFO estimates for NHP over the next 30 years. My own model assumes AFFO for 1997 of $1.89 per share, and a growth rate of 5.5% in years one through five, 5.5% in years six through 10 and 5% in years 11 through 30. With the help of my trusty computer, I learn that NHP

173

shares have a value today, based solely on this valuation method, of $23.22 (in late December 1996, NHP stock was trading at approximately $23, making it fairly valued under this valuation method).

A variation of the discounted cash flow growth model is the discounted dividend growth model. It is quite similar, but starts with the dividend rate over the past 12 months, rather than current FFO or AFFO, and projects the current value of all future dividends over the next, say, 30 years, based upon an assigned discount rate and an assumed dividend growth rate. A negative feature to this approach is that it penalizes those REITs whose dividends are low in relation to FFO or AFFO, unless the lower pay-out ratio is reflected in a higher assumed dividend growth rate. A positive feature is that it values only cash flow expected to be received by investors in the form of dividend payments.

No method of valuation is perfect, and discounted cash flow or dividend growth models certainly have their limitations. The net present value estimate is only as good as the accuracy of future growth forecasts; if we forecast 6% growth but the REIT delivers only 4%, our valuation will have been much too high. Another flaw in this method is that it doesn't take into account either the *qualitative* differences among the various REITs nor their net asset values; it takes into account only anticipated cash flow or dividend growth. Fans of this method should therefore adjust for qualitative differences by adjusting the total return required and thus the discount rate to be applied (*i.e.*, a riskier REIT will bear a higher discount rate), and by combining it with a net asset value model (and perhaps a P/FFO or P/AFFO model as well). The bottom line here is that discounted cash flow and dividend growth models, particularly if combined with other methods, can be very helpful in REIT evaluation, and should help us avoid paying too much for even the highest quality or fastest growing REIT.

Are REITs Cheap or Expensive as a Group?

Now that we've looked at some ways in which individual REITs can be valued, based on net asset values, P/FFO or P/AFFO ratios and discounted cash flow and dividend growth models, we should ask whether there is any way in which we can determine whether REITs, *as a group*, are cheap or expensive?

Investors who bought REITs in the Fall of 1993 learned, to their regret, that sometimes *all* REITs can be overvalued, and it may take one or two years (or even longer) before REITs' FFOs and dividends will "grow into" their stock prices. Fortunately, we REIT investors earn high current returns while we wait; nevertheless, it isn't much fun to watch the stock prices of our favorite REITs languish for a couple of years. In October 1993, New Plan Realty (NPR), at $23, was selling at 22.5 times estimated 1993 FFO of $1.02.

NPR's FFO has increased significantly since then, to an estimated $1.60 in 1996, but the stock price never rose above $24 until December 1996. We can see, with the benefit of hindsight, that the P/FFO ratio was much too high in 1993, despite NPR's rosy prospects, and has fallen from a P/FFO ratio of 22 then to less than 16 at the end of 1996. It would have done us little good to have bought United Dominion (UDR) instead of NPR in 1993, despite its lower P/FFO ratio of 19.8, as its P/FFO ratio also contracted, to 12.4 at the end of 1996, and its share price was still under $16 at that time as compared with $16.50 in October 1993. Meanwhile, UDR's FFO has increased from $.84 in 1993 to an estimated $1.25 for 1996. Admittedly, using 1993 to illustrate the point (a time when P/FFO ratios were unusually high) may be a bit unfair, but the message is pretty clear: Like virtually all investing, we must be careful not to get so carried away by REITs' prospects that we significantly overpay for them.

As we discussed in the prior section, if we use P/FFO ratios as our valuation method and a high-quality apartment REIT like UDR is selling at, say, 14 times expected FFO and one of comparable quality, such as Security Capital Pacific Trust (PTR), is selling at 12.5 times expected FFO, we may conclude that PTR is undervalued relative to UDR. But this doesn't tell us whether they're *both* cheap or *both* expensive. Similarly, UDR and PTR may be trading at premiums of 15% and 5%, respectively, over their net asset values, but this tells us nothing about what premiums over net asset values these REITs *should* sell for. Is there any way out of this dilemma?

The use of a well-constructed discounted cash flow or dividend growth model may be of some help here. When the REIT market is cheap, the current market prices of most REITs will be significantly lower than the "appropriate" prices indicated by such a model. For example, if 60 of the 70 REITs that we follow come out of the "black box" of our discounted AFFO or dividend growth models as significantly undervalued, this is likely to mean that REIT stocks are being undervalued by the market. Nevertheless, we cannot make such a decision in a vacuum. It may be that these models have failed to take into account fundamental negative changes in real estate or the economy that will cause future AFFO or dividend growth rates to be significantly lower than we've projected in our models. If we believe that such circumstances exist, we must revise our models and may find that REITs, as a group, are not undervalued at all.

How then do we get our bearings? Is there some "lodestar" by which we can compare our current valuations to what REITs "should" sell for? Unfortunately, no. If some all-knowing REIT man in the sky were to tell me that it's an absolute certainty that there would be no real estate overbuilding for the next 10 years, that the local economies all over the U.S. would be growing steadily at 3-4%

175

for such period of time with inflation at 3% and interest rates at 6%, that owners of real estate would continue to reap high and steady profits and that profitable acquisitions would continue without interruption for another decade or more, I'd conclude that we are in REIT heaven and should adjust our valuation models upward — but by how much? Furthermore, as no one can possibly *know* what the future will be, we are left no choice but to make our own oft-erroneous projections.

Yet all is not lost — we do have history as a guide, imperfect though it may be. If we know that REITs have historically provided dividend yields slightly above the yields available on 10-year U.S. Treasury notes we have at least one useful tool by which to measure current REIT valuations. It also would be useful to know whether REITs have historically traded at prices above or below their net asset values, and by how much; what has happened to REIT prices when the premiums have become large? A third method would be to review REITs' historical P/FFO ratios, and to compare the current average ratio with historical averages.

These tools will tell us, to the extent that the data is available (and assuming, of course, that it's meaningful[4]), where REITs are trading today in relation to historical 10-year Treasury note yields, net asset value premiums and P/FFO ratios. Once we have the historical data, we can then try to determine how REITs' growth prospects and safety profiles today compare with what they were in prior periods. For example, let's use historical P/FFO ratios. If REITs today trade at a P/FFO ratio of 12, compared with a historical average of 14, we can decide whether REITs' prospects today are a lot worse than they have been throughout much of their history. If we decide not, we may conclude that REITs, as a group, are cheap and may want to overweight them in our portfolios.

The T-Note Spread. Green Street Advisors publishes monthly several graphs comparing average REIT yields to the 10-year Treasury note (T-Note) yield going back to January 1990.

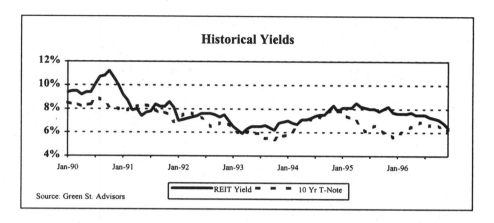

Historical Yields

Source: Green St. Advisors

REIT Yield ▬ ▬ ▬ 10 Yr T-Note

These graphs show *some* correlation between the two yields during certain time periods. Thus between the spring of 1991 and the spring of 1995, the dividend yield on the average REIT tracked quite closely with that of the T-Note. While the average yields ranged from 6% (5.5% for the T-Note) to 8.5% during that time period, the yield premium of the average REIT to that of the T-Note ranged from -10% to +20%. (The yield premium is the differential between the average REIT's yield and the T-Note yield expressed as a percentage of the latter; for example, if the average REIT yields 6% and the T-Note yields 5%, the yield premium would be (6%-5%)/5%, or 20%). However, it is interesting to note that the yield premium widened substantially in two periods: July 1990 to April 1991 (when it rose to almost 40%) and April 1995 to January 1996 (when it again hit 40%).

In these two latter periods REITs, based on their dividend yields, were either inordinately cheap relative to the T-Note or investors were discounting a difficult period ahead for REITs. As it turned out, 1991 and 1996 were extraordinarily good for REIT investors, as the NAREIT Equity REIT Index (on a total return basis) was up 35.7% in 1991 and 35.3% in 1996. Thus we know, after the fact, that investors were unduly concerned about REITs' future prospects from late 1990 to early 1991 and from April 1995 to early 1996 (or simply decided to ignore them as investments). To state it another way, the 40% premium was a strong "buy signal" for REITs. Near the very end of 1996, the T-Note was yielding 6.6% and the average REIT in Green Street's universe yielded 6.3%, for a discount of 5.1%. By this measure, REITs were at the more expensive end of the -10% to +20% band noted above, but didn't appear to be grossly expensive (by this measurement tool) as we entered 1997.[5]

The NAV Premium. Now let's consider another Green Street graph, this one charting, since January 1990, the average REIT's stock price in relationship to Green Street's estimate of its net asset value (NAV). Between January 1990 and the end of November 1996,

177

the average REIT traded at prices between 36% *below* NAV (October 1990) and 20% *above* NAV (February 1993 and November 1996); during most periods they ranged between a 9% discount and a 15% premium. Green Street's index reached a new high at the end of December 1996, reaching a 28% premium. Following the late 1990 period when the discount was unusually large, REITs stocks mounted a furious rally, as indicated by their 1991 total return of 35.7%. Conversely, 1994 (the year following the first time REIT stocks reached the 20% premium to NAV level) was very disappointing; in that year the Equity REITs managed a total return of only 3.17%.

What can we learn from this NAV approach to REIT industry valuation? Can this indicator tell us something despite its short sampling period? One obvious observation is that when REITs have traded at a significant discount to NAV (as they did near the end of 1990), they were extremely cheap, and when they've traded at a premium of 20% over NAV, as in 1993, they were quite expensive (as indicated by 1994's disappointing performance). As 1996 drew to a close, premiums were well over the 20% level, at 28%. Before we panic and sell all our REIT stocks, however, investors would be wise to consider whether the stunning total return of 35.3% posted by Equity REITs in 1996 was excessive exuberance which will lead to a poor year for REITs in 1997 or whether the market was "discounting" a significant increase in property values generally, or in REITs' NAVs, in particular, either of which would have the effect of significantly reducing the premium over NAV at which the average REIT traded at the end of 1996. My guess is that the latter development will occur. Furthermore, as REITs are increasingly seen by investors as highly active business corporations (rather than as passive investments in real estate), NAVs may become of lesser significance in the valuation process (at least with respect to the faster-growing REITs).

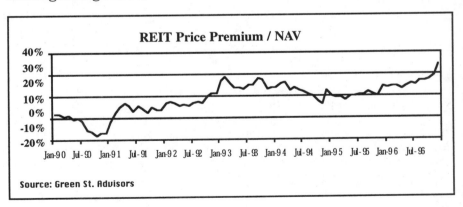

178

P/FFO Ratios. Let's take yet another look at historical vs. current valuations, this time from the perspective of P/FFO ratios. In a 1992 research publication,[6] Goldman Sachs reviewed average "price/cash flow ratios" for selected groups of REITs over long time periods. Assuming that Goldman Sachs' price/cash flow ratios are approximately equal to P/FFO ratios, we see that these ratios averaged 9.3 between 1963 and 1969, 7.6 between 1970 and 1979, 11.6 between 1980 and 1989 and 11.6 between 1989 and 1991.

Another such analysis, also done by Goldman Sachs,[7] contains a graph showing REIT P/FFO ratios from 1980 to 1996. According to that firm's data, the lowest P/FFO ratio was just under 8 between 1981 and 1982 and the highest was 19, between 1992 and 1993; the average over the entire time horizon of 1980 to 1996 was 13.0. My own analysis of a narrower list of arguably higher-quality REITs showed that P/FFO ratios averaged 14.0 between 1992 and 1996, with a high of 16.5 in 1993 and a low of 12.4 in 1995.

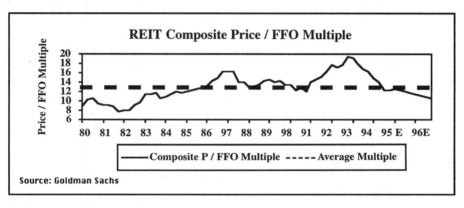

Ignoring the 1960s and 1970s, due to the very small total market cap of REIT stocks during those early time periods, we can determine from the foregoing that REITs have traded at average P/FFO ratios of between 13.0 and 14.0 over much of the last 15 years. If we average the 13.0 and 14.0 ratios, we can conclude that REITs have traded at an average P/FFO ratio of approximately 13.5 since 1980.

What are today's REITs' P/FFO ratios, based upon current prices? Let's look at P/AFFO ratios, as being more representative than P/FFO ratios. While this will result in higher ratios, they will tend to be more meaningful. Using an average of the highs and lows, and based upon trailing 12-month P/AFFO ratios provided, as of November 29, 1996, by Realty Stock Review, a widely respected REIT industry newsletter, we note the following:

Sector	P/AFFO Ratio
Apartmens	12.1
Shopping centers	11.3
Regional malls	11.7
Factory outlets	10.7
Manufactured homes	13.4
Health care	11.1
Hotels	11.1
Industrial	13.3
Office	13.5
Self-storage	12.1
Diversified/other	12.1
AVERAGE	**12.1**

In fairness, REIT prices have risen briskly in 1996 so let's take the *high* average P/AFFO ratio over the preceding 12 months, which was 13.6. We might note that this is still comparable to the long-term average of 13.5, and the latter was based upon FFOs rather than AFFOs; the ratio at November 1996 would have been significantly lower had we used P/FFO ratios. Accordingly, this valuation tool is telling us that REIT prices were not trading at exorbitant levels near the end of 1996, at least on a P/AFFO basis.

Summing it all up, we have seen that REITs, at the end of 1996, were trading at dividend yields within the range of the "normal" spread of 20% over to 10% under the 10-year Treasury note and at P/AFFO ratios at or below historical ratios (13-14 times expected AFFOs). However, REITs were also then trading at unusually high premiums over their net asset values. Accordingly, by two of these yardsticks REITs were fairly valued, but by the third (the NAV model) they were quite expensive.

The point of this exercise is not to forecast the direction of REIT stock prices in 1997 and beyond but to merely suggest some tools that REIT investors may find useful in trying to determine whether REIT stocks are, as a group, cheap or expensive at any particular point in time. Although all of these methods are clearly imprecise, they can alert REIT investors to periods when REITs are trading well below (or above) historical valuation levels, based upon their dividend yields relative to the 10-year T-note, their premiums or discounts to estimated asset values (which, in itself, will be only a rough approximation), and their P/FFO ratios. Whenever these measurements (or even two of them) suggest that REITs are not significantly overvalued, and if we don't expect a significant period of under-performance by real estate in general, we may have confidence that we aren't buying REIT stocks at excessive valuations.

For every investment strategy, there's an investor personality to match. While the number of individual foibles is potentially limitless, most investment styles can be boiled down to one of two types. Essentially, it's a case of hands-on, or hands-off.

180

Some investors will want to spend a great deal of time analyzing and applying historical and prospective valuation methodologies while others will just want to own high-quality REIT stocks, collect the fat dividends and watch 'em grow. While this chapter has hopefully provided some useful valuation tools for investors of a more active and analytical bent, investors who disdain models of the type suggested can also do very well with REIT stocks by either merely focusing on the blue-chip REITs via the criteria suggested in Chapter Seven and holding them for many years or buying shares in a mutual fund devoted to REIT ownership. Regardless of what strategy you pick, the REIT world will be a very hospitable place for all kinds of investors.

---

[1] One REIT industry analyst, Daniel P. Guenther (Managing Director of Lansdowne Research, an independent consulting firm), has suggested that a REIT might be valued by adding to its NAV another component of value (which he labels "Value Creation Ability and Capacity"), which is the capitalized value of the REIT's ability and capacity to produce earnings (and other sources of value) in excess of the growth in enterprise value already implied by the valuation of its existing properties.

[2] See, for example, the discussion of the significant fall-off in United Dominion's P/AFFO multiple between 1993 and 1996 in the next section.

[3] For example, in the Simon Property/DeBartolo Realty merger, the proxy statement, in discussing the methods used to determine the fairness of the exchange ratio of Simon shares for DeBartolo shares, did not even mention the asset values of either company.

[4] Some REIT observers don't trust REIT data going back more than a few years, due to the small size of the industry prior to 1992. But see note 4 of Chapter One.

[5] We must be particularly careful about using this model with historical data, as many (if not most) REITs have been reducing their dividend payout ratios in recent years. Thus there may be a secular decline in REIT yields (vis-a-vis FFO or AFFO), which could make the comparison with the 10-year T-note a bit misleading as an indicator of relative valuation. And, of course, we could make the argument that REITs are larger and stronger organizations today than they were as recently as five years ago, which could also have a bearing on the comparison with T-note yields.

[6] "Reit Redux," August 12, 1992.

[7] "Real Estate Stock Monitor," August 1995, p.1.

Part IV

How to Do It and What's Ahead

Chapter Nine

Building A REIT Portfolio

"You can never have too much of a good thing."
— *Mae West*

Or can you? Let's be optimistic. Let's assume that, having read this far, you are at least partially convinced that REITs are pretty good investments, you have some idea which types of REITs you like, whether you want to go for quality or chase high yields, and you are ready to do some serious REIT buying — or at least nibble a little bit. Before we get too far ahead of ourselves, though, let's put the whole concept of REIT investing into a larger perspective. And to do so intelligently we should ask a few critical questions. First, how much of one's total portfolio might be appropriate to invest in REITs? And how should we diversify among the various types of properties owned by REITs and the geographical areas in which they own them? Then, once we've determined all that, how should we jump into the market and build a REIT portfolio? The answers to these questions will provide investors with the solid footing needed to enter the realm of REIT investing.

How Much of a Good Thing Do We Want?

This is probably one of the most difficult questions to consider, as there are really no "right" answers. We've all seen financial columnists or brokerage firms declare that "the proper asset mix at this time is 65% stocks, 25% bonds and 10% cash" or some similar claim. This may work for the "average" investor, but how do you know if you're Mr. or Mrs. Average? The only "correct" answer is that the proper asset mix depends upon various factors unique to the individual, and the same answer applies to how much we should be investing in REITs.

One of the most important factors to consider is the individual's ability to invest over long periods of time without having to liquidate investments for short-term needs such as a child's college education, to buy a home or for some other purpose. If a significant amount of cash will be required within a relatively short period of time, that amount shouldn't be invested in stocks, bonds or REITs, as all such investments are subject to market forces. A bear market in any of these sectors could result in having to sell the investments at a loss notwithstanding their quality and favorable long-term prospects, and bear markets occur when least expected.

185

Let's assume that we have $100,000 available for investment, that we don't think we'll need any of it for many years and that we already have an "emergency fund" for rainy days. The allocation of this amount will then depend upon four other key variables: (a) How large a gain is the investor's objective? (b) How comfortable is the investor with market fluctuations? (c) How comfortable is the investor holding a stock that could decline (as well as rise) substantially? and (d) How much income from one's investments does the investor need to supplement other salary or retirement income?

Aggressive Investors Should Be Light on REITs

The aggressive investor looking for very large returns over fairly short time periods should not put a high percentage of his or her assets into REITs. While it is true that over long time periods REITs have been very competitive with the S&P 500 Index on a total return basis, in the short term REITs are a singles-hitters' game. Very few REIT investments will enable an investor to score a 50% gain in one year or rack up a "10-bagger," to use Peter Lynch's expression, within just a few years. Despite the views of some, real estate ownership is a low-risk venture if entered into without excessive debt leverage; conversely, the rewards are steady but don't usually offer huge short-term upside. Furthermore, the faster growing REITs will continue to raise additional equity capital with which to grow the business; this tends to eliminate any scarcity value for a REIT's shares, and prevents them from skyrocketing. Thus investors looking to double their net worth in 18 months should not be heavily invested in REITs.

REIT Prices Don't Fluctuate Much

On the other hand, as we discussed in Chapter One, price fluctuations of REIT shares are a fraction of what we see with most other common stocks. On a big day, a $45 REIT stock such as Reckson Associates may be up or down 3/8 or 1/2 a point, or about 1%. Compare this with the four and five point gyrations (4-5%) of such large cap stocks as Pfizer, Motorola or Proctor & Gamble (not to mention such high-tech favorites as Intel, Microsoft or Cisco Systems). If watching your stocks bounce up and down like a yo-yo makes you queasy and ready to call your broker with a "sell" order when they have a particularly bad day, you might be better off psychologically (and perhaps financially) owning a large portion of REITs to provide some ballast and stability to the portfolio.

REITs Contain Little Risk of Major Price Declines

One nice thing about REITs is that even those that turn out to be turkeys don't decline precipitously. Yes, there have been some big losers, but the prices of very few REIT shares have been chopped in half, except in extraordinary cases (such as where the REIT has allowed itself to become substantially overleveraged — and, even then, we don't see seven point one-day declines). Most of these big downers have occurred due, in large part, to significantly reduced dividends. By watching AFFO closely and comparing it with a REIT's regular dividend, we can usually spot a potential dividend cut well before it happens and get out in time (a REIT trading at a very high yield is often a tip-off). Investors need to be much more wary about other common stocks, where a single piece of negative news — whether it be a lost contract, an earnings "shortfall," a product liability claim or a new technology — can decimate a company's stock price virtually overnight. Accordingly, those investors who are highly loss-adverse should consider owning a substantial portion of REITs.

REITs Provide a High Current Income Level

Some financial planners advocate a large common stock weighting even for persons near or in retirement. They argue, with some justification, that over any significant measurement period, common stocks have provided more appreciation than virtually any other type of investment. If the investor-retiree needs additional income, all that's necessary is to sell off a small percentage of the portfolio.

It's hard to criticize that logic, but keep in mind that the last few years have been unusually free of bear markets. It will be difficult, both psychologically as well as financially, to sell off a significant chunk of the portfolio at a loss in the middle of a bear market when funds are needed. This potential problem becomes much less of an issue if a large portion of the investor's income requirements is generated from high current yields within a portfolio. It is for this reason that most financial planners continue to recommend a large segment of bonds for those investors requiring significant investment income.

To briefly illustrate the point, let's assume a hypothetical retiree who has a portfolio of $200,000 and needs to supplement $25,000 in annual pension and social security income with an additional $20,000 annually in order to take care of his or her living expenses. A 5% yield on the portfolio will generate $10,000 of that, and he or she will have to sell off only an additional $10,000 in stocks annually to net the required cash. Another investor in the same circumstances but owning a very low-yielding portfolio would have to sell close to $20,000, or 10% of the portfolio, each year. Doing this in a bear market that lasts a year or two would be painful indeed. Accordingly, it seems logical that persons needing to live off their investments would want to include a substantial number of high-yielding securities, such as REITs, in their portfolio.

Looking for the Appropriate REIT Allocation

The principles outlined above should help each investor make a personal decision as to the percentage of REITs that should be owned; there are just too many variables, in both personal financial planning and investor psychology, to use rigid formulae. One final and very important point should also be made. Assuming that the investor is not interested in home runs or even triples or doubles (home run hitters do tend to strike out a lot), is very uncomfortable with large price fluctuations, is highly loss-averse and needs a substantial current yield from his or her investments, does that mean that 50% or 75% of the portfolio should be in REITs?

No. The most fundamental principle of investing, which has been proven time after time over centuries, is that investment diversification is the key to stability of performance and preservation of capital over any significant period of time. While outstanding results might be obtained by putting a huge portion of one's assets in REITs, absolutely no one can foretell the future and even the most astute investors never score on *all* their investments. This principle of diversification is a very strong argument to the effect that investors should not go hog-wild on REITs even if they learn to love them as I do.

All right — if you threaten to boil me in hot oil, tar and feather me or ride me out of town on a rail unless I give you an "appropriate" percentage of one's "liquid" investment assets (primarily stocks, bonds and other securities) that "should" be invested in REITs by the "typical" conservative investor looking for steady (albeit unspectacular) returns with a modest degree of risk, I would suggest somewhere between 15% and 35%. I would adjust the portfolio between these two percentages on the basis of whether I believe the entire stock market is cheap (slide down toward the 15% floor) or expensive (increase toward the 35% ceiling). And, of course, these percentages might be adjusted to take existing REIT valuations into account as well. Why? Are such percentages supportable?

Admittedly, 15-35% is a significant overweighting of REITs in relationship to all publicly traded stocks. REITs had an equity market value of approximately $89 billion as of December 31, 1996, which is just slightly in excess of 1% of the estimated market value of all stocks traded on the New York, American and other stock exchanges and in the NASDAQ National Market System. REITs' relative market value would be smaller still if we included the vast U.S. and corporate bond markets. Such an overweighting reduces

188

the total potential diversification of one's portfolio and, to most financial planners and investment counselors, diversification is the Holy Grail of proper investment strategy. Consider, however, that in many respects REITs' investment prospects are related to their ability to acquire, manage and profit from real estate, and that the total value of commercial real estate in the United States has been estimated at between $3 trillion and $4 trillion (compared with approximately $9.3 trillion for stocks). From this perspective, a 15%-35% weighting in REITs is not like putting 15%-35% of one's assets into oil stocks or even technology stocks. Furthermore, price history has shown that over significant measurement periods (see the graph in Chapter One) Equity REITs have performed at least on a par with other common stocks on a total return basis, so having a significant percentage of one's assets in REITs should produce solid long-term performance, reduce volatility, diminish risk and provide substantial diversification in a balanced portfolio. Besides, I myself — an unabashed REIT supporter — have owned well over this percentage for many years, and I can guarantee you that I'm not a bit sorry!

Diversification Among REITs

The next logical question is, of course, once we know how much we want to invest in REITs, how many of them should we buy? To what extent shall we try to get property type and geographical diversification in our REIT portfolio? Shall we diversify by investment style?

Basic Diversification. Much depends, of course, on the absolute level of cash we want to invest. We will discuss later in this chapter the use of REIT mutual funds to obtain diversification for investors who don't want to worry about selecting a REIT portfolio and watching it closely. At some asset level, perhaps below $30,000, we just can't get enough diversification without getting clobbered on commissions. For most investors, an absolute minimum of six REITs is necessary to achieve a bare-bones level of property type and geographical diversification, as we'll discuss shortly. If we try to invest as little as $6,000 among six different REITs, we could put only $1,000 into each of them. If the brokerage firm has, say, a minimum commission of $50 per trade, the investor would pay a 5% commission on each purchase, which would mean giving up most of the first year's dividend. On the other hand, at $30,000, six trades would amount to $5,000 each, and the $50 commission would nick us for only 1% of the purchase price on each trade.

Six different REITs will provide a bare minimum of acceptable diversification by property type, but 10 REITs would enable the investor to obtain more reasonable diversification. With only six, I would suggest one in each of the following six different property types: apartments, retail, office, industrial, self-storage and health care. With additional funds, we might want to add a hotel or manufactured home community REIT. Investing even more funds could get us up to 10 REITs, which would enable us to own two REITs in each major sector (apartments, retail and office/industrial) and one in each of the other sectors (health care, self-storage, hotel and manufactured homes). With more funds, we could widen our *geographical* diversification within each sector. For example, we might want to add an apartment REIT whose properties are located on the Pacific Coast to those we already own that have apartment units in the Southeast and Northeast. Of course, we can similarly diversify geographically in other REIT sectors, such as neighborhood shopping centers and office/industrial properties. An alternative is to buy two or three of the well-managed diversified REITs, which own several different types of properties within a single geographical location — such as Washington REIT (Washington D.C./Virginia), Colonial Properties (the South) and Cousins Properties (the Southeast).

Overweighting and Underweighting. One of the key issues involving diversification is whether we should try to overweight or underweight our REIT holdings for particular property sectors. There is much difference of opinion on this topic, even among institutional REIT investors. Some of them don't try to adjust their portfolios in accordance with how much they like (or dislike) a sector, and simply use "market weightings." For example, if mall REITs make up 18% of all Equity REITs, such an investor will make sure that mall REITs will comprise 18% of his or her REIT portfolio. The theory here is similar to that of buying the S&P 500 Index rather than trying to select individual stocks: Advocates of this approach would argue that all stocks, including REITs, are usually efficiently priced, and it's unrealistic to assume that one can accurately forecast which sectors will do better than the others. Investors who prefer the "passive" and "market-weighting" strategies to REIT investing might want to consider simply purchasing shares of an indexed REIT fund, such as the Vanguard REIT Index fund. A breakdown of the market weightings among the major REIT sectors, as of December 31, 1996, can be found in Chapter Three.

Other investors, frequently those oriented toward maximum short-term performance, think that they can, indeed, figure out the "right" sectors to be in at any particular time. They will closely examine the "fundamentals" within the U.S. real estate markets and overweight the portfolio in those sectors where demand for space exceeds the supply, rents and occupancy rates are rising fastest or other factors convince the investor that investment returns will be maximized by emphasizing certain sectors over others. Kenneth Heebner, a well-known successful fund manager, uses this approach in his relatively new (but very successful) CGM Realty

Fund. This fund has been heavily invested in hotel, apartment and office/industrial REITs; retail REITs of all types and health care REITs have been conspicuously absent.

My suggestion is that, unless the investor is very confident that he or she knows which sectors will do best over the next couple of years, a portfolio bearing close to a market weighting would be most appropriate. Overweighting the "right sectors" is tricky, as other investors will often see the same thing, and all the REITs in that sector will be richly priced in anticipation of the rapid growth that is already expected by the market.

Diversification by Investment Style. Another very different approach to diversification is to give lesser consideration to owning different property types in different geographical areas and, instead, to own a package of REITs with different investment characteristics. Thus the investor could include in his or her portfolio a number of REITs generally thought to be of very high quality and low risk, and which offer highly predictable and steady growth (with little regard to their REIT "sector"); an additional number of REITs with low valuations (based upon, for example, a narrow "spread" between the price of the stock and the REIT's underlying net asset value or a low P/AFFO multiple); a few "gazelle" REITs for which the investor expects unusually rapid rates of growth; and, to round out the portfolio, a few "bond proxies," which have very high yields but minimal growth prospects. Such an approach may help to insulate the portfolio from major gyrations as institutional investors shift their REIT funds from one style of REIT investing to another.

Toward a Well-Balanced Portfolio. Which approach toward diversification is best? By property type? Geography? By investment characteristics? All of the above? Is it best to overweight some sectors and underweight others? There really isn't any statistical evidence that one approach to REIT investing or REIT diversification is better than any other; the recent extraordinary growth of the REIT world has been so sudden that the research has simply not yet been done — and would probably be inconclusive even if it had. The point here is that investors do need to be diversified in order to spread the investment risk among different managements and properties, but there is no right or wrong answer as to how best to accomplish this.

It's best to own at least one REIT in each property sector, and to seek some geographic diversification when owning more than one REIT within a sector. With respect to investment style, I personally prefer to put most of my REIT investment dollars in those blue-chip REITs whose managements have proven to be superb and whose long-term track records of FFO and dividend growth have been outstanding. REITs of this type should do well in all business and real estate climates, regardless of the prospects for the property sector in which they operate, and have shown that, rather than

191

being hurt by a problematic economy or difficult real estate market, they can find and take advantage of the numerous opportunities that present themselves when problems abound and hoards of distressed sellers suddenly want to dump properties at cheap prices. I'd then add some additional REITs that appear cheaply priced and misunderstood by the investment community, perhaps with higher yields and less well-defined growth prospects, together with a few REITs that look like they'll be rapid growers, due perhaps to their ability to access large amounts of capital and acquire tons of real estate at high cap rates. I'd be cautious about Mortgage REITs, as they've often been badly hurt by rising interest rates (but they can be extremely rewarding at times). Fortunately, the REIT industry is now so wide and deep that we have a large number of REITs of different investment characteristics from which to choose, while at the same time giving us the ability to invest in enough property sectors to provide proper diversification.

Although REIT investors shouldn't ignore the current actual or perceived problems and prospects applicable to each sector, we shouldn't take them too seriously either, particularly when investing in the blue-chip REITs. These REITs can do well in good climates and bad; when internal growth slows, perhaps due to overbuilding or declining demand for rental space, such a REIT (which has access to additional capital) is likely to find abundant acquisition opportunities that will provide good external FFO growth. Finally, we shouldn't become terribly concerned if we are overweighted in some sectors, particularly when we own REITs whose managements are adept at turning lemons into lemonade.

Here's just a sample of the kind of diversification that can be obtained within certain major sectors (where relevant, the areas of major geographical focus are included). The following list includes REITs having an equity market cap of at least $500 million as of December 12, 1996, based upon data provided by Realty Stock Review:

Property Type	REIT	Principal Location(s)
Apartments		
	Avalon	East Coast
	Bay, BRE and Irvine	California
	Charles Smith	Washington D.C.
	Equity Residential	Nationwide
	Evans Withycombe	Arizona & California
	Gables Residential	Texas, Tennessee and Georgia
	Merry and Summit	Southeast
	Post	Georgia/Florida
	Security Capital Atlantic	East Coast
	Security Capital Pacific	Western U.S
	United Dominion	Southeast/Southwest
Retail - Neighborhood Shopping Centers		
	Developers Diversified	Florida, Ohio
	Federal	East Coast

	Kimco	Eastern U.S.
	New Plan	New York, Ohio, Pennsylvania
	Vornado	East Coast
	Weingarten	Texas & Southwest
Retail - Factory Outlets		
	Chelsea/GCA	East and West Coasts
	Horizon	Midwest, West
Retail - Malls		
	CBL	Southeast
	General Growth	Nationwide
	Macerich	Nationwide
	Mills Corp	Nationwide
	Simon DeBartolo	Nationwide
	Taubman	Nationwide
	Urban Shopping	Illinois, Florida, California
Health Care - Long-Term Care, Medical Office and Rehabilitation		
	American Health	Not applicable
	Health Care Properties	Not applicable
	Health & Retirement Props	Not applicable
	MediTrust	Not applicable
	Nationwide Health	Not applicable
	Omega Healthcare	Not applicable
Office		
	Arden	California
	Beacon	Nationwide
	Cali Realty	New Jersey
	CarrAmerica	Nationwide
	Crescent	Nationwide
	Highwoods	Southeast
	Prentiss	Nationwide
	Reckson	New York & New Jersey
Industrial		
	Duke Realty	Midwest
	First Industrial	Midwest
	Liberty Property	Mid-Atlantic
	Security Capital Industrial	Nationwide
	Spieker Properties	West Coast
Self Storage		
	Public Storage	Nationwide
	Shurgard	East, Southwest, and West Coast
	Storage USA	Nationwide
Hotels		
	Felcor Suites	Nationwide
	Hospitality Properties	Nationwide
	Patriot American	East and Southwest
	RFS Hotel Investors	Nationwide
	Starwoods Lodging	Nationwide
Manufactured Homes		
	Manufactured Home	Nationwide
	Sun Communities	Midwest and Southeast

Unlike most sectors, *geographic* diversification isn't a major issue with respect to mall REITs, health care REITs and self-storage REITs, as detailed knowledge of the nuances, subtleties and opportunities peculiar to local markets isn't nearly as important in these sectors. A mall in Harrisburg, Pennsylvania, is pretty much like one in Eugene, Oregon, and the same skills are involved in acquiring or building the mall, locating quality tenants and operating it profitably. I'm oversimplifying, but the point is valid in most cases. Similar considerations apply to health care and storage properties. We don't miss a great deal by owning only one of these types of REITs, and most of the REITs that own properties in these sectors already are significantly diversified in their portfolio properties.

To summarize, we can obtain a good cross-section of REIT property types by investing in a minimum of six different REITs (one each in the apartment, retail, office, industrial, health care and self-storage sectors). Adding more will allow us to obtain more diversification geographically or to add additional property types. We can also invest in REITs with different investment characteristics. If comprised primarily of blue-chip issues, a well-diversified REIT portfolio will stand the investor in good stead for many years, regardless of the ever-changing preferences of professional REIT investors and the ebbs and flows of property cycles within each sector and within each geographical area of the United States.

How to Get Started

Investors might choose from four very different approaches in building a REIT portfolio. Selecting the "right" one depends upon the investor's temperament, willingness to spend a fair amount of time in the investment process and the availability of qualified professionals who are familiar with REITs and how to invest in them. Let's take a look at each, and review their pros and cons.

Do-it-Yourself

This approach is the most difficult and time-consuming but can be the most rewarding, at least psychologically. The tools required to build and monitor one's own REIT portfolio include the following: (a) willingness to spend at least a few hours a week following the REIT world and your own REIT portfolio and (b) if resources permit, a subscription to a good-quality REIT newsletter or research service. For example, Realty Stock Review, which is published semi-monthly, covers the entire REIT world with thoroughness and candor, and provides vital REIT data and information, dividend and financing news and excerpts from various research reports. It also contains a model REIT portfolio. Most retail brokerage firms provide research reports on individual REITs, many of which are very thorough. More information than ever before can be obtained "on-line," and many REITs (as well as NAREIT) have recently established their own web-sites. "Motley Fool," available on American On-Line, contains an excellent real estate "board" which contains abundant discussions of REITs and real estate issues.

As we discussed earlier, REITs are not complicated and their business prospects do not change quickly. As a result, REITs are less data-intensive or research-intensive than most other types of common stock investments. With just a bit of outside help, a willingness to ask questions of management and the discipline to carefully review the information publicly available (*e.g.*, annual reports, 10-Q's, etc.), most reasonably intelligent investors can do a pretty good job managing their own REIT portfolios.

The following table provides a very general description of the types of information which should prove valuable to REIT investors.

Sources for the Do-It-Yourselfer	Where to Find It	General Description
America On-Line ("Motley Fool" Real Estate Board)	American On-Line; keyword "Motley Fool"	General on-line discussion of real estate and REITs
Barron's Ground Floor	Barron's weekly magazine (available by subscription or on newsstands)	Frequently-appearing columns on real estate
Brokerage firms throughout the United States	Contact the appropriate broker or registered rep.	Research reports on REITs and related services
Green Street Advisors	Green Street Advisors: 110 Newport Center Drive, Newport Beach, CA. 92660	REIT research service (for institutional investors)
Korpacz Real Estate Investor Survey	Korpacz Company: 7470 New Technology Way, Frederick, MD. 21703	Information on institutional investment in real estate on a nationwide basis
National Real Estate Index	KOLL: 2200 Powell St., Emeryville, CA. 94608	Discussion and information on various real estate markets, including rental rates, cap rates, etc.
Penobscott Group	Penobscott Group: 160 State Street, Boston, MA. 02109	REIT research service (for institutional investors)
Real Estate Capital Markets	Institutional Real Estate, Inc.: 1475 N. Broadway, Suite 300, Walnut Creek, CA. 94596	Newsletter containing articles and statistics regarding real estate financing and capital flows
Realty Stock Review	Realty Stock Review: 179 Avenue at the Common, 2nd Floor, Shrewsbury, NJ 07702	Newsletter covering all facets of REITs and REIT investing
The SNL REIT Weekly	SNL Securities: 410 E. Main St., P.O. Box 2124, Charlottesville, VA. 22902	Newsletter containing condensed versions of REITs' press releases on earnings, deals, financings, etc..
Web-sites and home pages	Available from NAREIT (http://www.nareit.com) and numerous REITs	Data on individual REITs and the REIT industry available on-line

The "do-it-yourself" approach has several advantages. First, the investor will save substantially on management fees and brokerage commissions; neither a mutual fund nor an outside investment advisor will be needed, and a discount broker can be used. Second, the realization of capital gains and losses can be tailored to the investor's personal tax planning requirements. Third, as we discussed in Chapter One, a significant portion of most REITs' dividends are treated as a "return of capital," and is not immediately taxable to the shareholder. Owning REIT stocks directly allows the shareholder to take full advantage of this tax benefit. Finally, the knowledge and experience gained from managing one's own portfolio can, hopefully, lead not only to outstanding investment results, but also to a great deal of personal satisfaction.

Stockbrokers

Let's face it. By far the great majority of investors would prefer to spend their few free hours each week playing golf, taking the kids to a baseball game, reading a good novel or just sprucing up the garden or lawn. Only us oddballs actually enjoy poring over annual reports, calculating AFFOs or checking out absorption rates in the Long Island office market. A good solution to the problem of "OK, REITs are good — but which ones?" is to find a stockbroker who has a good familiarity with REITs and who has access to the research reports published by the major brokerage firms, many of which are outstanding.

Not that many years ago, when REITs were still occupying the sleepy backwaters of the investment world, it would have been very difficult to find such a broker. While today we may not find a REIT-knowledgeable broker by just walking into the nearest brokerage office, a few phone calls should solve the problem. REITs are gaining increasing publicity, in the personal financial magazines, business sections of major newspapers and elsewhere, and today most major brokerage firms employ at least one good REIT analyst (and several have entire staffs). REITs are now becoming recognized as a major investment alternative (along with electric utilities, preferred stocks and bonds) for yield-oriented investors, and it would be surprising indeed if at least one REIT-knowledgeable registered representative in any good-sized brokerage office couldn't be located.

Assuming a sympathetic broker can be found, the advantages of this approach include lots of personal attention, the ability to decide when, for tax purposes, we want to take capital gains (and the inevitable capital loss) and the relief of not having to research and worry about such issues as AFFO, apartment rental rates and other such REIT essentials. Of course, the brokerage commissions will be higher than for the do-it-yourself investor. Nevertheless, if you're careful to avoid too much trading and buy only those REITs that are consistent with your investment objectives, the higher commissions may be a small price to pay for the service provided. The watchwords here, as in much of life, are patience and selectivity.

Financial Planners and Investment Advisors

Today, as the average age of the population increases and lifespans become longer, more and more individuals are becoming serious about saving and investing toward a retirement free of financial worry. Whereas the huge baby-boomer cohort was most concerned about a new BMW or fancy restaurant as recently as the late '80s, today members of this generation are taking very seriously the responsibility of investing for their futures. Today employees of all ages are realizing that, even if Social Security will be there, it just won't be enough. While many of us are becoming knowledgeable investors and others are finding capable brokers or pouring savings into mutual funds, still others are retaining financial planners and investment advisors to devise, supervise and build individual investment portfolios in accordance with the individual's future goals and needs.

Financial planners provide general assistance in helping the individual to set up and organize a long-term financial plan, which would include retirement planning, estate planning, obtaining adequate insurance of all types and planning for major financial requirements such as the purchase of a home or funding a child's college education. As part of the process, some planners will manage and invest their client's funds, either directly or through mutual funds, and others will refer the client to an investment advisor. Some will be paid on the basis of commissions from insurance or other investments purchased, while others charge on the basis of a fee only.

Investment advisors, on the other hand, generally do little or no financial planning, and specialize in investing client funds in stocks, bonds and other securities. They are generally compensated only on the basis of a percentage of the assets they manage (generally between 1% and 2%). Thus if the portfolio grows, the advisor's fee will increase, and vice-versa. Some such firms provide a great deal of personal attention and "hand-holding," while others do not. These firms also vary a great deal in terms of the extent to which they will individualize a portfolio, and the extent to which they will take their client's personal tax situation into account when making buy and sell decisions.

The advantages of using a financial planner, alone or in conjunction with an independent investment advisor, include the similarity of interests between the firm and its clients, the personal attention given to the client, and the ability to structure portfolios on a highly individualized basis with due regard to the client's tax situation. The principal disadvantages to the would-be REIT investor include the difficulty locating a financial planner or investment advisor who is familiar with and experienced in investing in REITs, the payment of recurring fees whether or not any trades are made in the account, and the lack, by many such firms, of access to the relevant data essential for following the REIT world closely and carefully. Many investment advisors require a substantial portfolio size before undertaking to manage the account.

REIT Mutual Funds

As recently as five years ago only about five mutual funds were devoted to investing in real estate-related securities such as REITs. Today there are close to 30 of such funds. True, most of them are exceedingly small in size; according to Realty Stock Review,[1] on December 5, 1996, only nine of them had as much as $100 million in assets. The two giants, each with over $1 billion in assets, were Cohen & Steers Realty Shares ($1.7 billion) and Fidelity Real Estate ($1.4 billion). A list of the 10 largest REIT mutual funds, as of December 26, 1996, together with relevant information (courtesy of Realty Stock Review), is included in Appendix D. While some may scoff at the small size of these funds, most have done quite well during their relatively short histories. The Vanguard Group, which has a market niche in "index funds," has recently come out with the Vanguard REIT Index fund, a REIT mutual fund indexed to the Morgan Stanley REIT Index (which itself was launched at the end of 1994); the Morgan Stanley REIT Index, it should be noted, excludes Mortgage REITs and health care REITs. These exclusions could mean that this index could outperform or underperform a broader REIT index such as the NAREIT index. See Appendix E for a description of the various indices available for comparison purposes.

These REIT mutual funds provide an outstanding solution to the problem of how to obtain satisfactory REIT diversification when the dollar amount allocated to REITs is small. As we discussed above, the practical minimum required for even the most basic diversification, using individual companies, is at least $30,000. To take a purely arbitrary number, let's assume that the REIT investor wants to put 20% of his or her assets into REITs; this implies that the total portfolio would have to be $150,000 (20% of $150,000 = $30,000) in order to have a diversified portfolio of REITs. In contrast, not only can we obtain diversification through a REIT fund, but we can obtain lots of it. Most such funds own at least 20 or 30 different REITs, which will clearly insulate the investor against major financial damage should one or two of them suffer a meltdown; while this is much less likely to happen to a REIT than most other types of common stocks, such a situation is not out of the question.

Perhaps even most important, the investor gets the benefit of experienced professionals who have access to detailed information on each REIT and to REITs' top management when making investment decisions. Even active investors might want to invest a minimum amount in some of these funds in order to "benchmark"

198

their personal REIT investment track records and to get a window on what the "big boys" are doing from time to time.

Despite these significant strong points, REIT mutual funds aren't without their disadvantages. While no brokerage commissions are payable when investing in no-load funds, management fees can be sizable and typically range from 1% to 1.5% of total assets; in addition, the investor pays, indirectly through reduced dividend yields, for the fund's expenses such as legal and accounting fees and other expenses of operating a public company. Also, investors receive no individual attention and have no ability to time purchases or sales in order to engage in tax planning; any gains or losses realized by the fund during the year are passed through to the fund investor. Finally, the investor who frequently buys and sells shares in the same fund will have a devil of a time keeping current and accurate his or her cost basis and tax gain or loss information.

For the investor who doesn't have the resources to adequately diversify his or her REIT holdings, are these disadvantages so substantial as to offset the advantages the REIT funds provide? Clearly not, especially if the investor refrains from doing lots of trading. REIT funds are especially good for IRAs, as neither tax gains and losses nor cost basis is relevant in such accounts. They are the right answer for many investors who would otherwise have no safe and conservative way to own these terrific companies.

There are a plethora of ways for investors to enjoy the advantages and benefits of REIT investing, encompassing a full spectrum of investment styles. We can invest passively through one or more REIT mutual funds (even including an indexed fund). We can become more active (and obtain assistance) by using the services of a knowledgeable stockbroker, financial planner or investment advisor. Or, for those of us who are more adventurous, REITs can be individually researched, acquired and followed closely through a bit of diligence and patience, perhaps using some of the tools suggested in this chapter. If our REIT holdings are well-diversified, and particularly if we emphasize REITs with outstanding managements and good long-term strategies, patient investors should be able to reap the benefits of portfolio diversification and excellent total returns over many years.

---

[1] Realty Stock Review, December 16, 1996, p. 30.

Chapter Ten

What Can Go Wrong?

"There is nothing permanent except change."
— Heraclitus

I've spent the better part of this book singing the praises of REIT investing and trust that by this time I've been able to convince you that a passel of REITs belongs in every investment portfolio. However, no investment is perfect, and REITs are no exception. Any number of problems — some major, some minor — can threaten the health of our investments. Wise investors are aware of these potential problems and develop a keen eye to avoid being victimized. Here, we'll take a look at some of these unfortunate circumstances and learn how to spot them before they're able to make dents in our net worth.

In general, the risks of REIT investing can be divided into two categories: those that can affect virtually all REITs and those that may impact an individual REIT without causing problems for any others. We'll address that across-the-board threat first.

Issues Affecting All of REIT World

REITs, as investments, are subject to two major hazards: an excess supply of available rental properties and rising interest rates. Excess supply is, simply stated, a situation in which the amount of real estate available for occupancy exceeds the demand for rental space by tenants; this supply/demand imbalance is often referred to as a "renters' market," one in which tenants can extract very favorable lease terms from property owners. Whether excess supply results from more new construction than can be absorbed or a major fall-off in demand for space, it can be trouble for property owners. Rising interest rates likewise can create significant difficulties for those who own property. When interest rates skyrocket upwards, REITs' cost of borrowed funds can increase (thus reducing growth in FFO and net income), while the economy also can weaken (thus reducing demand for rental space). Furthermore, rising interest rates can have a negative effect on REITs' share prices.

Whatever the cause, instances of excess supply and rising interest rates are the most prominent threats to REITs' investment performance. While they aren't the only problems that can vex the REIT industry, they are easily the two most critical; let's talk about them in more detail.

Excess Supply and Overbuilding: The Bane of Real Estate Markets

We talked a bit in Chapter Three about cycles, and how the investment returns on real estate can change as we progress through the various phases of a typical real estate cycle. We also saw, and discussed briefly, how overbuilding in a property type or geographical area can influence (and exacerbate) the real estate cycle by causing occupancy rates and rents to decline, which in turn may cause property prices to fall; before long, to quote well-known real estate investor Sam Zell, the construction crane becomes an endangered species. Eventually demand catches up with supply, and the market ultimately recovers.

While excess supply often results from a temporary decline in demand for space (*e.g.*, due to a recession), the excess supply brought on by overbuilding can be a much larger and longer-lasting problem. "Overbuilding," simply stated, describes a local, regional or even nation-wide situation in which substantially more commercial or residential real estate is developed and offered for rent or sale than can be readily absorbed by the demand for such space within a reasonable period of time (*e.g.*, six to twelve months). Overbuilding puts pressure on rental and occupancy rates and negatively affects "same-store" operating income. It can cause cap rates in the affected sector or geographical region to increase, thus reducing the values of the REIT's properties. To the extent a REIT owns properties in an area or sector affected by overbuilding, we will often see the REIT's shareholders sell their shares in anticipation of the prospects of declining FFO growth. This can create a capital loss for shareholders who don't care to wait for an eventual improvement in the situation. In extreme cases, the reduced prospects for the REIT may cause lenders to shy away from renewing credit lines and could eliminate the REIT's ability to obtain new debt or equity financing, perhaps forcing a dividend cut.

Not a pretty picture. Of course, the excess supply monster comes in different degrees of ferocity. It can be just a bit impish, leaving discomfort in selected cities in just one property type (*e.g.*, apartments in Arizona and some cities in the Southeast in 1996). At the other extreme, our monster can be absolutely devastating, wreaking havoc for years in many sectors throughout the U.S. — we saw the effects of severe overbuilding in the late 1980s and early 1990s in office buildings, apartments, industrial properties, self-storage facilities and hotels. A mild excess supply condition will work itself out quickly, especially where job growth is favorable or improves, and absorption of space continues at a healthy rate or recovers in a rebounding economy. In these situations, investors may overreact, dumping REIT shares at unduly depressed prices and creating great values for investors with slightly longer time horizons. We must, however, be always on the alert for significant

202

overbuilding, which may cause severe excess supply problems; in such cases a REIT's share price may decline and stay depressed for several years, and the REIT may even have to cut its dividend.

The excess supply that results from a mild local, regional or national recession is apt to be temporary. While demand for commercial space and apartment units will soften, this situation usually rights itself quickly with the economic recovery. Serious excess supply resulting from chronic overbuilding, however, has often been a much more serious problem whose nasty consequences can last for several years. What lures the overbuilding monster? There are several possible culprits. Sometimes overbuilding results from overheated markets. When the operating profits from real estate are very strong, due to rising occupancy and rental rates, and property prices (reflecting these favorable conditions) are rising almost daily, the urge to build is overwhelming. Developers can easily make new projects "pencil out," and if banks, venture capital groups and other lenders and investors are ready, willing and able to supply the necessary capital, lots of new product rapidly comes on-stream. REITs themselves may be a major source of overbuilding, which could surface in the next property cycle. There are many more REITs today than in prior years that have the expertise and access to capital with which to develop new properties, and those that do business in hot markets will normally be able to flex their muscles and put up new buildings, whether they be apartments, offices, hotels or self-storage facilities.

A fertile breeding ground for overbuilding in the past was the Internal Revenue Code. When Congress amended the tax laws by enacting the Economic Recovery Act of 1981 — which accelerated real property depreciation — new projects were justified on the basis of tax savings alone, without regard to the operating performance of the new property. This was a large contributing factor to the overbuilt markets that commenced later in the 1980s. Tax legislation that induces overbuilding does not seem to be a danger today but, as one wag said, "no man's life, liberty or property is safe while Congress is in session." Even today, in view of the fact that REITs pay no taxes on their net income at "the corporate level," it may be said that Congress is "subsidizing" and "encouraging" real estate ownership.

While the large investment banking firms are essential in helping REITs raise the capital they need to grow, these firms can sometimes be a source of trouble. When a particular industry becomes very popular with investors hungry for additional growth, Wall Street is ready, willing and able to feed their voracious appetites. Businesses enjoying such attention are encouraged to expand rapidly, and this might include raising funds from the public for building additional commercial properties necessary to generate further rapid growth in sales and earnings. "Big-box" retailers such

203

as Wal-Mart, Ross and T.J. Maxx have been doing well for a number of years, and investors have thrown lots of money at them in order to encourage continued rapid expansion. Today some observers fear that "big-box" space is rapidly becoming excessive. On a smaller scale, this has been happening with large book stores such as Crown, Borders, BookStar and Barnes & Noble. A year ago we had but one small book store in my hometown of Westlake Village, California; we now have three large ones. Can we support them all?

One of the strange aspects of a period of overbuilding is that we can be in the midst of one, yet the building continues. This occurred in the office sector in the 1980s. By 1984 it was readily apparent to most observers that an overbuilt condition was rapidly in the making, yet the march of new offices continued well into the early 1990s. Although this could be explained by the long lead time necessary to complete an office project once it's started, more likely there's some subtle psychology at work here. Each developer justifies his own project on the basis that "it can't happen here — *my* project will be successful because it's designed better, offers more amenities and will be located in an underbuilt sub-market." Sometimes we have trouble recognizing changed realities, and this phenomenon can easily apply to tomorrow's builders and lenders just as it did in the office sector little more than 10 years ago.

The only sector that appears to be in excess supply today is retail. The problem was well stated by Milton Cooper, CEO of the highly regarded Kimco Realty: "Simply put, the USA is over-stored. Many retailers are increasing their square-footage without any regard for the relationship of space to the increase in population or disposable income." He predicted a significant increase in retailer bankruptcies, which has been borne out. Many of the usual effects of excess supply in this sector have occurred; thus we've seen declining occupancy rates and rising cap rates on many retail properties. Yet rental rates now seem to be stabilizing (and even rising modestly in certain mall and outlet center properties), and vacancies are slowly but surely being filled. However, it remains to be seen whether the problems caused by excess supply in the retail sector will again take a turn for the worse in the near future; much may depend upon the strength of the economy.

The problems in the retail sector notwithstanding, it is much less likely today than in prior years that a particular sector will become ravaged by substantial excess supply or as a result of severe overbuilding. Today the tax laws no longer subsidize development for its own sake; every project must offer the prospects of a sufficiently profitable return in order to obtain financing. Lenders, pension plans and other sources of development capital have been "once bitten, twice shy," and are demanding a very solid likelihood that their "hurdle rates of return" will be met by the new project.

Further, there is much more discipline in the real estate markets today. The savings and loans, a major culprit of the 1980s' overbuilding, are no longer major real estate lenders. The banks, which often funded 100-110% of the cost of a new "spec" development during many years of the last decade, have "gotten religion" and have much more stringent lending standards today, often limiting construction loans to 60-70% of the cost of the project; this requires a significant equity contribution from the developer. They are also looking at prospective cash flows much more carefully, relying less on appraisals. Banks and other lenders very often require a prescribed minimum level of pre-leasing before funding a construction loan. All of these requirements make it much less likely that ill-conceived projects will be started, or that the developer completes a deal merely to snag his development fee.

REITs may eventually become the dominant developers within particular sectors or geographical areas; this may already be happening in Texas and the Southeast, where several apartment REITs have been very active developers. Should this trend continue, the amount of new building that can be added to a particular sector or market may be limited by investors' refusal to provide additional equity capital to the REITs for use for such purposes. Furthermore, in view of the fact that management normally owns a significant amount of a REIT's shares and would thus be highly motivated to cause the REIT to do well, one would think that the REIT executives would avoid developing new properties when supply exceeds demand in its markets.[1]

Another reason not to fear major overbuilding over the next few years is that much more information is available today concerning the strength of markets, rental rates, occupancies and the sources of new demand for available space. Such data is readily available through consultants and others and may have the effect of closing down the development pipeline sooner than in the past. The number of permits issued for new apartment buildings has dropped precipitously in 1996 in the Phoenix and Tucson areas and in other parts of the U.S., quite likely in response to the rapid dissemination of apartment supply/demand data. It may very well be the case that the new market disciplines discussed above will be instrumental in moderating the number of new apartment units likely to be built in certain geographical areas in 1997-1998.

In the office sector, new development is starting to occur in response to gradually strengthening markets across the U.S. At the present time, however, the pace of new construction is quite subdued. Although new office buildings were reportedly under construction as early as 1995 in 27 of 42 markets reviewed in a 1996 Cushman & Wakefield survey, only 8.5 million square feet of new buildings were being developed, in comparison with more than 100 million square feet completed annually in the 1980s.[2] While the pace of new construction will undoubtedly pick up, advocates of the "milder cycles" theory may point out that lenders to office developers today loan no more than 60-70% on a new project and frequently require that at least 50% of the new space be pre-leased; they may further argue that, due to the monumental losses resulting from overbuilding in the '80s, these standards are unlikely to be significantly relaxed for a very long time.

Are these arguments valid? Barring a major and long-lasting recession, it seems unlikely that a *significant* condition of excess supply will occur in any sector in the near future; nevertheless, investors have lost lots of money betting that "this time it's different." As financial history has shown time and again, manias always seem to pop up like dandelions wherever we least expect them, whether they be for tulip bulbs in an earlier century, "one-decision" stocks in the early 1970s or California real estate in the late 1980s. Greed is a naturally occurring human trait, and we'd be foolish to assume that it's been abolished permanently. We should expect that otherwise intelligent lenders and investors will occasionally get carried away by the desire to make lots of bucks in a short time, and can thus expect to see excess supply in various property sectors at various times in the future, whether from excessive zeal on the part of the developers, investors or lenders or a major economic contraction. We just don't know how much. While this doesn't appear to be a major risk at the present time, we REIT investors need to always be well aware of the possibility.

Whither Interest Rates?

When investors talk about a particular stock or group of stocks as being "interest-rate sensitive," they usually mean that the stock's price performance is heavily influenced by interest-rate movements. For example, the shares of most electric utilities tend to rise when interest rates are falling, and vice-versa. There are many reasons why this occurs, almost all of which have to do with either the attraction of the stock for the investor or the impact of interest rates upon a company's business or profitability (or both).

Let's take that electric utility stock as an example. Utility stocks are most often bought for income and safety, with capital appreciation of lesser importance to the investor. Power companies are heavily regulated and grow very slowly; most of the investor's total return comes from the dividend that the utility pays. Accordingly, utility stocks compete, to a large extent, with bonds for the attentions of income-oriented investors. When interest rates rise, bond prices fall — resulting in a higher yield for new bond investors. Utility stocks will thus be similarly affected by rising interest rates. Their yields must rise in order to compete with the higher yields on bonds in a rising interest-rate environment, which will result in a price decline. Accordingly, rising interest rates result

206

in lower utility stock prices, independently of how the higher interest rates affect the utilities' profitability.

In fact, rising rates have historically put pressure on utilities' earnings, as most of them borrow very significantly in order to fund construction of new facilities. While a utility will usually be able to pass the cost of higher borrowing costs onto its consumers, this is not always the case. Regulators have been known to favor consumers at the expense of the utility and its shareholders and may, through various means, prevent the utility from recovering all of its higher borrowing costs. And even when they can, there is often a time delay. Furthermore, to the extent that utilities may eventually have to compete for business with other suppliers of gas and electricity, higher tariffs (reflecting the higher interest rates) may cause a drop in sales. Thus, for utilities, higher interest rates may adversely affect reported profits, which may also cause their stock prices to decline.

There are other market sectors that have generally been regarded as "interest-rate sensitive." These include banks, savings and loans, finance companies, insurance companies and even brokerage firms. It's beyond the scope of this book to review why such should be the case for these companies; the reasons are not as obvious as they are with the utility stocks and may vary with each such industry. Suffice it to say that investors perceive that rising interest rates will negatively affect the companies in these industries in one way or another and, as a result, investors expect the stocks of "interest-rate sensitive" companies to decline to a greater extent than most publicly traded shares during periods of rising interest rates.

How, then, are REIT shares perceived by investors? Are they "interest-rate sensitive" stocks? Is a significant risk in owning REITs that their shares will take a major tumble during periods when rates are rising briskly? Before we try to answer these questions, let's take a quick look at why REIT shares are bought and owned by investors, and how rising interest rates affect the REITs' expected profitability.

Traditionally, REIT shares have been bought by investors who are looking for large total returns, which includes a hefty dividend yield as well as potential price appreciation. Yields have traditionally made up about half of REITs' total returns; for example, a 7% yield and 7% annual price appreciation (resulting from 7% annual profit growth — assuming that the price/FFO ratio remains constant) results in a 14% total annual return. Because the dividend component of the expected return is so substantial, REITs must, to some extent, compete with bonds as well as other high-yielding stocks to attract investors. Thus when interest rates rise, bonds will fall in price to reflect the new yield requirements of the bond buyers; the more attractive bond yield can often mean that

REIT stock prices also will fall, which will increase their current yield to new buyers.

For example, let's assume that in January "long bonds" (with maturities of up to 30 years) yield 6.5% and the average REIT yields 7%. If the long bond drops in price in response to rising interest rates, causing it to yield 7%, the average REIT's price may also drop, causing its yield to rise to 7.5%. This kind of "price action" would preserve the relative yield differentials then in effect between bonds and REITs. In the real world, REIT prices do not always correlate well with bond prices (as we'll see below). However, the reality remains that REITs *do* compete with bonds and other high-yielding securities to attract yield-hungry investors, and most REIT buyers and owners assume that REIT prices will fall in response to higher interest rates (and vice-versa). The extent to which this occurs is more tenuous, but REIT investors should assume that REIT prices, like the prices for *all* common stocks, will weaken in response to higher rates; if this doesn't happen, so much the better.

A second related and very important question is whether a rise in interest rates causes significant problems for REITs by causing FFO to decline, weakening their balance sheets, diminishing their asset values or otherwise affecting their merit as an investment. It's difficult to generalize about this point, as much depends upon the individual REIT and the sector in which it owns properties and carries on its business, but let's take a look.

Higher interest rates are generally not good for any business, as they soak up purchasing power from the consumer and, if high enough, can cause recession. Thus retail and apartment REITs, which cater to individual consumers, may be hurt more than other sectors if rising rates slow the economy and reduce available consumer buying power. However, even REITs that lease properties to businesses, such as office and industrial property REITs, will be negatively affected to some extent, as businesses will also be affected by higher interest rates and a slowing economy. In general, property sectors which use longer-term leases (such as offices and industrial properties) will be hurt less by temporary recessions, as their lease payments will tend to be more stable.

REITs that carry variable-rate debt on their balance sheets will incur additional interest expense, and interest is usually a significant cost for a REIT as most REITs (as well as other property owners) normally use debt leverage to increase their investment returns. Thus if the debt is substantial and much of it is variable-rate in nature, FFO could be significantly affected by higher interest costs. In addition, REITs frequently must roll over a portion of their debt and, if interest rates are higher at maturity, the refinanced debt will carry a higher price tag. Furthermore, higher interest rates may reduce the amount of credit that can be obtained, due to prevailing lending standards. And new borrowings (to purchase additional properties) will cost the REIT more in interest expense.

Even when it comes to equity capital (as opposed to debt financing), higher interest rates can negatively affect REITs. REITs frequently come to the equity market and sell shares to raise funds for additional acquisitions or developments, and rising interest rates will often depress share prices generally and cause a REIT's nominal cost of equity capital to be higher than it would be if interest rates were low and share prices high.

Another negative relates to a REIT's asset values. Although cap rates are influenced by many factors, it's almost intuitive that a major increase in interest rates will exert upward pressure on cap rates. All things being equal, property buyers will generally insist on higher real estate returns when interest rates have moved up. Correspondingly, property values will tend to decline, which affects the asset values of the property owned by REITs. Although a large number of REIT buyers focus on FFO and other factors rather than the asset value of a particular REIT (based on the fact that REITs rarely sell their properties, that most REITs today are operating businesses and that operating results rather than asset values are more important to today's REIT investors), asset values are nevertheless very important in determining a REIT's intrinsic value. Any decline in such value could very well affect the share price of a REIT.

The foregoing discussion shows how rising interest rates can negatively affect a REIT's operating results, balance sheet, asset value and stock price. However, we might also note that in one important respect REITs may actually be *helped* by rising interest rates. This relates to the overbuilding threat. New competing projects, whether apartments, office buildings, outlet centers or any other type of property, must be financed. Clearly, higher interest rates will increase borrowing costs and cause the new project to become more expensive to develop, and may even make it *too* expensive. Higher rates may also affect the "hurdle rate" demanded by the developer's financial partners, causing many projects to be shelved or canceled. Obviously, the fewer new projects that get completed, the less existing properties will feel competitive pressure. Threats of overbuilding can rapidly fade when interest rates are rising briskly (although if the higher rates bring on a recession, an excess supply condition can arise due to a major fall-off in demand for space).[3]

We should keep in mind, of course, that we are talking in generalities here, and the extent to which rising interest rates will affect a particular REIT's business, profitability, asset values and financial condition must be analyzed individually. On balance, however, rising interest rates are generally not favorable for most REITs. Combined with the tendency of the shares of *all* companies (including REITs) to decline in response to rising interest rates, REIT investors need to be very much aware of the interest-rate environment.

For these reasons, it is generally assumed by most investors that REIT share prices are highly sensitive to interest rates, rising when they decline and declining when they rise. Observers have often compared REIT prices and yields to the 10-year Treasury note, and graphs of this type show a striking correlation between them. For example, an August 1995 research report from Goldman Sachs[4] shows a strong correlation between the 10-year T-note yield and the annualized NAREIT Equity REIT dividend yield, particularly since July 1986. The following graph extends the Goldman Sachs data through November 1996.

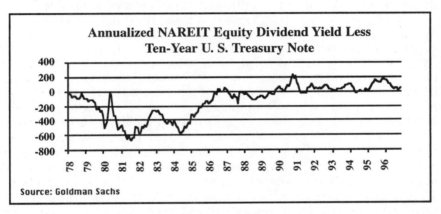

Source: Goldman Sachs

A similar study done by PaineWebber[5] shows a similar high correlation between long-term Treasury bond yields and REITs' dividend yields between 1982 and the end of 1995. These studies make a persuasive argument that rising interest rates correlate rather well with declining REIT stock prices. If yields have to go up to compete with higher Treasury yields, the most direct way for this to occur is for REIT prices to decline.

Nevertheless, REIT stocks may be no more interest-rate sensitive than are other commons stocks. A study done in 1995 by Lehman Brothers focused on the question of *proportional* changes in interest rates and corresponding changes in the prices of REIT shares and the S&P 500 index. [6] This firm's study concluded that "during all time periods analyzed, NAREIT total return sensitivity to interest rates is about the same as the S&P 500" and that "REIT prices are highly sensitive to interest rate changes, however, no more so than is the case with the broader stock market." If Lehman Brothers' conclusion is correct, we REIT investors should be wary of rising interest rates, but no more so than other common stock investors — many bull markets have been choked to death by rising interest rates.[7]

Hostile Capital-Raising Environments

As we've discussed earlier, REITs must pay dividends each year to their shareholders equal to at least 95% of taxable income and, as a practical matter, they almost always pay out more than that (based upon higher FFOs and AFFOs). Thus they cannot retain very much of their annual cash flows with which to grow their businesses. Therefore, REITs are much more dependent than other businesses upon their ability to access the capital markets. Without the ability to raise new capital, REITs will not be able to acquire or develop additional properties, and FFO growth will be highly dependent on improved results from *existing* properties.

As a result of this inherent limitation, investors must be mindful that even the highest-quality REIT may not always have access to additional equity capital. Johnny-come-latelys to the stock market, as well as recently-minted MBAs handling their first portfolios for institutions, may not be aware that there *is* such a thing as a bear market — that fierce creature with the strong sharp claws does make his presence known every now and then. More particularly, the REIT world has been subject to this critter's wrath, most recently in 1990. While no one can predict when the next major downer will occur, for the broad market or for REIT stocks only, it will clearly happen again. During these horrible periods, many (if not most) REITs will find it extremely difficult to find buyers for any new shares they'd like to sell in order to raise funds for new investments. This, in turn, will retard FFO growth until such time as the markets return to "normalcy."

We REIT investors should also be aware that the access-to-capital door may be slammed in our favorite REIT's face even in the absence of a general market, or REIT market, decline. This could occur in any sector of the REIT market where investors perceive that the overbuilding monster is about to rear its ugly head; this happened to a significant number of apartment REITs in mid-1995, which would have liked to raise new equity capital by selling additional shares but found no takers. It could also occur for individual REITs whose growth prospects are deemed lackluster by REIT investors generally, or where other concerns (such as excessive debt, conflicts of interests or other such issues) are significant enough to scare away potential investors.

Attracting new capital is the life-blood of healthy, growing REIT organizations. External and even internal events over which managements may have little or no control may cut off a REIT from this essential new capital and, at least for a period of time, cause FFO growth to be much slower than what investors had been expecting. This, in turn, will often cause significant erosion in a

211

REIT's stock price. This is one reason why investors are willing to pay a premium price for those REITs whose perceived quality and growth prospects are such that they will almost always be able to attract additional equity capital, even in bear markets.

Legislation

If the cynic's view that "no man's life, liberty or property is safe when Congress is in session" is correct, we must recognize that what Congress giveth, Congress may also taketh away. Is there any risk that the favorable tax attributes of REITs may be rescinded by legislators greedy for additional tax revenues? Are there any other legislative dangers that REIT investors ought to worry about?

It is highly unlikely that Congress would enact legislation that would rescind REITs' tax deduction for the dividends paid to their shareholders, thus subjecting REITs' net income to taxation at the corporate level. There are several public policy reasons for this. First, due to REITs' high dividend payments and lower debt leverage, they probably generate as much income for the Federal government as they would if they were conventional real estate corporations (it's just that the taxes are paid by the individual shareholders rather than the corporate owner). Second, REITs most likely provide more tax revenues than if they held real property in partnership form (which is a typical format for the ownership of real estate). Finally, REITs have shown that real estate ownership and management can be quite profitable without using excessive debt leverage (which might become more popular in the absence of the REIT format); encouraging greater financing with debt could have the effect of substantially exacerbating the swings in the normal business and real estate cycles and thus harm the economy over the long term.

Another risk, with perhaps a slightly higher chance of occurring, is that UPREITs and DownREITs may, at some time in the future, be precluded from acquiring real estate through an exchange of their operating partnership units in transactions which defer the recognition of capital gain taxes. This could negatively affect those REITs which are highly active in this method of financing property acquisitions.

I'm not aware that anyone, inside or outside of the halls of Congress, has ever even suggested that REITs should be taxable in the same manner as regular corporations. Congress has deemed it advisable to encourage real estate ownership through the REIT vehicle and, in fact, NAREIT has done a very commendable job in persuading Congress over the years to liberalize the REIT laws in a manner that has expanded the scope of REITs' authorized business activities. Nevertheless, I would be remiss in writing a book of this type if I didn't remind readers that legislation adverse to REITs is always a possibility, and cannot be dismissed out of hand.

Potential Problems Affecting Individual REITs

Thus far in this chapter we've been discussing potential adverse developments that can plague REITs generally. But REITs — like virtually any other investment — can be victimized on an individual basis; one REIT can become mighty sick without contaminating its brothers or sisters.

As a preliminary note, we REIT investors will find it very helpful to be able to distinguish between a widespread epidemic and a very localized, albeit serious, illness. In early 1995, two of the newly created factory outlet center REITs, McArthur/Glen and Factory Stores of America, got themselves into a heap of trouble, the former by being unable to deliver the large number of additional developments it promised Wall Street and the latter by expanding too aggressively and taking on too much debt in the process. The market, which is often prone to shoot first and ask questions later, assumed that the illness was sector-wide, and destroyed the stock prices of such steady performers as Chelsea/GCA and Tanger Factory Outlet Centers as well as the problem-plagued outlet REITs. However, by the end of 1995, Chelsea/GCA's stock was back near its all-time high, and Tanger stock was in the process of recovering as well. Investors who dumped their Chelsea/GCA stock in the low $20s because of their inability to distinguish between a major sector problem and problems with individual REITs have swallowed a bitter pill and, hopefully, have learned a valuable lesson.

Recessions

We've discussed earlier how a recession can lead to declining demand for leased space, resulting in markets with excess supply even when little new construction has been completed. However, recession can also hurt specific real estate owners (including, of course, REITs) even when property supply and demand are in equilibrium. Tenant sales may suffer, resulting in lower "overage rentals" (additional rents paid on a lease, based on sales exceeding a pre-set minimum) for owners of retail properties, and even declining occupancies. Apartment units, especially those being developed, may be slow to lease, perhaps as a result of declining job growth. Generally speaking, during recessionary conditions, both consumers and businesses will cut back on their spending patterns, and it will be difficult to raise rents and keep occupancy rates high. As discussed earlier, focus on a specific geographical area is usually a favorable attribute of a REIT. However, the flip side is that local or regional recessions can have significant adverse consequences for such a geographically focused REIT.

We've learned over the last decade or two that economic conditions in the U.S. aren't always the same in every geographic area. We can have an oil industry depression in the Southwest, while the rest of the country is doing fine; the Northeast can be in the dumper, while residents of other states are doing well; and, more recently, the economic rebound that started in 1992 seemed to have bypassed California until recently. Many REITs own real estate concentrated in one specific area of the country, particularly apartment REITs. Accordingly, investors must be watchful for deteriorating local economic conditions in the areas in which their REITs' properties are located. Such conditions will often result in much slower FFO growth and REIT stock price declines as nervous REIT investors bail out of their holdings.

We might note here, however, that due to the continuous need for health care services and reimbursement of delivery costs by Federal and state governments, health care REITs have been largely immune from recessionary conditions, and this favorable circumstance isn't likely to change in the near future. Recent forays into assisted-living facilities by many health care REITs, however, could make their businesses more economically sensitive due to the fact that government reimbursement for health care expenses is much less prevalent for this newer type of facility.

Changing Consumer and Business Preferences

Like recessions, changing consumer and business preferences can reduce renters' demands for a property type, causing supply of space to substantially exceed demand, or, by reducing the profitability of the tenants, make the business of the property owner less profitable — or both.

Beginning with the first point, today self-storage facilities are quite popular with many consumers in an increasingly mobile population; will they always be so? Will a large segment of the U.S. population continue to either prefer or require apartments, or will single-family home ownership attract a higher percentage of the population in the first decade of the 21st century? Will manufactured home communities continue to enjoy the success they've had in recent years? Will businesses continue to need the types of industrial properties they've been happily using, or will some new form of doing business render many of these facilities obsolete? Will companies continue to absorb space in large office buildings as they have in the past? These are questions no one may be able to answer with assurance, but which REIT investors will ignore at their peril.

With respect to the second aspect of this topic, some businesses may desire to rent less space in certain types of properties in the future as a result of changing societal preferences. If we own these types of properties, we must be aware of these changes. The most obvious example is seen in consumers' reluctance today to spend as much time in large shopping malls as they did in the '80s; mall sales have been flat for several years, as we discussed in an earlier chapter, and this is making it difficult to

214

obtain the types of rental increases from tenant-retailers as could be had earlier. Will "big-box" retailers continue to make life hard on the occupants of neighborhood shopping centers? Will outlet centers prove more appealing to consumers than either malls or traditional discounters or, conversely, are they just a temporary phenomenon? In a different but related area, will changes in the health care delivery system in the United States cause health care providers to become less interested in leasing the types of health care facilities they do today?

These are difficult questions to answer, but their importance to REIT owners is very clear: If we guess wrong, we may be owners of a REIT whose asset values and future growth rates may be significantly diminished.

Credibility Issues

Probably the most common type of REIT-specific problem that can cause headaches for a REIT investor is the ordinary, garden-variety mistake in judgment or execution that can lead to significant management credibility issues. The types of actions that can cause problems of this type are widely varied. They include paying too much for a portfolio of properties and later having to write them down (*e.g.*, American Health Properties); expanding too quickly and taking on too much debt in the process (*e.g.*, Factory Stores of America); underestimating the difficulty of assimilating a major portfolio acquisition (*e.g.*, Manufactured Home Communities); and providing investors with "bad" information, such as by underestimating the expenses of operating a public company (*e.g.*, Holly Residential Properties), overpromising the number of new development properties that will be completed in the next 12 months (*e.g.*, McArthur/Glen) or overestimating future FFO growth prospects (*e.g.*, Crown American Realty).

Other types of mistakes can include expanding into new areas without adequate management in place, buying properties that ultimately provide less-than-expected operating income, raising more funds than can be invested within a reasonably short period (thus causing FFO dilution as the funds are "parked" in short-term, low-interest-bearing securities) and increasing the dividend faster than growth in FFO (thus raising concerns about the adequacy of dividend coverage).

Another type of problem investors sometimes encounter really has nothing at all to do with mistakes of judgment or execution, but stems from material conflicts of interest between management and the shareholders. REITs that are not internally managed (*i.e.*, those that have entered into management agreements with outside advisors) are always subject to such conflicts, but those that are fully managed internally can also sometimes greatly disappoint investors as well. Perhaps some of the most serious of such

215

problems have to do with the REIT buying one or more properties from an executive officer (fortunately, this does not occur anywhere near as often as it used to), allowing an executive officer to compete with the REIT with respect to the purchase of available properties, and allowing high-profile CEOs to spend much of their time on other ventures and business interests. On the other hand, excessive compensation given to executives despite mediocre operating results, while annoying to shareholders, is not usually as damaging as the other types of conflicts mentioned.

Many investors are wary of the "UPREIT" format, which poses knotty conflict-of-interest issues. UPREITs, as you may recall from Chapter Two, are REITs whose assets are held by a limited partnership in which the REIT owns a controlling interest and in which REIT "insiders" may own a substantial interest. Thus these insiders may own few shares in the REIT itself, and their usually low tax basis in their partnership interests create a conflict of interest should it be desirable to sell a property or in the event a purchase offer is made for the entire REIT. This conflict surfaced in 1996 when an offer was made to acquire Chateau Properties, an UPREIT; the existence of this type of conflict and the uncertainties of how it will be resolved can create credibility issues for a REIT's management.

Most of these types of problems can be remedied by a REIT's management if it is forthright with investors, quickly recognizes any mistakes made and promptly takes action to rectify the situation. In 1996 Highwoods Properties (HIW) agreed to acquire the assets of Crocker Realty, and advised investors that the acquisition would be very accretive to FFO. However, it did not sufficiently highlight the fact that most of that accretion would result from the substantial additional debt HIW would be taking on in order to pay for Crocker. Investor concern over the prospects of a highly leveraged balance sheet helped to depress HIW's shares shortly after the deal was announced. Management reacted promptly, however, and announced a major equity financing so that most of the debt could be repaid. With that financing completed, investor confidence was soon restored and eventually HIW's stock hit new all-time highs. The key issue resulting from most of these problems is management's loss of credibility with investors. Investors will assume that management is significantly flawed and will continue to make mistakes. Unless prompt action is taken, it can be very hard to regain investors' confidence; in extreme cases, the only alternatives for such a REIT are to become acquired (*e.g.*, Holly Residential and McArthur/Glen) or to obtain new management (*e.g.*, American Health Properties).

There is obviously no way for REIT investors to avoid all such problems. The most conservative strategy is to invest only in those "blue chip" REITs that have posted strong track records over many

216

years, where management's reputation is of the highest order. Of course, we will often be paying substantial premiums, in terms of pricing, in order to own these companies, and will miss out on those REITs which have gotten into trouble but which are primed for a rebound. Another strategy is to avoid those REITs which have not been public companies for several years, as large numbers of these management credibility issues seem to have arisen in REITs which were "unseasoned." However, using this approach will cause us to miss out on some very promising newcomers. There is no "right" strategy; it all depends upon how much risk the investor is comfortable with and how much research he or she is willing to do.

Balance Sheet Woes

Another major problem that can trouble a REIT investor may arise if management over-burdens the REIT's balance sheet with excessive debt. Investors must be particularly careful here, as high debt levels often go hand in hand with impressive FFO growth and high dividend yields; such attributes, which can lure investors, are often "purchased" or "subsidized" by excessive debt on a REIT's balance sheet. Too much debt, particularly if it bears a short-term maturity, can virtually destroy a REIT. We've discussed earlier, in Chapter Seven, the importance of a strong balance sheet in determining which REITs merit "blue-chip" status. Unfortunately, those REITs that have allowed their balance sheets to deteriorate will not only fall into disfavor with investors, but may, if their property markets deteriorate, have to be sold or, at worst, dismembered.

A weak balance sheet subjects a REIT to all sorts of unforeseen events, and none of them are pleasant. Such weakness could stem from very high debt levels in relation to the REIT's market capitalization or net asset value, a low coverage of interest expense from property cash flows, a large portion of the debt maturing within just a year or two, or much of the debt being exposed to fluctuations in short-term interest rates. The consequences of such sins, most of which we've reviewed earlier, include the following: The inability to obtain new debt or equity financing in order to expand and grow FFO; the magnifying effects that excessive debt leverage can have in the event of declining net operating income; the danger that lenders will refuse to "roll over" existing debt at maturity; the increased risk that covenants in credit agreements will not be complied with; and exposure to significantly higher operating costs, and reduced FFO, should interest rates rise substantially.

These kinds of potential problems are often discounted by investors well before they are actually experienced by the REIT. Thus a REIT that is perceived to be over-leveraged or have other balance sheet problems that could spin out of control will see its shares trade at a low price/FFO ratio in relation to its peers and to other REITs generally. The steady decline in the stock price of Factory Stores of America (since re-named FAC Realty Trust) is a good case in point. The debt on FAC's balance sheet was well over 50% of its total market capitalization during much of 1995, and investors worried that it had simply over-expanded during the prior two years. This REIT's share price fell from $21.625 at the end of 1994 to $13.125 at the end of 1995 (and was trading at under $7 at the end of 1996), thus anticipating significant problems ahead. (FAC announced early in 1996 that FFO had declined significantly in 1995, and cut its dividend.)

Other REITs whose share prices may have been depressed during 1995 and 1996 in substantial part because of a relatively weak balance sheet include Burnham Pacific Properties, Town & Country, Crown American Realty, Kranzco Realty, Tucker Properties and Horizon Group (Tucker was acquired by Bradley Real Estate in 1996, but at no premium to its market price.) Of course, there are often many reasons why investors are negative on a particular REIT, as evidenced by a low price/FFO ratio; most of the REITs mentioned above have given investors concern in more than one area. Nevertheless, balance sheet issues have played a substantial part in putting these REITs in the investor's dog-house.

Small Market Valuations

REIT investors need to be aware that, despite REITs' 35-year history, very few REITs are large companies in relationship to major U.S. corporations. Let's take Hewlett-Packard, for example. As of the end of its 1996 fiscal year, H-P had more than 1 billion shares outstanding; at its market price of $50.25 per share at the end of 1996, H-P's total outstanding shares had a market value of $50.2 billion. Getting a bit smaller, General Motors, as of the end of 1996, had shares outstanding worth approximately $42 billion. Getting away from the real giants, Genuine Parts, a supplier of automotive parts and accessories (but clearly not a household name), had common stock outstanding, in December 1996, with a market value of $5.5 billion.

Compare these market caps to those inhabiting the REIT world. Simon DeBartolo Group, whose common shares had the largest market value in the REIT world in late 1996, could muster an equity market cap of only $4.8 billion (as of December 19, 1996). As 1996 drew to a close, only a handful of REITs could boast of equity market caps in the $1 billion to $2 billion range and the average REIT equity market cap was just slightly above $500 million. The following are average "implied" equity market caps (outstanding common shares and operating partnership units convertible into common shares, multiplied by the market price) for the REITs covered by Green Street Advisors as of September 1996 (Green Street emphasizes those REITs with the largest market caps).[8]

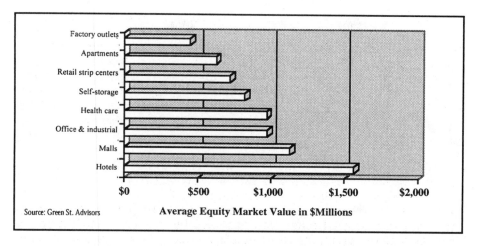

Source: Green St. Advisors **Average Equity Market Value in $Millions**

This data provides us with a pretty clear picture. While the "typical" REIT is by no means a tiny company, it is hardly a major U.S. corporation. As Kimco's Milton Cooper noted in March 1995, "The present market cap of all REITs (approximately $40 billion at the time he made the statement) is less than the market cap of either Wal-Mart or Microsoft."[9]

The market cap of the entire REIT industry, as well as many of the individual REITs within it, has been growing rapidly during the last few years, as we'll discuss in more detail in the next chapter. Nevertheless, the still relatively small market caps of most REITs present potential problems (as well as opportunities). The opportunities relate to the fact that many REITs are too small to fall within the radar screens of major investment firms, particularly those catering to institutions, and may be inefficiently priced. This, of course, may create significant investment bargains for the investor willing to do his or her own research. Further, a small amount of growth, on an absolute basis, can have a very substantial impact upon a small REIT's percentage FFO growth. Chelsea/GCA doesn't have to add too many additional outlet centers each year in order to post significant percentage gains in FFO.

On the other hand, the potential problems that can result from small size are several: a REIT with a small market cap may not be able to obtain the public awareness and sponsorship necessary to enable it to raise the equity capital necessary for its growth. Further, to the extent that pension and institutional ownership of REITs could be a new trend fostering the growth of the entire REIT industry or an individual REIT, a small market cap is likely to discourage such entities from investing in such a REIT due to its lack of market liquidity. Finally, a minor misjudgment on the part of

219

management of a small REIT (see "Credibility Issues" above) could have a major impact upon the REIT's future business prospects, FFO growth and reputation with investors.

Depth of Management and Management Succession Issues

Perhaps a more serious potential problem related to the relatively small size of many REITs is the issue of management depth and succession. Smaller companies (whether REITs or other businesses), due to their limited financial resources, are often unable to develop the type of extensive organization found in a major corporation such as General Electric. We must ask ourselves whether the REIT will be at a competitive disadvantage if, for example, it cannot afford to hire a staff of employees of the highest caliber or to obtain the very best market information available concerning supply and demand for properties in its targeted market area. Other questions might relate to the depth and experience of the REIT's property acquisition or property management department, or perhaps the sophistication and strength of the REIT's financial reporting, budgeting and forecasting systems. These are issues that must be addressed separately for each REIT, but small size can limit any company's ability to attract high-quality resources, including capable middle management.

Assuming that we investors are comfortable with a REIT's management capabilities notwithstanding its modest size, it's nevertheless often the case that we must rely upon a few very outstanding individuals to manage the REIT for the best long-term results with the least risk. Let's face it: while we sometimes see "superstar management" in the large corporations (e.g., Warren Buffett at Berkshire Hathaway, Michael Eisner at Disney, Jack Welch at General Electric or Roberto Goizueta at Coca-Cola), investors often see a higher percentage of such high-profile management in smaller companies such as REITs. Knowledgeable investors are attracted to such REITs as Crescent Real Estate Equities, Kimco Realty, Manufactured Home Communities, Simon DeBartolo Group and Vornado Realty Trust, to name a few, because they are managed by such well-known real estate investors and managers as Richard Rainwater, Milton Cooper, Sam Zell, the Simons and Steven Roth, respectively.[10]

The problem for REIT investors, therefore, is to determine whether such individuals have been able to develop highly capable managerial talent that can take over in the event of retirement (or a sudden unexpected event such as death or disability). A related problem is determining the extent to which such a REIT's stock price reflects the "star" status of top management. For example, if Richard Rainwater were to decide next week that he was tired of managing Crescent (or, God forbid, something should prevent him from actively managing that REIT), what would happen to Crescent's share price? In other words, is the price of a REIT's stock based so much upon the ability and reputation of just one individual that a sudden departure of such person will cause the price to collapse by 20-25%? A REIT's stock price would be less likely to tumble if senior management has done a good job bringing along talented younger management, and has convinced investors that such is the case.

One recent, though unfortunate, example might prove instructive. Mr. Larry Miller was Chief Executive Officer of Bradley Real Estate, a well-regarded shopping center REIT, for approximately 10 years when he was struck down by a heart attack in his mid-50s. Mr. Miller was an extremely capable CEO who was well-respected by both REIT investors and his peers. Nevertheless, apparently due to his foresight in developing additional high-quality managerial talent, Bradley's stock price moved very little immediately following his untimely death.

Management succession is a sensitive issue that is, for obvious reasons, difficult for both investors and REIT managements to discuss, but is of vital concern to investors. Genius is tough to replace in any organization, no matter how large, but it's even tougher to replace in small- to medium-sized companies such as most REITs.

Perspective

The lesson to be learned here is twofold. On the one hand, true disasters in the REIT world have been few and far between; yes, there have been plenty of errors and misjudgments by managements, but REIT bankruptcies have been rare over the last 35 years, and there have been very few major share price collapses. Even such troubled REITs as American Health Properties, Burnham Pacific Properties, Holly Residential, Dial REIT (since re-named MidAmerica Realty), McArthur/Glen and Tucker Properties have either turned themselves around, obtained new management or been sold on a basis that retained some significant value for their shareholders. In the absence of a major abuse of management's fiduciary duties to its shareholders (for example, fraud or egregious instances of self-dealing) or an extremely leveraged balance sheet, most mistakes by REIT management can inflict only limited damage.

On the other hand, we do need to understand the risks involved in REIT investing. Despite the fact that REITs have done very well for their investors during their 35 years of existence, many REIT managements have made plenty of mistakes that have cost their shareholders dearly. Bearing these costs can be particularly tragic for REIT investors, who usually seek safety of principal and high (and gradually increasing) income. Dividend cuts come particularly hard to REIT investors.

So, while I have always been upbeat and confident about REIT investing (and, in fact, my own REIT investment experience over the past 20+ years has justified this attitude), it's a fact that problems will inevitably arise from time to time, usually when and where least expected. REITs are companies run by mortals who engage in business in an economy that refuses to remain stationary; REITs are no different from other companies in this regard. Accordingly, we investors must be ever watchful for things that can go wrong; furthermore, because none of us can be assured of spotting all problems ahead of time, ascertaining their importance and adjusting our portfolios appropriately, we must be well-diversified in our REIT investments so that one major unexpected problem can't ruin our entire financial plan.

---

[1] According to Glenn Mueller, national director of real estate research at Price Waterhouse, "When REITs develop a property, they need to have it occupied right away. Otherwise their cash flow is affected negatively, which will hurt their stock price. A REIT cannot afford to develop a spec building and let it sit vacant." See "More Capital Fuels Competition, Pumps Up Prices," in Institutional Real Estate Universe, September 1996, p. 1.

[2] Wall Street Journal, February 16, 1996, p. B3, citing a Cushman & Wakefield survey.

[3] Nevertheless, such a result is not assured, as the last great period of overbuilding got started during a period of high interest rates. One would think, however, that in most economic environments developers will be less motivated to construct new properties when interest rates are high, particularly if the high rates are believed likely to significantly slow the growth of the economy or cause a recession.

[4] U.S. Research, Real Estate Stock Monitor, August 1995, p. 17.

[5] PaineWebber REIT Index Monthly Review and Commentary, January 1996, p. 3.

[6] Lehman Brothers, "Interest Rates and REITs: Understanding the Question is Half the Battle," November 6, 1995.

[7] Interestingly enough, although interest rates rose in 1996 (as evidenced by the 30-year Treasury bond, whose yield rose from 5.95% to 6.64% between December 31, 1995 and December 31, 1996), REIT stocks turned in a smashing performance. What does that tell us about the correlation of REITs' stock performance with interest rates? That sometimes they correlate and sometimes they don't?

[8] Green Street Advisors, Inc., Real Estate Stock Index, September 25, 1996.

[9] Kimco Realty Corporation's 1994 Annual Report to Shareholders, p. 3. Mr. Cooper, however, went on to suggest that the market capitalization of the REIT industry could at least quintuple in future years. See the discussion on this point in Chapter Eleven.

[10] In late 1996, Vornado Realty hired well-known real estate executive Mike Fascitelli away from a major investment banking firm. While his compensation package was the talk of the REIT world for a couple of weeks, investors gave Steven Roth a vote of confidence by boosting Vornado's shares substantially in the days immediately following the announcement.

Chapter Eleven

Tea Leaves

"Forecasts may tell you a great deal about the forecaster;
they tell you nothing about the future."
—*Warren Buffett*

Will we continue to draw blank stares from real estate and common stock investors when we mention the word "REIT" at cocktail parties? Or is the REIT industry now poised to emerge from the backwaters of the investment world? Will the continuing securitization of real estate draw billions of investment dollars from institutions and individuals who come to realize that investing in strong real estate organizations with innovative managements can provide outstanding total returns? Here, we'll break out the crystal ball and look at some of the issues that could affect the size and landscape of the REIT industry over the next several years.

Before we get to the fortune-telling, though, let's start by looking at the past and the present. The total equity market cap (defined as the number of shares outstanding multiplied by the market price) of the Equity REITs did not reach $1 billion until 1968, five years after the first REIT was organized. By the end of 1996, almost 30 years later, such equity market cap stood at $78.3 billion, an increase of 57%, or approximately 17% annually. Most of this growth occurred recently; at the end of 1992, the Equity REITs' equity market cap was only $11 billion, but increased to $26 billion and $39 billion at the end of 1993 and 1994, respectively, primarily as a result of the IPO binge in those two years. The growth in 1995 and 1996 came primarily from secondary offerings and price appreciation. There were only 34 publicly traded Equity REITs at the end of 1971. By the end of 1996, 25 years later, there were 166.

Despite this impressive growth, as we discussed briefly in the last chapter the REIT industry remains small in comparison with both the stock market and the total value of commercial real estate in the United States. General Electric, Exxon, Philip Morris, Merck, Intel and Microsoft, at the end of 1996, each had a market cap that was in excess of the equity market cap of the entire REIT industry ($89 billion). Furthermore, it has been estimated that, at the beginning of 1996, REITs owned less than 10% of the $1.22 trillion institutionally owned commercial real estate market,[1] and a much smaller percentage of the total value of all commercial real estate in the U.S. (which has been estimated at between $3 trillion and $4 trillion).

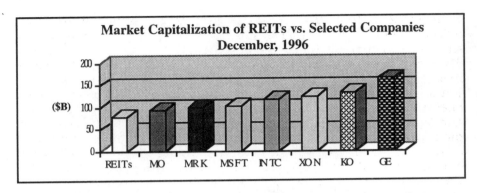

Market Capitalization of REITs vs. Selected Companies December, 1996

($B)

REITs MO MR K MSFT N TC XON KO GE

REITs' property ownership percentage is low, not only on an absolute basis, but also in relationship to that of other countries. NAREIT has estimated that in the U.K., for example, more than 50% of the market value of that country's commercial real estate has been securitized and is publicly traded. Should securitization become as prevalent here as in the U.K., the market cap of the U.S. REIT industry would expand by more than five-fold, to over $500 billion. *Can* this happen? *Will* it happen? In order to hazard a guess, we will need to consider two key questions: (a) will a significant number of additional real estate owners and developers want to become REITs, and (b) will a much greater number of investors want to own them?

Supply Side: Why Property Companies Will Want to REIT-ize

A successful and growing real estate organization could list several reasons why it might be motivated to become a public company in the form of a REIT. In fact, as recent history illustrates, the trend toward going public is becoming more and more prevalent. Perhaps one of the most obvious reasons is that, unlike most corporations, REITs pay no taxes at the corporate level, thus enabling them and their shareholders to avoid double taxation. This is clearly a prime motivating factor for many real estate companies. Furthermore, becoming an UPREIT or a DownREIT (see Chapter Two) gives the real estate organization a significant advantage in the acquisition of properties from sellers who, by accepting "operating partnership" units, can defer capital gains taxation.

Two prime examples of outstanding real estate companies that went public within the past few years include Kimco Realty, which completed its initial public offering in November 1991 after 25 years of highly successful real estate operations as a private company, and Post Properties, another outstanding real estate organization, which

224

went public in July 1993. Reasons given by the principal executive officers of both of these highly successful companies are remarkably similar, and include those discussed below. This is not merely a coincidence; both Kimco and Post exemplify the type of innovative real estate organizations that went public within just the last few years. They both have developed long track records of successful operations in their respective fields (neighborhood shopping centers and apartments, respectively), have managements that have been pioneers in their field in terms of innovation (and which continue to own a significant portion of the outstanding stock of each REIT) and are devoted to strengthening their organizations and motivating their employees in order to attain well above average long-term growth for their shareholders.

Access to Capital

A primary inducement for going public is the much greater access to capital and financing flexibility that an organization enjoys as a publicly traded company. Successful and growing real estate organizations constantly need additional capital with which to build and acquire real estate, to improve and upgrade individual properties and to continue to strengthen the ranks of management. Further, as we discussed earlier, successful REITs must constantly return to the capital markets for the resources necessary to grow at above-average rates. However, as Kimco CEO Milton Cooper reminds us, lenders have been manic-depressive over the years when it comes to lending to owners, developers and operators of real estate; during some periods they are eager to virtually throw money at these enterprises, while at others they are absolute skinflints. It's difficult to finance and manage a growing business under such stop-and-go conditions.

That's not to say that the traditional sources of financing will be discarded when a REIT is formed. Successful REITs normally obtain traditional short-term financing from banks and longer-term financing from other lenders, such as insurance companies, in the same way that they've done earlier as private companies. Joint-venture deals with financial partners can also be obtained, whether the company is public or private. But what provides so much more flexibility and financial resources to a publicly traded REIT is its access to the public markets through the issuance of "equity" (common and convertible preferred stock), non-convertible preferred stock and debentures (both regular and convertible).

The issuance of common stock, while expensive (see Chapter Six), provides the most permanent type of financing, as there is never any obligation to repay it. Furthermore, it allows the REIT to leverage this additional capital by adding debt to it; most lenders insist that the borrower have a substantial cushion of shareholders' equity before becoming eligible for certain types of loans, as well as certain minimum "coverage" of interest payment obligations. Thus selling common stock provides permanent capital and allows the REIT to borrow more. The sale of preferred stock is another avenue normally open only to publicly traded companies. Although preferred stock adds financial leverage to a REIT's balance sheet and investors should therefore treat it as debt in analyzing the REIT's financial strength, such a security is not recorded as "debt" on the company's balance sheet and is not treated as such by lenders. Furthermore, non-convertible preferred stock does not dilute the shareholders' equity interest in the REIT.

Finally, a significant number of REITs (some of the health care REITs being notable examples) have been able to raise capital by the issuance and sale of convertible debentures; these securities are often issued without having to pledge properties as collateral, which allows companies more flexibility to use their properties as collateral for other types of private or public financing. Assuming that the stock price rises and the convertibles are later converted into common stock, the effective sale price of the underlying common shares will be higher than if the REIT merely issued the stock directly and at a lower price at an earlier date.

The broader mix of available financing options is of significant value to a real estate company. It is likely that at various times the public markets will be foreclosed to a REIT due to depressed market conditions or other reasons; private financing may then be readily available. Conversely, at other times private lenders may be exceedingly tight-fisted, while the public markets readily beckon. Thus greatly expanded access to capital will be a key reason why many well-run and growing real estate companies will become REITs in the years ahead.

Ability to Strengthen and Motivate the Organization

Today, more than ever before, owning and operating commercial real estate successfully — whether it be apartments, office buildings, retail properties or any other type — is a *business.* As such, a strong organization is essential to success; competition is fierce everywhere, and only the strong real estate organizations are likely to survive and prosper.

Truly successful organizations are not dependent upon the leadership skills and abilities of any one individual, no matter how capable and dynamic. Successors must be carefully hired and groomed. Furthermore, depth of management is essential to long-term success; highly skilled and motivated individuals will be required at all levels. While there are ways in which private companies, even those that are large in scope, can build strong organizations and motivate employees and management at all levels, it is clearly easier to accomplish these objectives if the company is publicly held. Stock options have long been a widely accepted

226

motivational tool for a company's management, in some cases reaching all the way down to the newest hire. Programs such as stock option plans, stock purchase plans (allowing employees to buy their employer's stock at a discount from market) and other compensation plans based upon company performance are prevalent in almost all publicly held companies today.

Discipline and control is becoming increasingly important to managements in their efforts to stay a step ahead of the competition. Many public companies find that the disciplines imposed upon them, while often costly, strengthen the organization in the long run. These disciplines include having a Board of Directors that consists of several outside directors with whom business plans and projects must be discussed and justified; having to answer to the shareholders with respect to expense control, compensation programs and other shareholder concerns; and implementing strong financial systems and controls.

These factors, by strengthening the organization and its financial disciplines, allow public REITs to become more efficient owners and managers of real estate. As such, they will be able to continue to take tenants and market share from the smaller, less well-capitalized and less disciplined real estate owner.

Liquidity and Estate Planning

Another key factor likely to induce many outstanding real estate companies to go public is the ability of the public markets to provide liquidity for the ownership interests of management and employees. In all businesses, whether they're real estate companies, manufacturers or service providers, management changes from time to time, and individuals who have devoted years to a successful operation may desire to "cash out," whether upon retirement or otherwise. Furthermore, key personnel who own an interest in the business often need to convert some of their capital to cash, whether to provide for retirement needs, buy a new home, fund children's college education or other reasons. Having a readily available public market into which shares can be sold from time to time is invaluable in such situations, as transfers of privately held shares or partnership interests are either costly and time-consuming or are simply not available to private organizations.

Estate planning concerns may also induce successful real estate companies to "REIT-ize." Uncle Sam is quite avaricious when it comes to folks who leave this earth with more than $600,000 in assets; when Uncle Sam is paid his due, assets exceeding that amount can be taxed at rates beyond 50%. This is not to say that becoming a public company will enable a successful real estate entrepreneur to avoid estate taxes (although gifts from time to time may be made much easier). Rather, taking one's company public may enable such a person's successor to avoid having to sell all or a significant part of the business in order to obtain the funds to pay the estate taxes. Shares in such a company can be sold in the public markets to obtain the necessary funds, and the business itself can remain undisturbed.

On the Other Hand: The Virtues of Remaining Private

Admittedly, there are some negatives to becoming a public company, whether a REIT or otherwise. Management will be operating in a "fish bowl," as almost every major decision must be explained to the investors, who will be constantly looking over management's shoulder. Independent directors will need to be consulted on all major projects. There will be significant pressure to "perform," often on a very short-term basis. The costs of running a public company will be large, and include premiums for directors' and officers' insurance, expensive audit fees, costs of maintaining an investors' relations department, transfer agent fees, and legal and other costs to comply with SEC requirements.

Nevertheless, it's quite likely that the benefits of becoming a public company in the form of a REIT will greatly outweigh these negatives for many, if not most, successful real estate organizations who want to have the maximum opportunity for long-term success. There is talk of legendary real estate investor Sam Zell putting his office properties into a new REIT during 1997. Highly respected California real estate investor Donald Bren, who organized Irvine Apartment Communities a few years ago, may form at least one new REIT to own and manage his office, industrial and retail properties. William Sanders' Security Capital Group may soon be taking public its Pacific Retail organization. If these whispers are any indication of what the "best and the brightest" real estate entrepreneurs intend to do over the next several years, the entire REIT industry has a very bright future ahead.

Demand Side: Why More Investors Will Want to Own REITs

It obviously won't matter how many great real estate companies want to become REITs if there is insufficient demand for their shares by investors. Following the end of the IPO boom of 1993-1994, many well-run and experienced real estate organizations were told that investor enthusiasm for REITs had chilled and that the IPO window had slammed shut. Will enough new investment interest in REITs be created in the future in order to allow these successful companies to go public while at the same time provide for the capital needs of existing REITs?

As we've discussed in Chapter Four, investor interest in REITs has been retarded by the "neither fish nor fowl" syndrome (real estate investors believe that REITs are *not* real estate and thus don't trust them, while common stock investors believe they *are* real estate and thus are not much interested in them). Furthermore, many individual investors and financial planners have been burned badly by the real estate limited partnerships of the '80s and by buying real estate with the use of excessive leverage, and assume that REITs aren't much different. Finally, many myths surrounding real estate in general and REITs in particular have been difficult to dispel. Nevertheless, it would be ludicrous for investors, both individual and institutional alike, not to develop a strong affinity for REITs, due to their excellent attributes as long-term investments. Indeed, if the strong demand for REIT shares in 1996 is any indication, this is already happening.

Individual Investors

A perceptive observer once noted that the baby-boomer generation is like a rather large rat that has just been swallowed by a snake — it greatly changes the form of the snake as it wends its way down the snake's long torso. The baby-boomers created overcrowded classes when they started school and spiraling tuition rates as they pursued higher education, stoked demand for houses, BMWs and brie as they got jobs and ascended the corporate ladder and more recently inspired an awesome growth rate in mutual funds as they began to contemplate future retirement. These boomers are now between ages 35 and 50, and seem to be serious indeed about investing.

Although these new investors have channeled billions of dollars into mutual funds, they are also exploring other alternatives. Many are investing on their own, and both the full-service and discount brokerage firms have benefited from their business. Others are turning to financial planners and investment advisors.

Some of this new money is already flowing into REITs. According to data provided by NAREIT, there were 89 publicly traded Equity REITs at the end of 1992, having an equity market cap of $11 billion; by the end of 1996, their number had swollen to 166, with an equity market cap of $78 billion. The number of mutual funds devoted primarily to REIT investing has grown from 6 to 27 from 1992 to mid-November 1996, and their assets increased from $342 million to $4.4 billion, according to a PaineWebber report.[2] By January 16, 1997, real estate mutual fund assets had swollen to over $6.5 billion.[3] There are now even REIT "indexed" mutual funds readily available. But will REITs be able to capture more than a tiny portion of the new investment funds that will be deployed through the end of the '90s and into the 21st century?

All signs say yes. New investors start with small investments, and the mutual fund is one obvious beneficiary; a mutual fund is a cost-effective way for new investors to get into a regular investment program. The investor need only send in checks; he or she need not become a student of the financial markets nor keep detailed records of every transaction. The popular "401k" plans encourage employees to invest, also, through mutual funds. However, over time these investments will grow larger, and investors' needs will grow and become more complex. Many investors will want to get more personally involved. They will want to time their financial transactions for tax reasons. They will use individual stock brokers to help them review specific investments. They will seek out financial planners and investment advisors as a means of obtaining outside professional help. They will want to diversify their investments among different "asset classes" to minimize the adverse effects of the occasional crash in a particular market.

Therein lies a golden opportunity for REITs and NAREIT, their trade organization, to attract new investors. Back in Chapter One I told you why I love REITs; if they are as terrific as I think they are, REITs will become a very attractive method of diversification for these serious new investors. They need not, of course, park all or even the lion's share of their investment dollars in REITs; even a small portion, such as 10%-15%, would result in huge additional demand for REIT shares.

From an investor's standpoint, the justification for banking on REITs is clear: REITs have, over many years, delivered total returns to their investors that approximate those of the S&P 500 index; they have low "betas," which means that the REIT sector of one's portfolio won't move in lock-step with the rest of the market and they have been (and are expected to remain) less volatile; they provide substantial dividend yields; and they respond to different economic conditions and developments than do other common stocks. As investors' assets become larger and the investors themselves become more knowledgeable about the investment world, they will want to diversify into REIT investments. We are already seeing this; financial publications catering to individual investors are even now publishing articles that extol the benefits of REIT investing.[4] America On-line's "Motley Fool" has a very popular real estate industry discussion group that focuses primarily on REITs. And more will come.

Brokerage firms likewise are expanding their coverage of REIT investments. At the end of 1992, 39 investment firms covered REITs; this number had expanded to 59 in 1996.[5] NAREIT has an ongoing program to educate financial planners in the virtues of REIT investing as an excellent form of diversification for their clients' assets. Investment advisors, more than ever before, are looking at REITs as a strong alternative to utility stocks and perhaps even bonds.

As these forms of investor education continue, new converts to REIT investing will be won over. Bonds and utility stocks will continue to have a place in many portfolios, but REITs' virtues in relation to other yield-oriented investments will become more widely known and accepted. The stigma of the real estate limited partnerships will fade from investors' memories, and they will look to acquire real estate investments with high liquidity. And as the baby-boomers get longer in the tooth and near retirement age, the high, steady and growing dividend income provided by REITs will become more and more attractive to them.

Institutional Investors

In Chapter Four we noted that institutions and pension funds have been slow to embrace REITs in a big way. These multi-billion dollar organizations tend to "earmark" a modest portion of their assets for real estate investment in order to obtain further diversification. Historically these funds have invested in real estate directly or in funds organized and managed by large insurance companies; these investments have been supervised by separate real estate divisions within their organization or by outside real estate advisors. The personnel of these organizations tend to be real estate experts rather than common stock investors, and thus traditionally haven't been comfortable owning publicly traded, real estate-oriented securities such as REITs, even if allowed to do so.

Other factors also had the effect of discouraging institutions from investing in REITs. The REIT stocks' volatility (relative to directly owned real estate) was regarded as a negative. Further, until just a few years ago, the number of quality REITs in which large institutional investors could invest was very small; they could easily dismiss the REIT industry as insignificant, and many desirable types of properties (e.g., offices, industrial properties, malls and hotels) weren't even represented in the REIT world. Objections have been raised with respect to the small market caps of the REITs, which has made it difficult to buy and sell REIT shares in large blocks without affecting their market price. Finally, even if an institution found a REIT it would like to own, it couldn't buy a significant position without finding itself the owner of practically a controlling position in the REIT.

Despite these obstacles, institutional investors have been steadily and significantly increasing their ownership of REIT shares. Based upon the findings of Michael Giliberto,[6] institutions owned approximately 25% of the aggregate market cap of the stocks within the Lehman Brothers Equity REIT Index, together with the health care REITs, from the second quarter of 1990 to mid-1992 (his survey doesn't go back further in time, but it's very unlikely that the percentage exceeded 25% in any earlier period). Kenneth D. Campbell, who has followed REITs since 1961, refers to a CRA Securities study[7] that estimates that institutions (including pension funds, mutual funds and investment advisors) held approximately 45% of the market value of all Equity REITs at the end of 1994. In the spring of 1996, PaineWebber reviewed the institutional ownership of the 117 REITs included in that firm's REIT index and concluded that institutional ownership was 51% as of March 3, 1996; the majority of such ownership was held by investment advisors and mutual funds. (The amount of such institutional ownership varied widely by sector, the highest being hotel REITs at 72% and the lowest being triple net lease REITs at 27%). And the significant amount of funds going into REIT shares in 1996 would indicate that the ownership of REITs by institutions is increasing weekly (if not daily).

Nevertheless, compared with the size of the entire common stock universe (approximately $9.3 trillion at the end of 1996), the aggregate market cap of all publicly traded REITs ($89 billion at the end of 1996) remains very small. Can REITs lure more investment dollars out of the huge institutional investors? Yes indeed. REITs will accomplish this on the basis of the quality of their organizations, the consistency of their earnings growth, their larger market caps (as the best-known REITs continue to raise capital) and the increasing market liquidity of their shares. Let's look at each of these important factors.

REITs' quality. Between the time that the REIT industry was born in the early 1960s and until just a few years ago, most REITs were managed in a fairly passive way by small real estate staffs. Not until the 1980s did most REITs become internally managed; before then the REITs had advisory agreements with outside companies that provided for the various real estate services that the REIT would need, such as leasing and property management. To speak of most REITs as "organizations" would have been dubious. Insider stock ownership was nil, conflicts of interest were numerous and most REITs had limited access to capital. Most real estate professionals employed by the large institutions would have found investing in such REITs almost laughable.

All of this has changed since Kimco Realty quietly became a public company in 1991, followed by scores of additional high quality real estate organizations in the following years. Sophisticated and powerful real estate companies that had been operating very successfully for many years and that had developed well-earned reputations as leaders in their field became REITs. A partial list of such companies includes DeBartolo Realty, Simon Property Group and Taubman Centers (malls); Developers Diversified and Vornado (neighborhood shopping centers); Bay Apartment Communities, Evans Withycombe, Irvine Apartment Communities, Post Properties and Summit Properties (apartments); and Cali Realty, Reckson Associates, Spieker Properties and Weeks Corp. (office and industrial). Yes, there were some REITs that were outstanding organizations prior to 1991 (such as Federal, New Plan,

232

United Dominion, Washington REIT and Weingarten), but their number was small indeed.

The increasing number of quality organizations with excellent management depth that have become REITs, such as the REITs named above as well as others, has been a major factor encouraging many institutions to give the REIT world some serious time and attention. Furthermore, the number of real estate sectors in which these REITs hold properties has expanded significantly, as we've seen earlier. This also has encouraged a number of institutions to take a very close look at REIT investing. Indeed, many of them have already begun.

Earnings growth. A second factor that will increase the amount of institutional funds flowing into REIT investments is their recognition of the strength of many REITs' past and prospective earnings growth accomplishments and capabilities. Many institutions learned to their sorrow in the late 1980s and early 1990s that "management" can be as important as "location" as a determinant of success for a portfolio of properties, and many REITs have outstanding property management skills. Furthermore, many REITs (whether due to their management's extensive tenant contacts, their strong financial resources, their in-house research capabilities or even their ability to issue operating partnership units in order to allow the seller to defer capital gains taxes) are often able to acquire outstanding properties at discount prices. These capabilities all add up to steady and impressive earnings growth, and institutions will realize that they are likely to generate better real estate-related investment returns by buying REITs rather than by buying and owning properties directly.

The track records of many real estate management firms that have managed directly owned properties for institutional investors or the large pools of properties put together as "funds" by large insurance companies have not been impressive,[8] and many institutional investors have, since the early '90s, been reducing their investments in this area. These institutions may look with envy at the outstanding track records put together over many years by the folks at Kimco, Simon, Post and other REITs, and wonder why they shouldn't just own their stocks as a replacement for a significant portion of their directly owned real estate portfolios.

Increased market caps and share liquidity. The third factor that will drive increased institutional ownership of REIT shares is the increased liquidity that will result from the increasing market caps of many REITs. Before the 1993-1994 IPO boom, not a single REIT could boast an equity market cap of as much as $1 billion. By mid-December 1996, a total of 27 REITs had passed that milestone, and another 10 were within $200 million of that number.[9] Rapidly-growing REITs continue to expand their property holdings; due to the factors discussed earlier, they must continue to sell additional shares. While this reduces the ownership interests of the existing shareholders, it has the favorable side effect of increasing the REIT's equity market cap and the public "float" of available shares. Furthermore, property acquisitions are often made through the issuance of stock and operating partnership units convertible into shares. Finally, mergers are resulting in more shares outstanding and larger market caps for many REITs. The trading volume of many REITs today matches that of many "mid-cap" companies, and such volumes will expand with their increasing market caps. The institutions, if patient, should be able to establish sizable positions without causing them to own "too large" a percentage of a single REIT or unduly affecting the current market price. Further, as the institutions become more comfortable with REITs, they may not find it all that important to be able to dump hundreds of thousands of shares within 20 minutes.

One experienced REIT observer, William Campbell, an analyst with Equity Research Collaborative (a Boston-based real estate research and consulting firm), has noted several other advantages to pension funds and other institutions owning REITs rather than directly owned properties. These include the use of leverage in real estate investing (which is often not legally permitted in direct investments by pension funds); the greater ability of REITs to assemble multiple properties in a single geographical area, which can increase operating efficiencies (and thus total returns); the ability (for most pensions and institutions) to obtain greater diversification by way of management, geography and property type; and the ease with which management can be "replaced" should the investment prove disappointing (merely by selling shares).

Finally, a study by Professor Lynne B. Sagalyn of Columbia University (referred to in footnote 8), suggests reasons why the rapid securitization of real estate (principally in the form of REITs) has "created the first viable opportunity for institutional investors to consider investing in real estate through the public markets." These include ease of diversification, acquisition of exposure to different forms of real estate, enhanced liquidity, more efficient pricing of risk and better monitoring of real estate management.

In what form will the institutions invest in REITs? There are several. They can, of course, simply buy REIT shares in the open market. They can negotiate private placements directly with a REIT, whether in the form of common stock or a special issue of convertible preferred, and they can buy shares in "spot offerings" that are completed within just a few trading days. They can form joint ventures with a REIT, putting up the funds for the acquisition of significant property portfolios or for the development of one or more new properties. They can swap properties which they own for

REIT shares. It is not terribly important which type of investment is chosen. What *is* important for REIT investors is that the institutions and huge pension funds are finding that REITs are a strong alternative to direct or "pooled funds" ownership of real estate, and will be investing in them at a greatly accelerating pace.[10] This will augment the credibility of REITs as excellent investments, provide them with needed capital at reduced costs and enable many more privately held successful real estate companies to become REITs.

The move towards greater institutional ownership of REIT shares has already begun in earnest. In a June 14, 1996, Wall Street Journal article titled "Dutch Fund Makes Splash in U.S. REITs," the REIT investment activities of Stichting Pensioenfonds ABP (ABP), a pension fund for almost one million Netherlands public employees, were highlighted. The article said that ABP, which manages $125 billion in assets, has already invested more than $1 billion in U.S. REITs and intends to "quadruple the size of its $1.2 billion U.S. real estate portfolio" by the year 2000. Further, the California State Teachers' Retirement System announced in mid-1996 that it is looking to exchange all or a large portion of its $1.8 billion worth of properties for REIT shares. In the fall of 1996, Prudential Insurance Co. of America announced that it would sell almost all of its remaining $5.6 billion worth of hotels, office buildings and other properties and, in connection with such new strategy, plans to swap some of its properties for shares of REITs. Well-known REIT observer Barry Vinocur, writing in Barron's,[11] stated that "it's estimated that tax-exempt pension funds own some $150 billion worth of properties" and noted that Douglas Abbey, a principal with real estate advisor AMB Investments, "expects the funds to shift gradually toward a mix of 80% publicly traded real estate stocks and 20% direct real estate investments." It has been estimated that institutions may swap as much as $10-15 billion in real estate for REIT shares by the middle of 1998.

Changes in the Nature of REITs

Throughout this book I've tried to emphasize a crucial point concerning the nature of today's REITs. Until the IPO boom of 1993-1994, most REITs were fairly small companies and had limited capabilities. They were able to acquire real estate, and most were able to manage it quite well. Many were able to refurbish, renovate and upgrade their properties, which enabled them to add value to their portfolios and increase FFO at a pace quicker than could be achieved with a purely passive "buy-and-hold" strategy. But very few were able to *develop* properties.

This all changed with the REIT cohort of 1993-1994. A very large number of these new REITs came public with well-established development capabilities. There are times in various real estate cycles where it is simply uneconomical to develop new properties; existing rental rates during these periods are simply insufficient to justify the costs of land acquisition, property entitlement and construction. However, at other times (*e.g.*, apartments in 1994-1995) new development is clearly warranted. REITs with this added capability clearly have an advantage over the others, as they will be able to take advantage of favorable development opportunities when conditions are appropriate and thus have the opportunity to grow their FFO faster than their less-endowed siblings.

In the future, much of the available real estate capital will flow to those REITs that "can do it all." While solid real estate companies without development capabilities will continue to attract capital on the basis of their track records and managerial skills, the lion's share of the new capital will be captured by those organizations that can create the most additional value for their shareholders. These companies (most of which are likely to be REITs) will have the acquisition skills to buy properties at bargain prices, the research abilities to ascertain where growth at the property level will be strongest, the staff necessary to manage existing properties in the most creative and efficient manner, the capability of developing the types of properties most in demand by tenants (and in the best locations) and the foresight to create highly incentivized managements and well thought-out succession plans. These types of real estate organizations, by continuing to attract lots of new capital, will become significantly larger than most of today's REITs, and will attract large institutional followings.

As the securitization of real estate in the U.S. continues to grow, these companies will become increasingly more powerful and will become national in scope. They will account for an ever-increasing percentage of the new properties that are being developed, and (assuming that they remain disciplined) will help to moderate the severity of the real estate cycles that have plagued real estate owners over the years.

We are already seeing this process evolve, particularly in certain real estate sectors. A good example of this trend is in the office sector, where Beacon, CarrAmerica and Crescent are building their organizations and going nationwide in scope. Other REITs will follow the same pattern (perhaps first expanding regionally, such as Highwoods (offices), Weeks (industrial), United Dominion (apartments) and Weingarten (retail shopping centers)). Those REITs that do not follow suit will have to become either very savvy "local sharpshooters" or will fall into the shadows of REITdom, perhaps eventually being acquired by the larger REITs.

Legislation on the Horizon

On the legislative front, one change on the REIT horizon might include an expansion of REITs' legal authority to operate related businesses. As you may recall from Chapter Two, at least 75% of a REIT's gross income must come from rents, mortgage interest or gains from the sale of real property, and the receipt of "non-real-estate-related" income, such as from an "operating business," is not permitted. The proposed Real Estate Investment Trust Simplification Tax Act ("REITSA"), which was introduced in Congress but had not yet been enacted at the time this book went to press, would relax and simplify certain operational, organizational and income restrictions. It's unlikely that REITs would be able to directly earn income from clearly "non-real-estate-related" sources, but perhaps that definition might be relaxed a bit to allow REITs to generate income from sources very closely related to owning and managing real estate.[12] Further, REITs' ability to form *taxable* subsidiaries, enabling them to engage in certain "non-real-estate related" businesses indirectly (albeit at the cost of paying taxes on the income earned by such subsidiaries), could be clarified and perhaps even expanded.

The proposed REITSA legislation would contain a "de minimus" rule that would allow a REIT to earn up to 1% of a property's gross income from presently impermissible (non-real estate) services without "tainting" the underlying rental income. This feature would allow a REIT to provide additional services which, although not generating a significant amount of revenue, could be of substantial value to its tenants (such as a concierge service at an apartment or office building) without losing its favorable tax status. Such flexibility could enable the property-owning REIT to maintain its competitive edge vis-à-vis its non-REIT competitors.

REITSA would also modernize certain rules and regulations applicable to REITs, and allow them greater operational flexibility in certain areas. It would remove certain "traps for the unwary" that could result in the inadvertent loss of status as a REIT. It would also allow a REIT to retain capital gains upon the sale of one or more properties, pay the capital gains tax and pass through a tax credit to the shareholders; this would merely mirror the tax law applicable to mutual funds.

Consolidation within the Industry

Despite the likelihood that many well-run privately held real estate companies will become REITs in the years ahead, a counter-trend has begun to appear. Several REITs have recently been acquired by, or merged with, larger real estate organizations. Some of these transactions include Wellsford's acquisition of Holly Residential, McArthur Glen's acquisition by Horizon Group, the merger of REIT of California with BRE Properties, the buyout of Tucker Properties by Bradley Real Estate and Highwoods' purchase of Crocker Realty Trust. Three significant apartment REIT mergers were either completed or announced in late 1996 and early 1997, including the merger of South West Properties into United Dominion Realty, and the agreements of Camden Property to acquire Paragon Group and of Equity Residential to acquire Wellsford Residential. These deals, however, pale in comparison with the 1996 merger between DeBartolo Realty and Simon Property Group, which has created the largest retail real estate organization in the U.S. As a result of these developments, there has been some speculation in the REIT industry that the modest pace of mergers and acquisitions we've seen recently will accelerate in the years ahead. According to Barry Vinocur, editor and publisher of Realty Stock Review, "There's been more merger activity in REIT land in the last 12 months (March 1995 to March 1996) than in the prior five or 10 years combined."[13]

As we've discussed earlier, REITs clearly need capital if they want to grow FFO at a significant pace, but many REITs that came public in 1993-1994, as well as some older, smaller REITs, may not be able to raise such capital. This unfortunate situation has come about because an individual REIT may be just too small to attract a significant investment following, it fails to convince investors that it has a sound growth strategy or its management has failed to earn a reputation with REIT investors for skill and creativity. Investors have thus wondered, in such situations, whether the shareholders would be better served if the REIT were to be acquired by a stronger organization.

The potential advantages to the shareholders of both the acquiring and acquired REITs are significant. A premium to the previous market price might be paid to the acquired company's shareholders, either in cash or stock of the acquiring company; this occurred in the Holly/Wellsford, Simon/DeBartolo, United Dominion/South West Properties, Camden/Paragon and Equity/Wellsford deals, among others. The acquiring company might have the financial resources and management expertise to improve the profitability of the acquired company's properties. Redundant costs, particularly with respect to operating a public company, may be eliminated, thus enhancing the profitability of the combined company. These factors alone might justify paying a premium to the acquired company's shareholders, as they often enhance the FFO growth of the acquiring REIT.[14] Finally, as in the case of the Simon/DeBartolo merger, the new larger company may have a stronger bargaining position with tenants and an increased likelihood of attracting low-priced investment capital.

To what extent will these mergers actually happen? It appears they will continue steadily, but perhaps not at the rapid pace that some expect. Yes, a substantial number of REITs *ought* to be acquired by larger, stronger organizations. But there are several impediments to this occurring with regularity. Many, if not most, of

238

the potential acquirees do not own properties with enough upside potential to make them interesting to a major buyer. They may consist of apartment units in poor locations or retail centers that are barely holding their own against the malls and "power centers."

Another reason may be that those REITs that *ought* to be acquired are controlled by individuals with large egos who may have no intention of selling their "crown jewels," or even giving up their compensation packages. Some of these REITs even have restrictions in their bylaws or charter documents that give existing major shareholders an effective veto power over any merger proposal.

Finally, the stocks of most REITs today — even those that seem to be going nowhere in terms of significant FFO growth — are selling at prices that are significantly above their net asset values. For example, Green Street Advisors has noted that the average premium over net asset value at which their universe of REITs traded near the end of December 1996 was a whopping 28%. Acquiring a mediocre performer at a price significantly exceeding net asset value might be accretive to FFO if paid for with shares selling at an even higher premium above net asset value. However, it's not clear that all such deals create long-term value for the acquiring company's shareholders when the true cost of equity capital is factored into the equation. One reason why the Simon/DeBartolo deal was well-received is that DeBartolo's shares were selling well below estimated net asset value at the time the deal was announced.

Nevertheless, mergers *will* occur regularly in the REIT industry. Those that are well-conceived and that offer many of the potential advantages discussed earlier will be greeted with enthusiasm and will benefit the shareholders of both the acquiring and the acquired companies. However, it will be very difficult for REIT investors to spot these ahead of time. It is noteworthy that the shares of other mall and retail REITs barely budged in the wake of the Simon/DeBartolo merger announcement, and the same shrugging of shoulders occurred immediately following the late 1996 announcements regarding South West Properties and Paragon Group. Investors do not seem to believe that a period of hyper-active merger activity is at hand.[15]

Summary

The future of the REIT industry is very bright indeed, for both real estate companies and their shareholders. The REIT vehicle allows successful and far-sighted real estate organizations tremendous new access to needed capital and affords them the type of financing flexibility they've never had before. It provides their owners with liquidity for their major assets and enables them to more easily attract and motivate quality management. The availability of ever-larger and more capable REITs enables individual investors and large institutions alike to diversify their investment portfolios, while offering the prospects of outstanding total returns on their investments.

Due to the forces discussed in this chapter, it would not be surprising 10 years from now to see REITs own at least $500 billion of commercial real estate. That would still be less than half of the nation's institutionally-owned real estate, and would still not exceed the percentage of securitized ownership that prevails in many other major world economies such as the U.K. As the well-known real estate investor Sam Zell recently stated, "we're only in the top of the second inning in the 'equitization' of real estate in the United States." Mr. Peter Aldrich, Founder and Co-chair of Aldrich Eastman Waltch, a well-known real estate advisory firm, has stated that "The industry's right on track now for 25 percent compounded growth rate of market cap. Nothing should slow it now, unless there's bad public policy."[16]

For the prospective REIT investor, the argument to join in the blossoming field is a compelling one. REITs allow investors to enjoy the substantial benefits of high, stable dividend yields that will grow steadily over the years, together with significant opportunities for capital appreciation. Investors already have a wide choice in both the real property sectors in which they can invest and the investment strategies being pursued by REIT managements, and their choices will multiply as additional REITs are organized in future years. For yield-oriented investors, REIT investing in the past has been glorious, but the best is yet to come.

---

[1] NAREIT, "The REIT Investment Summary," January 1996.

[2] PaineWebber, Real Estate Research, November 15, 1996.

[3] Realty Stock Review, January 31, 1997, p. 20.

[4] See, for example, "The REIT Stuff," Financial World, January 2, 1996, "REIT Investing in the 1990's," Journal of the American Association of Individual Investors, May 1995, "Amid an Improving Climate, REITs Grow Steadily, The New York Times, October 27, 1996, and "Seeking Shelter in Real Estate Trusts," The New York Times, January 19, 1997.

[5] See note 3 above.

[6] See "Institutional Ownership and Equity REIT Performance," in The Journal of Real Estate Investment Trusts, November 1996, p. 43.

[7] "The REIT Report," Autumn 1995, p. 49.

[8] Professor Lynne B. Sagalyn, of Columbia University, states that "For the 1975-1993 period, public real estate has outperformed private real estate investments — by nearly 400 basis points — even after making the requisite statistical adjustments to both public and private real estate data." See "Institutional Options: Publicly Traded REITs and Privately Held Real Estate Investments," reprinted in The Journal of Real Estate Investment Trusts, July 1996.

[9] Realty Stock Review, December 26, 1996, p. 16-20.

[10] We should note that many institutions' interest in owning REITs as an alternative to direct real estate investment would be very limited unless they come to believe that REITs' performance and total returns correlate well with that of real estate as an asset class. While there have been many studies seeking to track REITs' performance vis-à-vis that of real estate (and although it is this author's belief that "REITs aren't real estate" for many of the reasons discussed in this book), current opinion seems to be that REITs' performance, over significant time periods, will track closely with the performance of real estate. See, for example, "A Behind-the-Scenes Look at the Investment Performance of REITs," by Daniel P. Guenther and T. Ritson Ferguson, in The Journal of Real Estate Investment Trusts, November 1996, p. 31. The authors suggest, based upon their study, that "savvy investors will continue to take advantage of the high long-term correlation and short-term counter-cyclicality of REIT and real estate asset returns to enhance portfolio returns."

[11] Barron's, July 1, 1996, p. 40.

[12] Mr. Sanford Alexander, Chairman and CEO of Weingarten Realty and former Chairman of NAREIT, notes that NAREIT was successful in 1996 in "convincing the IRS to rule that revenues from providing cable television services to multifamily REIT tenants are qualifying income for the REIT tax tests." See "Chair's Message," in The REIT Report, Autumn 1996, p. 5.

[13] Realty Stock Review, March 29, 1996, p.3.

[14] Green Street Advisors calculated the cost savings resulting from eight REIT mergers done between October 1994 and October 1996, noting that "the net increase in FFO resulting from savings achieved by reducing overhead have averaged 3.0%." See Green Street Advisors, Inc., "Real Estate Stock Index," October 25, 1996, p. 1.

[15] For an interesting perspective on mergers and acquisitions in the REIT industry, see "The Future of Consolidation," by W. Blake Baird and Paul J. Donahue, in The REIT Report, Autumn 1996, p. 28.

[16] The REIT Report, Autumn 1996, p. 35.

APPENDIX A

Taxation of Dividends for Equity REIT Shareholders

An interesting (and potentially rewarding) nuance of the Equity REIT kingdom is that a portion of the dividends received by the shareholder is frequently tax-deferred. This situation arises because most REITs pay dividends on the basis of their funds from operations (or adjusted funds from operations), which is invariably greater than net income.

For income tax purposes, distributions paid to shareholders can consist of ordinary income, long-term capital gains, and return of capital. The distributions attributable to return of capital will reduce the shareholder's cost basis by an equivalent amount. Only the portion of the dividends attributable to ordinary income and capital gains will be currently taxed. The reduction in cost basis will then be recaptured for tax purposes, upon sale of the stock, as capital gain. A good example of this dividend allocation is the 1995 distributions for United Dominion Realty (UDR).

	Dividend per Share	Percent of Total
Ordinary Income	$0.715	82.2%
Capital Gains	$0.003	0.3%
Return of Capital	$0.152	17.5%
Total	$0.870	100.0%

Shareholders cannot predict the amount of the dividend that will be tax-deferred merely by looking at *financially-reported* net income, as the tax-deferred portion is based upon *taxable* income. The differences between net income available to common shareholders for financial reporting purposes and taxable income before dividend deductions relate primarily to:

1) differences between taxable depreciation (usually accelerated) versus book (usually straight-line) real estate depreciation;
2) accrual on preferred stock dividends; and
3) deferral for tax purposes of certain capital gains on property sales (*e.g.*, tax-deferred exchanges); all realized gains or losses on sales of investments are distributed to shareholders if and when they are recognized for income tax purposes.

There is generally no publicly available information to determine, ahead of time, the portion of distribution that will be taxed as ordinary income. The primary problem is that, for tax purposes, certain income and expense items are calculated differently than what appears in the financial statements, as explained above. Without extensive tax disclosure by the company, this number must be generated at the company level and the shareholder will have to wait until year-end to obtain the final figures.

EXAMPLE:

Let's assume the investor purchased 100 shares of UDR at $15.00 in 1997 for a total cost of $1,500. For simplicity, we will ignore commissions. By year-end, he or she will have received $0.96 a share in dividends (assuming no dividend increase during the year) for a total of $96. Let us further assume the ratios of ordinary income, capital gains, and return of capital in effect for 1995 (as stated in the table above) still apply. Therefore, $78.91 will be taxed as ordinary income, $0.29 will be taxed as long-term capital gain, and $16.80 will be tax-deferred as a return of capital. The investor must then reduce his or her cost basis by the equivalent amount of the return of capital component ($16.80) so that the "new" cost basis of the 100 shares of UDR is now $1,483.20. Let us finally assume that the 100 shares are sold one year and one day later for $16.00 per share, for a total of $1,600 (again ignoring commissions). The investor will then report a total long-term capital gain of $116.80 on Schedule D.

An important note is that state tax laws may differ from federal law. Investors should confirm the status of their dividends under Federal and state tax laws with their accountant or financial advisor.

APPENDIX B

Example of Income Statement Derivation of Adjusted Funds from Operations (AFFO) and Funds or Cash Available for Distribution (FAD or CAD).

Post Properties (PPS): Third Quarter, 1996		
Revenue		
Rental—owned property	$40,583	
Property management	722	
Landscape services	1,199	
Interest	50	
Other	1,661	
Total Revenue		$44,215
Expenses:		
Property operating & maintenance	$15,115	
Depreciation - real estate assets	5,877	
Total Property Expenses		$20,992
Corporate & Other Expenses		
Property management - third party	$558	
Landscape management	1,013	
Interest	5,970	
Amortization of financing costs	293	
Depreciation - non real estate assets	197	
General and administration	1,769	
Minority interest	0	
Total Corporate & Other Expenses		$9,800
Total Expenses		$30,792
Income before minority interests and extraordinary items		$13,423
Gain on sale of assets		$693
Minority interest in operating partnership		(2,535)
Net Income		$11,581
Add:		
Depreciation and amortization - real estate assets		$5,877
Minority Interest		2,696
Less:		
Net gain on sale		$ (854)
Amortization of financing costs		(55)
Funds from Operations (FFO)		$19,245
FFO per share		$0.71
Less:		
Recurring Capital Expenditures		$(692)
Adjusted funds from operations		$18,553

AFFO per share	**$0.69**
Less:	
Non-recurring capital expenditures	(687)
Funds or cash available for distribution	$17,866
FAD or CAD per share	**$0.66**
Weighted average number of shares/operating units	26,928,896

Notes:

1. Depreciation of "hard assets" like apartment buildings and other structures can be deceptive. The property (including the underlying land) could actually appreciate in value, particularly if well maintained; however, for accounting purposes, depreciation must be deducted in order to derive net income. Funds from operations is calculated by adding back real estate depreciation and amortization to net income. However, property owners incur recurring expenditures that are certainly real and which need to be taken into account to provide a true picture of the owner's cash flow from the property. Examples include the necessary replacement, from time to time, of carpets and roofs. In some cases, property owners may make tenant improvements (and/or provide tenant allowances) which are necessary to retain the property's competitive position with existing and potential tenants, and may pay leasing commissions. Since many of these expenditures are capitalized, they must be deducted from funds from operations (FFO) in order to determine "adjusted funds from operations," or AFFO, which is the "truest" picture of economic cash flow.

Funds (or Cash) Available for Distribution (FAD or CAD) is sometimes calculated in a slightly different manner. Unlike AFFO, which deducts the amortization of *normal and recurring* real-estate related expenditures from FFO, FAD or CAD is often derived by deducting *non-recurring* (as well as normal and recurring) expenditures. Unfortunately, there is no widely-accepted standard for making these adjustments.

2. Another major consideration is the use of variable rate debt. If the balance sheet reflects a significant portion of variable rate debt bearing short-term maturities, there is a significant risk of increasing interest costs in the future should interest rates rise. An assessment of this risk can be made by adjusting the cost of the variable rate debt coupon to fixed rate levels in order to make an "apples to apples" comparison with other REITs and operating companies. This adjustment can also be made for operating entities with substantial levels of tax-exempt financing.

3. When reviewing a REIT's revenues, it is a good idea to analyze lease expirations and existing rents and compare them to market rates. This approach may help in determining whether rental revenues may decrease when leases are renewed at market rates.

4. Always distinguish revenues from services as opposed to revenues from rents. Rental revenue tends to be of higher quality and more stable, as service clients can easily terminate the relationship.

5. Always analyze the type of debt and debt maturities. REIT investors would obviously prefer long-term debt to short-term and fixed-rate debt to variable rate.

6. Look for recurring "capital expenditures" which do not improve or prolong the life of the property, as well as financing traps (*e.g.*, "buydowns" of loan interest coupons).

APPENDIX C

Cost of Equity Capital

There is no general agreement on how to calculate a REIT's "cost of equity capital." There are, however, several ways to approach this issue. One "shorthand" method, which can be used to determine a REIT's "nominal" equity capital cost, is to first estimate the REIT's per share FFO earned in the most recent quarter and annualize it or, perhaps more appropriate, the per share FFO expected to be earned over the next 12 months. This per share FFO should then be adjusted for (a) any additional shares to be issued, and (b) the expected incremental FFO to be earned from the investment of the sale proceeds. Finally, we would then divide such "pro forma" FFO per share by the price the REIT receives for each new share sold (after deducting underwriting commissions).[1]

Let's assume, for example, that "Apartment REIT USA" has 10 million shares outstanding and is expected to earn $10 million in FFO over the next 12 months. It intends to issue an additional 1 million shares and receive net proceeds of $9 per share (after underwriting commissions), which will be used to buy additional apartments providing an initial yield of 9%; this investment of $9 million will thus provide $810,000 of additional FFO (9% of $9 million). Therefore, on a pro forma basis, this REIT will have $10.81 million in FFO which, when divided by 11 million shares outstanding, will produce FFO of $.98 per share. Dividing this by the $9 net offering price results in a nominal cost of equity capital of 10.88%. Note that this is higher than the entry yield (9%) available on the new apartment investments, as a result of which this stock offering would be dilutive to FFO. However, if we tweak the numbers a bit and hypothesize that Apartment REIT USA is able to sell its new shares at a net price of $12, its nominal cost of equity capital becomes 8.4%. Thus, the higher the price at which a REIT can sell new shares, the cheaper its nominal cost of capital will be, thus making it more likely that the offering will be accretive to FFO.

Many observers believe that the above approach measures only a REIT's *nominal* cost of equity capital, and that its *true* cost of equity capital should be measured in a very different way. In the first approach, we divided pro forma expected FFO per share by the net sale proceeds per share, using expected FFO only for the next 12 months. But what about the *additional* FFO that will be generated by the REIT for many years into the future? This additional FFO will be forever diluted by the new shares being issued and, for this reason, it may not be appropriate to use expected FFO for just the next 12 months (*i.e.*, why not 24 months? 36 months?) How can longer time periods be taken into account?

A REIT's *true* cost of equity capital may be best measured by the total return expected by investors on their investment in the REIT. For example, if investors "price" a REIT's shares in the trading market such that 12% total annual returns are demanded — and expected — well into the future (on the basis of existing and projected dividend yields, anticipated FFO or

AFFO and expected growth rates), why isn't the REIT's true cost of equity capital the same 12%? A few REITs may be so conservative, and their FFO and dividend growth so predictable, that mere 10% annual returns might be demanded by investors; in such a case, the REIT's true cost of equity capital might very well be 10%. A difficulty with this approach is to determine the total returns that are demanded by investors; this isn't as easy as it might appear. All of this gets us into capital asset pricing models, "modern portfolio theory" and the like, which are topics beyond the scope of this book. Nevertheless, REIT investors who want to delve into this issue might want to try to determine the total returns expected by investors in particular REITs, and use those figures to determine the REIT's true cost of equity capital. Keep in mind, however, that in view of REITs' historical total returns of close to the mid-teens, very few REITs (if any) would have expected total returns of less than 12%.

REITs' legal requirement to pay out 95% of net income to their shareholders each year in the form of dividends makes it very difficult to grow externally (e.g., through acquisitions or new development) without frequently coming back to the markets for more equity capital. Keeping payout ratios low certainly helps reduce the overall cost of equity capital, as does periodically selling off properties with less-than-exciting long-term potential. However, innovative REIT managements who continue to find attractive opportunities will undoubtedly need to raise additional equity capital from time to time. It is thus important for REIT investors to understand how to analyze a REIT's nominal cost of equity capital and its true longer-term cost of equity capital as well.

---

[1] Some investors have looked simply at a REIT's dividend yield, which is quite misleading; FFO and AFFO are far more important than dividend payments in the context of determining most REITs' valuations and thus the dilution from issuing additional shares.

APPENDIX D

10 Largest REIT/ Real Estate Mutual Funds

Fund	Assets ($MM)	1996 YTD Return	3 Yr. Return	5 Yr. Return	Phone Number
Cohen & Steers Realty Shares	1,809.0	31.93	17.42	19.49	(800) 437-9912
Fidelity Real Estate	1,536.7	30.71	15.01	16.71	(800) 544-8888
Vanguard REIT Index *	382.7	24.92			(800) 662-7447
Heitman Real Estate	194.6	31.86	15.83	17.84	(800) 435-1405
Morgan Stanley U.S. Real Estate	184.1	34.80			(800) 548 7786
CGM Realty	142.6	36.35			(800) 345-4048
Templeton Real Estate Securities	141.4	16.54	5.30	11.41	(800) 237-0738
Longleaf Partners Realty	139.6	38.60			(800) 445-9469
Franklin Real Estate	112.7	27.65			(800) 342-5236
DFA/AEW Real Estate Securities	64.0	28.59	10.65		(310) 395-8005

* Inception date 5/13/96

Source: Realty Stock Review, Dec. 26, 1996

Note: Not all of these funds invest exclusively in REITs; many invest in other real estate-related securities as well.

APPENDIX E

Equity REIT Indices

The significant growth in the market cap of Equity REITs has increased the need for a reliable indicator of market values. Appraisal-based valuations are too limiting since property valuations occur infrequently and appraisals, even if obtained, are usually very subjective; perhaps even more important, REIT stocks normally trade at prices well above asset values (reflecting their often-significant external growth prospects). Therefore, NAREIT (the REIT industry organization), institutional consultants and many of the brokerage firms have developed their own indices to measure the changes in real estate company market valuations, as measured by a basket of real estate equities that trade on the New York Stock Exchange (NYSE), American Stock Exchange (ASE), and the NASDAQ. The indices can include up to four types of real estate-related companies: (1) equity real estate investment trusts (REITs), (2) real property operating companies not organized as REITs, (3) developers, and (4) general contractors. Equity REITs comprise the largest portion of most indices. Some of the more widely followed indices include:

(A) Russell-NCREIF (National Council of Real Estate Investment Fiduciaries) Property Index. Also known as RNPI. This index is, historically, the oldest real estate index. It is a widely known and acknowledged appraisal-based series of commercial properties. Only quarterly returns are available for this series, beginning in the first quarter of 1978.

(B) NAREIT Total Return Series Index. All data is based on the last closing price of the month for all tax qualified REITs listed on the NYSE, ASE, and NASDAQ National Market System. The data is market capitalization weighted. Prior to 1987, REITs were added to the Index the January following their listing. Since 1987, newly formed or listed REITs are added to the Index in the month in which they come public. Newly issued shares of existing REITs are added to the total shares outstanding in the month that the shares are issued. Only common shares issued by the REIT are included in the index. The total return calculation is based upon the weighting at the beginning of the period. Only those REITs listed for the entire period are used in the total return calculation. Dividends are included in the month, based upon their payment date. There is no smoothing of income. Liquidating dividends, whether partial or full, are treated as income. This has the effect of negatively biasing the price appreciation component of the index, but results in accurate realized income and total return numbers. Equity REITs are defined as REITs with 75% or greater of their gross invested book assets invested directly or indirectly in the equity ownership of real estate. Equity REITs excluding Health Care REITs is a return series created by deleting REITs that invest in health care facilities from the Equity REIT total return series starting in 1985 when the first health care REIT was formed; this series was terminated in 1996. Mortgage REITs are defined as REITs with 75% or more of their gross invested book assets invested directly or indirectly in mortgages.   Hybrid REITs are defined as not meeting the Equity or Mortgage REIT definitions.

(C) Morgan Stanley REIT Index.   This index is a market capitalization weighted total return index of 93 selected REITs. It is listed on the ASE and trades under the symbol "RMS." The index includes only those REITs that pass a liquidity test.   This is intended to allow for investing, hedging, trading, and sector allocation activities by institutional investors. The index is calculated by summing the market capitalization (share price multiplied by the total common shares outstanding) of each component stock and dividing the sum by a divisor.   The dividends are reinvested into the index portfolio.   Therefore, at the close of trading each day, the prices of the component securities which will trade ex-dividend the next day will be adjusted downward by the value of the dividend amount to reflect the impact on the stock as it trades without the dividend on the following day. The initial divisor was chosen to yield an initial index value of 200 as of December 31, 1994.   To ensure index continuity, the divisor will be recalculated as necessary to accommodate new share issuances, share repurchases, special cash dividends, rights offerings, spin-offs, and the deletion or addition of component stocks to the index.   The current components, weightings and the divisor can be obtained at any time from the ASE.

The minimum criteria for inclusion is: (1) minimum market cap of $100 million, (2) minimum of 7 million shares outstanding, (3) minimum trading volume of 1.2 million shares over the preceding six months and (4) minimum market price of $7.50 per share for the majority of business days in the preceding three calendar months.   If the market capitalization falls below $75 million or the minimum float drops below 6.3 million shares, the stock will be deleted. Also, if trading volume drops below 0.9 million shares for the preceding six months or the share price drops below $5.00 per share for a majority of the business days during the preceding three calendar months, the stock will be dropped. The index will be rebalanced on both a quarterly and daily basis. Each quarter, tests for inclusion or deletion are applied for each stock. The divisor will be adjusted accordingly.   The index may also be rebalanced daily as necessary to deal with mergers and acquisitions, LBOs, bankruptcy, loss of REIT status, or a fundamental change in business of the component stock, and the divisor will be adjusted accordingly.

The Index excludes Mortgage REITs and health care REITs. By leaving out the health care REITs, the index is ignoring roughly 12% of the total Equity REIT market. Each of the 93 Equity REITs included in the Morgan Stanley Index is included in the NAREIT index. A comparison of these two indices, by sector weighting, is as follows:

Sector (all figures in %)	NAREIT	Morgan Stanley
Apartments	20	26
Manufactured Homes	2	2
Self-Storage	6	7
Office/Industrial	16	19
Regional Malls	9	13
Shopping Centers	13	16
Factory Outlets	2	2
Hotels	7	6
Net Lease	4	4
Mortgage/Mixed Use/Misc.	10	5
Healthcare	12	0
Total	100	100

(D) Wilshire Real Estate Securities Index.   In September, 1991, Wilshire Associates, a leading institutional consulting firm, introduced the Wilshire Real Estate Securities Index as a broad measure of the performance of publicly traded real estate related equities. The primary purpose was for the institutional investment community to use the index for asset allocation, performance comparison and research. The index is a market capitalization weighted index of publicly traded real estate securities such as REITs, real estate operating companies (REOCs), and partnerships.   The index is comprised of companies whose charter is the equity ownership and operation of commercial real estate. The beginning date, January 1, 1978, was selected because it coincides with the Russell/NCREIF Property Index start date. The index is rebalanced monthly and returns are calculated on a buy and hold basis. The index has been constructed to avoid survivor bias, and currently includes 111 companies.

Companies are added to the index at the end of the next quarter if all of the following conditions are satisfied: (1) The company is an equity owner of certain commercial real estate; security types excluded from consideration are Mortgage REITs, health care REITs, real estate finance companies, home builders, land owners, and subdividers. Also, Hybrid REITs (companies with more than 25% of their assets in direct mortgage investments) will not be included. (2) The company has a book value of real estate assets of at least $100 million. (3) Market capitalization is at least $100 million.   (4) 75% of the company's total revenue comes from ownership and operation of real estate assets. (5) The liquidity of the company's stock is commensurate with that of other institutionally held equity securities.

New issues are added to the index on the first day of the quarter following a new offering. A company may be removed if: (1) direct mortgages represent more than 25% of the company's assets for two consecutive quarters or if NAREIT reclassifies an Equity REIT as a Mortgage REIT, (2) less than 50% of the company's total revenues is generated from the ownership and operation of real estate assets for two consecutive quarters, or (3) the company's stock becomes uninvestable due to illiquidity for two consecutive quarters or if the security fails to qualify for listing on its exchange.   The criteria are treated as "guidelines" and will be evaluated on an individual basis for application.

(E) Individualized Indices. Many of the large "sell-side" brokerage firms have their own proprietary indices or "lists" of REITs which they follow and measure. There is no formal index tracking process for many of these indices or lists.

The attached is a current list of securities for each of the major indices described above; they will, of course, change over time.

NAREIT

Sector	Subsector	REIT	Ticker
IND/OFF	INDUSTRIAL	AMERICAN INDUSTRIAL PROPERTIES REIT	IND
IND/OFF	INDUSTRIAL	CENTERPOINT PROPERTIES	CNT
IND/OFF	INDUSTRIAL	FIRST INDUSTRIAL REALTY TRUST	FR
IND/OFF	INDUSTRIAL	MERIDIAN INDUSTRIAL TRUST	MDN
IND/OFF	INDUSTRIAL	MERIDIAN POINT REALTY TRUST VIII CO.	MPH
IND/OFF	INDUSTRIAL	MERIDIAN POINT REALTY TRUST '83	MPTBS
IND/OFF	INDUSTRIAL	MONMOUTH REAL ESTATE INVESTMENT CORP	MNRTA
IND/OFF	INDUSTRIAL	SECURITY CAPITAL INDUSTRIAL TRUST	SCN
IND/OFF	INDUSTRIAL	WEEKS CORP	WKS
IND/OFF	OFFICE	ARDEN REALTY	ARI
IND/OFF	OFFICE	BEACON PROPERTIES CORP	BCN
IND/OFF	OFFICE	BRANDYWINE REALTY TRUST	BDN
IND/OFF	OFFICE	CALI REALTY TRUST	CLI
IND/OFF	OFFICE	CARRAMERICA REALTY CORP.	CRE
IND/OFF	OFFICE	COUSINS PROPERTIES	CUZ
IND/OFF	OFFICE	CRESCENT REAL ESTATE EQUITIES	CEI
IND/OFF	OFFICE	G&L REALTY	GLR
IND/OFF	OFFICE	HIGHWOODS PROPERTIES	HIW
IND/OFF	OFFICE	KOGER EQUITIES	KE
IND/OFF	OFFICE	NOONEY REALTY TRUST	NRTI
IND/OFF	OFFICE	PRENTISS PROPERTIES	PP
IND/OFF	OFFICE	REALTY REFUND TRUST	RRF
IND/OFF	MIXED	BEDFORD PROPERTY INVESTORS	BED
IND/OFF	MIXED	DUKE REALTY INVESTMENTS	DRE
IND/OFF	MIXED	LIBERTY PROPERTY TRUST	LRY
IND/OFF	MIXED	RECKSON ASSOC. REALTY	RA
IND/OFF	MIXED	SPIEKER PROPERTIES	SPK
SPECIALTY		CALIFORNIA JOCKEY CLUB	CJ
SPECIALTY		NATIONAL GOLF PROPERTIES	TEE
SPECIALTY		SANTA ANITA	SAR
SPECIALTY	TRIPLE NET LEASE	COMMERCIAL NET LEASE REALTY	NNN
SPECIALTY	TRIPLE NET LEASE	FRANCHISE FINANCE CORP AMER	FFA
SPECIALTY	TRIPLE NET LEASE	LEXINGTON CORP PROPERTIES	LXP
SPECIALTY	TRIPLE NET LEASE	ONE LIBERTY PROPERTIES	OLP
SPECIALTY	TRIPLE NET LEASE	PITTSBURGH WV RAILROAD	PW
SPECIALTY	TRIPLE NET LEASE	REALTY INCOME CORP	OLP
SPECIALTY	TRIPLE NET LEASE	TRINET CORP REALTY	TRI
SPECIALTY	HOTELS	AMERICANA HOTELS AND REALTY CORP	AHR
SPECIALTY	HOTELS	AMERICAN GENERAL HOSPITALITY CORP	AGT
SPECIALTY	HOTELS	BOYKIN LODGING	BOY
SPECIALTY	HOTELS	EQUITY INNS	ENN
SPECIALTY	HOTELS	FELCOR SUITE HOTELS	FCH
SPECIALTY	HOTELS	HOSPITALITY PROPERTIES TRUST	HPT
SPECIALTY	HOTELS	HOST FUNDING	HFD
SPECIALTY	HOTELS	INNKEEPERS USA TRUST	KPA
SPECIALTY	HOTELS	JAMESON INNS	JAMS
SPECIALTY	HOTELS	PATRIOT AMERICAN HOSPITALITY	PAH
SPECIALTY	HOTELS	RFS HOTEL INVESTORS	RFS
SPECIALTY	HOTELS	STARWOOD LODGING TRUST	HOT
SPECIALTY	HOTELS	SUNSTONE HOTEL ADVISORS	SSI
SPECIALTY	HOTELS	WINSTON HOTELS	WINN
MORTGAGE		ASSET INVESTORS CORP	AIC
MORTGAGE		CAPSTEAD MORTGAGE	CMO
MORTGAGE		CWM MORTGAGE HOLDINGS	CWM
MORTGAGE		HOMEPLEX MORTGAGE INV	HPX
MORTGAGE		IMPERIAL CREDIT MORTG	IMH
MORTGAGE		RESOURCE MORTGAGE CAPITAL	RMR
MORTGAGE		RYMAC MORTGAGE CAPITAL	RMR
MORTGAGE		THORNBURG MORTGAGE ASSET	TMA
MORTGAGE		TIS MORTGAGE INVESTMENT CO	TIS

RETAIL	STRIP CENTERS	AGREE REALTY CORP.	ADC
RETAIL	STRIP CENTERS	ALEXANDER HAAGEN PROPERTIES	ACH
RETAIL	STRIP CENTERS	ALEXANDER'S	ALX
RETAIL	STRIP CENTERS	BRADLEY REAL ESTATE TRUST	BTR
RETAIL	STRIP CENTERS	BURNHAM PACIFIC PROPERTIES	BPP
RETAIL	STRIP CENTERS	DEVELOPERS DIVERSIFIED REALTY CORP.	DDR
RETAIL	STRIP CENTERS	EXCEL REALTY TRUST	XEL
RETAIL	STRIP CENTERS	FEDERAL REALTY INVESTMENT TRUST	FRT
RETAIL	STRIP CENTERS	FIRST WASHINGTON REALTY TRUST	FRW
RETAIL	STRIP CENTERS	GLIMCHER REALTY TRUST	GRT
RETAIL	STRIP CENTERS	HRE PROPERTIES	HRE
RETAIL	STRIP CENTERS	IRT PROPERTY CO.	IRT
RETAIL	STRIP CENTERS	JDN REALTY CORP.	JDN
RETAIL	STRIP CENTERS	KIMCO REALTY CORP.	KIM
RETAIL	STRIP CENTERS	KRANZCO REALTY TRUST	KRT
RETAIL	STRIP CENTERS	MALAN REALTY INVESTORS	MAL
RETAIL	STRIP CENTERS	MARK CENTERS TRUST	MCT
RETAIL	STRIP CENTERS	MID-AMERICA REALTY INVESTMENTS	MDI
RETAIL	STRIP CENTERS	MID-ATLANTIC REALTY TRUST	MRR
RETAIL	STRIP CENTERS	NEW PLAN REALTY TRUST	NPR
RETAIL	STRIP CENTERS	PRICE REIT (CLASS B)	RET
RETAIL	STRIP CENTERS	RAMCO-GERSHENSON PROPERTIES TRUST	RPT
RETAIL	STRIP CENTERS	REGENCY REALTY CORP.	REG
RETAIL	STRIP CENTERS	SAUL CENTERS	BFS
RETAIL	STRIP CENTERS	VORNADO REALTY TRUST	VNO
RETAIL	STRIP CENTERS	WEINGARTEN REALTY INVESTORS	WRI
RETAIL	STRIP CENTERS	WESTERN INVESTMENT REAL ESTATE TRUST	WIR
RETAIL	OUTLET	CHELSEA GCA REALTY	CCG
RETAIL	OUTLET	FAC REALTY TRUST	FAC
RETAIL	OUTLET	HORIZON GROUP	HGI
RETAIL	OUTLET	PRIME RETAIL	PRME
RETAIL	OUTLET	TANGER FACTORY OUTLET CENTERS	SKT
RETAIL	REGIONAL MALLS	ARBOR PROPERTY TRUST	ABR
RETAIL	REGIONAL MALLS	CBL & ASSOCIATES	CBL
RETAIL	REGIONAL MALLS	CROWN AMERICAN REALTY TRUST	CWN
RETAIL	REGIONAL MALLS	GENERAL GROWTH PROPERTIES	GGP
RETAIL	REGIONAL MALLS	JP REALTY	JPR
RETAIL	REGIONAL MALLS	MACERICH COMPANY, THE	MAC
RETAIL	REGIONAL MALLS	MILLS CORP.	MLS
RETAIL	REGIONAL MALLS	SIMON DEBARTOLO GROUP	SPG
RETAIL	REGIONAL MALLS	TAUBMAN CENTERS	TCO
RETAIL	REGIONAL MALLS	URBAN SHOPPING CENTERS	URB
SELF STORAGE		PUBLIC STORAGE	PSA
SELF STORAGE		PUBLIC STORAGE XI	PSM
SELF STORAGE		PUBLIC STORAGE XIV	PSP
SELF STORAGE		PUBLIC STORAGE XV	PSQ
SELF STORAGE		PUBLIC STORAGE XVI	PSU
SELF STORAGE		PUBLIC STORAGE XVII	PSV
SELF STORAGE		PUBLIC STORAGE XVIII	PSW
SELF STORAGE		PUBLIC STORAGE XIX	PSY
SELF STORAGE		PUBLIC STORAGE XX	PSZ
SELF STORAGE		SHURGARD STORAGE CENTERS	SHU
SELF STORAGE		SOVRAN SELF STORAGE	SSS
SELF STORAGE		STORAGE TRUST REALTY	SEA
SELF STORAGE		STORAGE USA	SUS
DIVERSE		ALLIED CAPITAL COMMERCIAL CORP	ALCC
DIVERSE		ANGELES MORTGAGE INVESTMENT TRUST	ANM
DIVERSE		ARIZONA LAND INCOME CORP.	AZL
DIVERSE		BANYAN STRATEGIC REALTY TRUST	VLANS
DIVERSE		BODDIE-NOELL PROPERTIES	BNP
DIVERSE		BRT REALTY TRUST	BRT
DIVERSE		CALIFORNIA REIT	CT
DIVERSE		CHICAGO DOCK AND CANAL TRUST	DOCKS
DIVERSE		COLONIAL PROPERTIES TRUST	CLP
DIVERSE		COMMERCIAL ASSETS	CAX

DIVERSE		CONTINENTAL MORTGAGE & EQUITY TRUST	CMETS
DIVERSE		CV REIT	CVI
DIVERSE		EASTGROUP PROPERTIES	EGP
DIVERSE		EQK REALTY INVESTORS I	EKR
DIVERSE		FRANKLIN SELECT REALTY TRUST	FSN
DIVERSE		FIRST UNION REAL ESTATE INVESTMENTS	FUR
DIVERSE		GLENBOROUGH REALTY TRUST	GLB
DIVERSE		HMG/COURTLAND PROPERTIES	HMG
DIVERSE		INCOME OPPORTUNITY REALTY INVESTORS	IOT
DIVERSE		MGI PROPERTIES	MGI
DIVERSE		NATIONAL INCOME REALTY TRUST	NIRTS
DIVERSE		PACIFIC GULF PROPERTIES	PAG
DIVERSE		PENNSYLVANIA REIT	PEI
DIVERSE		PMC COMMERCIAL TRUST	PCC
DIVERSE		PROPERTY CAPITAL TRUST	PCT
DIVERSE		SIZELER PROPERTY INVESTORS	SIZ
DIVERSE		TRANSCONTINENTAL REALTY INVESTORS	TCI
DIVERSE		VALUE PROPERTY TRUST	VLP
DIVERSE		WASHINGTON REAL ESTATE INVESTMENT TRUST	WRE
HEALTH		AMERICAN HEALTH PROPERTIES	AHE
HEALTH		CAPSTONE CAPITAL CORP	CCT
HEALTH		HEALTH CARE PROPERTIES	HCP
HEALTH		HEALTH CARE REIT	HCN
HEALTH		HEALTH & RETIREMENT PROPERTIES TRUST	HRP
HEALTH		HEALTHCARE REALTY TRUST	HR
HEALTH		LTC PROPERTIES	LTC
HEALTH		MEDITRUST	MT
HEALTH		NATIONAL HEALTH INVESTORS	NHI
HEALTH		NATIONWIDE HEALTH PROPERTIES	NHP
HEALTH		OMEGA HEALTHCARE INVESTORS	OHI
HEALTH		UNIVERSAL HEALTH REALTY INCOME TRUST	UHT
RESIDENTIAL	MAN HOMES	CHATEAU PROPERTIES	CPJ
RESIDENTIAL	MAN HOMES	MANUFACTURED HOME COMMUNITIES	MHC
RESIDENTIAL	MAN HOMES	ROC COMMUNITIES	RCI
RESIDENTIAL	MAN HOMES	SUN COMMUNITIES	SUI
RESIDENTIAL	MAN HOMES	UNITED MOBILE HOMES	UMH
RESIDENTIAL	APARTMENTS	AMBASSADOR APTS	AAH
RESIDENTIAL	APARTMENTS	AMERICAN REAL ESTATE INVESTMENT CORP.	REA
RESIDENTIAL	APARTMENTS	AMLI RESIDENTIAL PROPERTIES TRUST	AML
RESIDENTIAL	APARTMENTS	APARTMENT. INVESTMENT & MANAGEMENT CO.	AIV
RESIDENTIAL	APARTMENTS	ASR INVESTMENTS CORP.	ASR
RESIDENTIAL	APARTMENTS	ASSOCIATED ESTATES REALTY CORP.	AEC
RESIDENTIAL	APARTMENTS	AVALON PROPERTIES	AVN
RESIDENTIAL	APARTMENTS	BAY APARTMENT PROPERTIES	BYA
RESIDENTIAL	APARTMENTS	BERKSHIRE REALTY CO.	BRI
RESIDENTIAL	APARTMENTS	BRE PROPERTIES	BRE
RESIDENTIAL	APARTMENTS	CAMDEN PROPERTY TRUST	CPT
RESIDENTIAL	APARTMENTS	CHARLES E SMITH RESIDENTIAL REALTY	SRW
RESIDENTIAL	APARTMENTS	COLUMBUS REALTY TRUST	CLB
RESIDENTIAL	APARTMENTS	CRI LIQUIDATING REIT	CFR
RESIDENTIAL	APARTMENTS	CRIIMI MAE	CMM
RESIDENTIAL	APARTMENTS	EQUITY RESIDENTIAL PROPERTIES TRUST	EQR
RESIDENTIAL	APARTMENTS	ESSEX PROPERTY TRUST	ESS
RESIDENTIAL	APARTMENTS	EVANS WITHYCOMBE RESIDENTIAL	EWR
RESIDENTIAL	APARTMENTS	GABLES RESIDENTIAL TRUST	GBP
RESIDENTIAL	APARTMENTS	HOME PROPERTIES OF NY	HME
RESIDENTIAL	APARTMENTS	IRVINE APARTMENT COMMUNITIES	IAC
RESIDENTIAL	APARTMENTS	MERRY LAND & INVESTMENT COMPANY	MRY
RESIDENTIAL	APARTMENTS	MID-AMERICA APARTMENT COMMUNITIES	MAA
RESIDENTIAL	APARTMENTS	OASIS RESIDENTIAL	OAS
RESIDENTIAL	APARTMENTS	PARAGON GROUP	PAO
RESIDENTIAL	APARTMENTS	POST PROPERTIES	PPS
RESIDENTIAL	APARTMENTS	PRESIDENTIAL REALTY CORP.	PDL.A
RESIDENTIAL	APARTMENTS	PRESIDENTIAL REALTY CORP. (CLASS B)	PDL.B
RESIDENTIAL	APARTMENTS	REDWOOD TRUST	RWTI

RESIDENTIAL	APARTMENTS	SECURITY CAPITAL ATLANTIC TRUST	SCA
RESIDENTIAL	APARTMENTS	SECURITY CAPITAL PACIFIC TRUST	PTR
RESIDENTIAL	APARTMENTS	SUMMIT PROPERTIES	SMT
RESIDENTIAL	APARTMENTS	SOUTH WEST PROPERTY TRUST	SWP
RESIDENTIAL	APARTMENTS	TOWN & COUNTRY TRUST, THE	TCT
RESIDENTIAL	APARTMENTS	UNITED DOMINION REALTY TRUST	UDR
RESIDENTIAL	APARTMENTS	WALDEN RESIDENTIAL PROPERTIES	WDN
RESIDENTIAL	APARTMENTS	WELLSFORD RESIDENTIAL PROPERTY TRUST	WRP

Morgan Stanley

Sector	Subsector	REIT	Ticker
IND/OFF	INDUSTRIAL	CENTERPOINT PROPERTIES	CNT
IND/OFF	INDUSTRIAL	FIRST INDUSTRIAL REALTY TRUST	FR
IND/OFF	INDUSTRIAL	SECURITY CAPITAL INDUSTRIAL TRUST	SCN
IND/OFF	INDUSTRIAL	WEEKS CORP	WKS
IND/OFF	OFFICE	BEACON PROPERTIES CORP	BCN
IND/OFF	OFFICE	CALI REALTY TRUST	CLI
IND/OFF	OFFICE	CARRAMERICA REALTY CORP.	CRE
IND/OFF	OFFICE	COUSINS PROPERTIES	CUZ
IND/OFF	OFFICE	CRESCENT REAL ESTATE EQUITIES	CEI
IND/OFF	OFFICE	HIGHWOODS PROPERTIES	HIW
IND/OFF	OFFICE	KOGER EQUITIES	KE
IND/OFF	MIXED	DUKE REALTY INVESTMENTS	DRE
IND/OFF	MIXED	LIBERTY PROPERTY TRUST	LRY
IND/OFF	MIXED	SPIEKER PROPERTIES	SPK
SPECIALTY		NATIONAL GOLF PROPERTIES	TEE
SPECIALTY	TRIPLE NET LEASE	COMMERCIAL NET LEASE REALTY	NNN
SPECIALTY	TRIPLE NET LEASE	FRANCHISE FINANCE CORP AMER	FFA
SPECIALTY	TRIPLE NET LEASE	LEXINGTON CORP PROPERTIES	LXP
SPECIALTY	TRIPLE NET LEASE	TRINET CORP REALTY	TRI
SPECIALTY	HOTELS	EQUITY INNS	ENN
SPECIALTY	HOTELS	FELCOR SUITE HOTELS	FCH
SPECIALTY	HOTELS	INNKEEPERS USA TRUST	KPA
SPECIALTY	HOTELS	PATRIOT AMERICAN HOSPITALITY	PAH
SPECIALTY	HOTELS	RFS HOTEL INVESTORS	RFS
SPECIALTY	HOTELS	STARWOOD LODGING TRUST	HOT
SPECIALTY	HOTELS	WINSTON HOTELS	WINN
RETAIL	STRIP CENTERS	ALEXANDER HAAGEN PROPERTIES	ACH
RETAIL	STRIP CENTERS	BRADLEY REAL ESTATE TRUST	BTR
RETAIL	STRIP CENTERS	BURNHAM PACIFIC PROPERTIES	BPP
RETAIL	STRIP CENTERS	DEVELOPERS DIVERSIFIED REALTY CORP.	DDR
RETAIL	STRIP CENTERS	EXCEL REALTY TRUST	XEL
RETAIL	STRIP CENTERS	FEDERAL REALTY INVESTMENT TRUST	FRT
RETAIL	STRIP CENTERS	GLIMCHER REALTY TRUST	GRT
RETAIL	STRIP CENTERS	IRT PROPERTY CO.	IRT
RETAIL	STRIP CENTERS	JDN REALTY CORP.	JDN
RETAIL	STRIP CENTERS	KIMCO REALTY CORP.	KIM
RETAIL	STRIP CENTERS	KRANZCO REALTY TRUST	KRT
RETAIL	STRIP CENTERS	MARK CENTERS TRUST	MCT
RETAIL	STRIP CENTERS	NEW PLAN REALTY TRUST	NPR
RETAIL	STRIP CENTERS	SAUL CENTERS	BFS
RETAIL	STRIP CENTERS	VORNADO REALTY TRUST	VNO
RETAIL	STRIP CENTERS	WEINGARTEN REALTY INVESTORS	WRI
RETAIL	STRIP CENTERS	WESTERN INVESTMENT REAL ESTATE TRUST	WIR
RETAIL	OUTLET	CHELSEA GCA REALTY	CCG
RETAIL	OUTLET	FAC REALTY TRUST	FAC
RETAIL	OUTLET	HORIZON GROUP	HGI
RETAIL	REGIONAL MALLS	CBL & ASSOCIATES	CBL
RETAIL	REGIONAL MALLS	CROWN AMERICAN REALTY TRUST	CWN
RETAIL	REGIONAL MALLS	GENERAL GROWTH PROPERTIES	GGP

RETAIL	REGIONAL MALLS	JP REALTY	JPR
RETAIL	REGIONAL MALLS	MACERICH COMPANY, THE	MAC
RETAIL	REGIONAL MALLS	MILLS CORP.	MLS
RETAIL	REGIONAL MALLS	SIMON DEBARTOLO GROUP	SPG
RETAIL	REGIONAL MALLS	TAUBMAN CENTERS	TCO
RETAIL	REGIONAL MALLS	URBAN SHOPPING CENTERS	URB
SELF STORAGE		PUBLIC STORAGE	PSA
SELF STORAGE		SHURGARD STORAGE CENTERS	SHU
SELF STORAGE		STORAGE TRUST REALTY	SEA
SELF STORAGE		STORAGE USA	SUS
DIVERSE		COLONIAL PROPERTIES TRUST	CLP
DIVERSE		MGI PROPERTIES	MGI
DIVERSE		PENNSYLVANIA REIT	PEI
DIVERSE		WASHINGTON REAL ESTATE INVESTMENT TRUST	WRE
RESIDENTIAL	MAN HOMES	MANUFACTURED HOME COMMUNITIES	MHC
RESIDENTIAL	MAN HOMES	ROC COMMUNITIES	RCI
RESIDENTIAL	MAN HOMES	SUN COMMUNITIES	SUI
RESIDENTIAL	APARTMENTS	AMBASSADOR APTS	AAH
RESIDENTIAL	APARTMENTS	AMLI RESIDENTIAL PROPERTIES TRUST	AML
RESIDENTIAL	APARTMENTS	APARTMENT. INVESTMENT & MANAGEMENT CO.	AIV
RESIDENTIAL	APARTMENTS	ASSOCIATED ESTATES REALTY CORP.	AEC
RESIDENTIAL	APARTMENTS	AVALON PROPERTIES	AVN
RESIDENTIAL	APARTMENTS	BAY APARTMENT PROPERTIES	BYA
RESIDENTIAL	APARTMENTS	BERKSHIRE REALTY CO.	BRI
RESIDENTIAL	APARTMENTS	BRE PROPERTIES	BRE
RESIDENTIAL	APARTMENTS	CAMDEN PROPERTY TRUST	CPT
RESIDENTIAL	APARTMENTS	CHARLES E SMITH RESIDENTIAL REALTY	SRW
RESIDENTIAL	APARTMENTS	COLUMBUS REALTY TRUST	CLB
RESIDENTIAL	APARTMENTS	EQUITY RESIDENTIAL PROPERTIES TRUST	EQR
RESIDENTIAL	APARTMENTS	EVANS WITHYCOMBE RESIDENTIAL	EWR
RESIDENTIAL	APARTMENTS	GABLES RESIDENTIAL TRUST	GBP
RESIDENTIAL	APARTMENTS	IRVINE APARTMENT COMMUNITIES	IAC
RESIDENTIAL	APARTMENTS	MERRY LAND & INVESTMENT COMPANY	MRY
RESIDENTIAL	APARTMENTS	MID-AMERICA APARTMENT COMMUNITIES	MAA
RESIDENTIAL	APARTMENTS	OASIS RESIDENTIAL	OAS
RESIDENTIAL	APARTMENTS	PARAGON GROUP	PAO
RESIDENTIAL	APARTMENTS	POST PROPERTIES	PPS
RESIDENTIAL	APARTMENTS	SECURITY CAPITAL PACIFIC TRUST	PTR
RESIDENTIAL	APARTMENTS	SUMMIT PROPERTIES	SMT
RESIDENTIAL	APARTMENTS	SOUTH WEST PROPERTY TRUST	SWP
RESIDENTIAL	APARTMENTS	TOWN & COUNTRY TRUST, THE	TCT
RESIDENTIAL	APARTMENTS	UNITED DOMINION REALTY TRUST	UDR
RESIDENTIAL	APARTMENTS	WALDEN RESIDENTIAL PROPERTIES	WDN
RESIDENTIAL	APARTMENTS	WELLSFORD RESIDENTIAL PROPERTY TRUST	WRP

Wilshire

Sector	Subsector	REIT	Ticker
IND/OFF	INDUSTRIAL	CENTERPOINT PROPERTIES	CNT
IND/OFF	INDUSTRIAL	FIRST INDUSTRIAL REALTY TRUST	FR
IND/OFF	INDUSTRIAL	SECURITY CAPITAL INDUSTRIAL TRUST	SCN
IND/OFF	INDUSTRIAL	WEEKS CORP	WKS
IND/OFF	OFFICE	BEACON PROPERTIES CORP	BCN
IND/OFF	OFFICE	CALI REALTY TRUST	CLI
IND/OFF	OFFICE	CARRAMERICA REALTY CORP.	CRE
IND/OFF	OFFICE	COUSINS PROPERTIES	CUZ
IND/OFF	OFFICE	CRESCENT REAL ESTATE EQUITIES	CEI
IND/OFF	OFFICE	HIGHWOODS PROPERTIES	HIW
IND/OFF	OFFICE	KOGER EQUITIES	KE
IND/OFF	MIXED	DUKE REALTY INVESTMENTS	DRE

IND/OFF	MIXED	LIBERTY PROPERTY TRUST	LRY
IND/OFF	MIXED	RECKSON ASSOC. REALTY	RA
IND/OFF	MIXED	SPIEKER PROPERTIES	SPK
SPECIALTY	HOTELS	AMERICAN GENERAL HOSPITALITY CORP	AGT
SPECIALTY	HOTELS	EQUITY INNS	ENN
SPECIALTY	HOTELS	FELCOR SUITE HOTELS	FCH
SPECIALTY	HOTELS	HOSPITALITY PROPERTIES TRUST	HPT
SPECIALTY	HOTELS	PATRIOT AMERICAN HOSPITALITY	PAH
SPECIALTY	HOTELS	RFS HOTEL INVESTORS	RFS
SPECIALTY	HOTELS	STARWOOD LODGING TRUST	HOT
SPECIALTY	HOTELS	WINSTON HOTELS	WINN
RETAIL	STRIP CENTERS	ALEXANDER HAAGEN PROPERTIES	ACH
RETAIL	STRIP CENTERS	BRADLEY REAL ESTATE TRUST	BTR
RETAIL	STRIP CENTERS	BURNHAM PACIFIC PROPERTIES	BPP
RETAIL	STRIP CENTERS	DEVELOPERS DIVERSIFIED REALTY CORP.	DDR
RETAIL	STRIP CENTERS	FEDERAL REALTY INVESTMENT TRUST	FRT
RETAIL	STRIP CENTERS	GLIMCHER REALTY TRUST	GRT
RETAIL	STRIP CENTERS	IRT PROPERTY CO.	IRT
RETAIL	STRIP CENTERS	JDN REALTY CORP.	JDN
RETAIL	STRIP CENTERS	KIMCO REALTY CORP.	KIM
RETAIL	STRIP CENTERS	KRANZCO REALTY TRUST	KRT
RETAIL	STRIP CENTERS	MARK CENTERS TRUST	MCT
RETAIL	STRIP CENTERS	NEW PLAN REALTY TRUST	NPR
RETAIL	STRIP CENTERS	PRICE REIT (CLASS B)	RET
RETAIL	STRIP CENTERS	REGENCY REALTY CORP.	REG
RETAIL	STRIP CENTERS	SAUL CENTERS	BFS
RETAIL	STRIP CENTERS	VORNADO REALTY TRUST	VNO
RETAIL	STRIP CENTERS	WEINGARTEN REALTY	WRI
RETAIL	STRIP CENTERS	WESTERN INVESTMENT REAL ESTATE	WIR
RETAIL	OUTLET	CHELSEA GCA REALTY	CCG
RETAIL	OUTLET	FAC REALTY TRUST	FAC
RETAIL	OUTLET	HORIZON GROUP	HGI
RETAIL	OUTLET	TANGER FACTORY OUTLET CENTERS	SKT
RETAIL	REGIONAL MALLS	ARBOR PROPERTY TRUST	ABR
RETAIL	REGIONAL MALLS	CBL & ASSOCIATES	CBL
RETAIL	REGIONAL MALLS	CROWN AMERICAN REALTY TRUST	CWN
RETAIL	REGIONAL MALLS	GENERAL GROWTH PROPERTIES	GGP
RETAIL	REGIONAL MALLS	JP REALTY	JPR
RETAIL	REGIONAL MALLS	MACERICH COMPANY, THE	MAC
RETAIL	REGIONAL MALLS	MILLS CORP.	MLS
RETAIL	REGIONAL MALLS	SIMON DEBARTOLO GROUP	SPG
RETAIL	REGIONAL MALLS	TAUBMAN CENTERS	TCO
SELF STORAGE		PUBLIC STORAGE	PSA
SELF STORAGE		SHURGARD STORAGE CENTERS	SHU
SELF STORAGE		SOVRAN SELF STORAGE	SSS
SELF STORAGE		STORAGE TRUST REALTY	SEA
SELF STORAGE		STORAGE USA	SUS
DIVERSE		COLONIAL PROPERTIES TRUST	CLP
DIVERSE		FIRST UNION REAL ESTATE INVESTMENTS	FUR
DIVERSE		MGI PROPERTIES	MGI
DIVERSE		PENNSYLVANIA REIT	PEI
DIVERSE		SIZELER PROPERTY INVESTORS	SIZ
DIVERSE		WASHINGTON REAL ESTATE INVESTMENT TRUST	WRE
RESIDENTIAL	MAN HOMES	CHATEAU PROPERTIES	CPJ
RESIDENTIAL	MAN HOMES	MANUFACTURED HOME COMMUNITIES	MHC
RESIDENTIAL	MAN HOMES	ROC COMMUNITIES	RCI
RESIDENTIAL	MAN HOMES	SUN COMMUNITIES	SUI
RESIDENTIAL	APARTMENTS	AMBASSADOR APTS	AAH
RESIDENTIAL	APARTMENTS	AMLI RESIDENTIAL PROPERTIES TRUST	AML
RESIDENTIAL	APARTMENTS	APARTMENT. INVESTMENT & MANAGEMENT CO.	AIV
RESIDENTIAL	APARTMENTS	ASSOCIATED ESTATES REALTY CORP.	AEC
RESIDENTIAL	APARTMENTS	AVALON PROPERTIES	AVN
RESIDENTIAL	APARTMENTS	BAY APARTMENT PROPERTIES	BYA
RESIDENTIAL	APARTMENTS	BERKSHIRE REALITY CO.	BRI
RESIDENTIAL	APARTMENTS	BRE PROPERTIES	BRE

RESIDENTIAL	APARTMENTS	CAMDEN PROPERTY TRUST	CPT
RESIDENTIAL	APARTMENTS	CHARLES E SMITH RESIDENTIAL REALTY	SRW
RESIDENTIAL	APARTMENTS	COLUMBUS REALTY TRUST	CLB
RESIDENTIAL	APARTMENTS	EQUITY RESIDENTIAL PROPERTIES TRUST	EQR
RESIDENTIAL	APARTMENTS	ESSEX PROPERTY TRUST	ESS
RESIDENTIAL	APARTMENTS	EVANS WITHYCOMBE RESIDENTIAL	EWR
RESIDENTIAL	APARTMENTS	GABLES RESIDENTIAL TRUST	GBP
RESIDENTIAL	APARTMENTS	HOME PROPERTIES OF NY	HME
RESIDENTIAL	APARTMENTS	IRVINE APARTMENT COMMUNITIES	IAC
RESIDENTIAL	APARTMENTS	MERRY LAND & INVESTMENT COMPANY	MRY
RESIDENTIAL	APARTMENTS	MID-AMERICA APARTMENT COMMUNITIES	MAA
RESIDENTIAL	APARTMENTS	OASIS RESIDENTIAL	OAS
RESIDENTIAL	APARTMENTS	PARAGON GROUP	PAO
RESIDENTIAL	APARTMENTS	POST PROPERTIES	PPS
RESIDENTIAL	APARTMENTS	SECURITY CAPITAL PACIFIC TRUST	PTR
RESIDENTIAL	APARTMENTS	SOUTH WEST PROPERTY TRUST	SWP
RESIDENTIAL	APARTMENTS	SUMMIT PROPERTIES	SMT
RESIDENTIAL	APARTMENTS	TOWN & COUNTRY TRUST, THE	TCT
RESIDENTIAL	APARTMENTS	UNITED DOMINION REALTY TRUST	UDR
RESIDENTIAL	APARTMENTS	WELLSFORD RESIDENTIAL	WRP
OPERATING		AMERICAN REAL ESTATE PARTNERS	ACP
OPERATING		BRISTOL HOTEL CO	BH
OPERATING		CATELLUS DEVELOPMENT CORP	CDX
OPERATING		FOREST CITY ENTERPRISES	FCE.A
OPERATING		HOST MARRIOTT CORP	HMT
OPERATING		LA QUINTA MOTOR INNS	LQI
OPERATING		NEWHALL LAND & FARMING	NHL
OPERATING		PROMUS HOTEL CORP	PRH
OPERATING		RED LION HOTELS INC	RL
OPERATING		RED ROOF INNS INC	RRI
OPERATING		ROUSE CO	RSE
OPERATING		STUDIO PLUS HOTELS I	SPHI

GLOSSARY

The following terms are used in one or more chapters of this book:

AFFO or Adjusted Funds From Operations FFO, less normalized recurring expenditures which are capitalized by the REIT and then amortized but which are necessary to maintain a REIT's properties and its revenue stream (e.g., new carpeting and drapes in apartment units, leasing expenses and tenant improvement allowances). Any "straight-lining" of rents is usually eliminated when determining AFFO.

Base Year In a commercial lease, the year which is used as a reference against which revenues or expenses in subsequent years are measured for purposes of determining additional rent or the tenant's sharing of additional operating expenses of the building.

Basis Point One one-hundredth of one percent (.01%). Thus a one basis point increase in the yield of a 10-year bond would result in a yield increase from, say, 6.81% to 6.82%.

Beta The extent to which a stock's price moves with an index of stocks, such as the S&P500.

Bond Proxy Describes the shares of a REIT which provide a high dividend yield to its shareholders but where FFO/AFFO and dividend growth is expected to be quite low, e.g., 2-4% annually.

Book Value The net value of a company's assets less its liabilities, as reflected on its balance sheet pursuant to GAAP (see "GAAP" in this Glossary). Book value will reflect depreciation and amortization, which are expensed for accounting purposes, and may have little relationship to a company's "net asset value" if evaluated at market prices (see "Net Asset Value" in this Glossary).

Cap Rate The unleveraged return expected to be received by the buyer of a property, expressed as the percentage determined by dividing the expected net operating income from the property (before depreciation) by the purchase price. Generally, high cap rates indicate greater perceived risk by the buyer. A "nominal" cap rate excludes, in determining the expected net operating income from a property, such often-capitalized expenses as new carpeting or drapes (i.e., in apartment units) or tenant improvements or leasing commissions; an "effective" or "economic" cap rate includes such expenditures.

Cash Flow With reference to a property (or group of properties), the owner's rental revenues from the property less all property operating expenses. The term ignores depreciation and amortization expenses, as well as interest on loans incurred to finance the property. Sometimes referred to as "EBITDA."

Cash-on-Cash Return The yield an investor would receive as a result of buying a specific property for a specific purchase price, assuming a given level of rental income and operating expenses but without taking into account the additional leverage provided by debt. For example, if an investor buys an office building for $2 million, expects the first year rental income from tenants of the building to be $500,000 and operating expenses to be $300,000, the net operating income would be $200,000 and the investor's "cash-on-cash return" would be $200,000 divided by $2 million, or 10%.

Cost of Capital The cost to a company, such as a REIT, of raising capital in the form of equity (common or preferred stock) or debt. The cost of *equity* capital takes the form of diluting the interests of the existing equity holders in the company; see Appendix C. The cost of *debt* capital is merely the interest expense on the debt incurred.

Debt Capital The amount of debt that a REIT carries on its balance sheet from time to time. This could be long-term mortgage debt, secured or unsecured debentures issued to public or private investors, borrowings under a bank or insurance company credit line or any other type of indebtedness. It does not include equity capital, such as common or preferred stock.

Discounting In financial markets, the process by which expected future developments and events which will affect an investment are anticipated and taken into account by the price at which such investment currently trades.

DownREIT A DownREIT is structured much like an UPREIT (see "UPREIT" in this Glossary), but has been formed after the REIT has become a public company and generally does not include members of management among the partners in the controlled partnership.

EBITDA See "Cash Flow" in this Glossary.

Equity Capital Permanent capital which has been raised through the sale and issuance of securities which have no right to repayment by the issuing company. This normally takes the form of common stock. Preferred stock is also sometimes regarded as equity capital, although often the company has an obligation to redeem such shares at certain times or under certain conditions.

Equity Market Cap	The total "equity value" of a public company, such as a REIT, determined by multiplying the company's total common shares outstanding by the market price of the shares as of a particular date. See also "Market Cap" in this Glossary. The term "Implied Market Cap" is sometimes used to refer to the market cap of an UPREIT or a DownREIT which has operating partnership units outstanding that are convertible into common shares; the "Implied Market Cap" takes the value of these units into account.
Equity REIT	A REIT which owns, or has an "equity interest" in, real estate (rather than making loans secured by real estate collateral).
FFO or Funds From Operations	Net income (determined in accordance with GAAP), excluding gains (or losses) from debt restructuring and sales of property, plus depreciation of real property, and after adjustments for unconsolidated entities, such as partnerships and joint ventures, in which the REIT holds an interest.
GAAP	Generally accepted accounting principles, as in effect from time to time, to which financial statements of public companies must conform.
GLA	Acronym for "gross leaseable area," which measures the total amount of leaseable space in a commercial property.
Hybrid REIT	A REIT which both owns real estate and makes loans secured by real estate collateral.
Interest Coverage	The ratio of a company's operating income (before amortization, depreciation and interest expense) to total interest expense. This ratio measures the extent to which interest expense on existing debt is "covered" by existing cash flow.
Leverage	Process by which the owner of a property may expand both the economic benefits and the risks of property ownership by adding borrowed funds to the owner's own funds committed to the venture.
Market Cap	The total market value of a REIT's (or other company's) outstanding securities and indebtedness. For example, if 20 million shares of a REIT are trading at $20 each, 2 million shares of the REIT's preferred stock are trading at $10 each and the REIT has $100 million of debt, its "market cap" would be $520 million ($400 million in common stock, $20 million in preferred stock and $100 million in indebtedness). See also "Equity Market Cap" in this Glossary.
Mortgage REIT	A REIT which makes and holds loans and other obligations which are secured by real estate collateral.

NAREIT National Association of Real Estate Investment Trusts, the REITs' trade organization.

Net Asset Value, or NAV The net "market value" of all a REIT's assets, including but not limited to its properties, after subtracting all its liabilities and obligations. Such net asset value (which is usually expressed on a "per share" basis) must be estimated by analysts and investors, as REITs generally don't obtain appraisals on their properties (and investors have become skeptical of appraisals even when available).

Net Income An accounting term which measures the profits earned by a business enterprise after all expenses are deducted from revenues; under GAAP (see "GAAP" in this Glossary), depreciation of real estate owned is treated as an expense of the business.

Overage Refers to a typical provision in a retail lease which requires the payment of rent payments in addition to the base rental prescribed in the lease if the store's sales exceed certain specified levels during the measurement period.

Overbuilding A situation in which so much new real estate has been recently completed in a particular area that the supply of available space significantly exceeds the demand by renters and users; the normal consequences of overbuilding are falling rental and occupancy rates.

Payout Ratio The ratio of a REIT's annual dividend rate to its FFO or AFFO, on a per share basis. For example, if FFO is $1.00 per share and the current dividend rate is $.80 per share, the payout ratio would be 80%.

PSI- Positive spread investing The ability to raise funds (both equity and debt) at a cost significantly less than the initial returns that can be obtained on real estate acquisitions.

Profitless Prosperity Describes a situation whereby either the owner or the tenant of a property enjoys higher rentals or sales, respectively, due to a strong economy, but where higher costs offset virtually all the benefits of the higher rentals or sales.

Real Estate Investment Trust Act of 1960 Legislation passed by Congress and signed into law which authorized REITs; the purpose of the new law was to allow individuals to "pool their investments" in real estate in order to get the same benefits as might be obtained by direct ownership.

REIT or Real Estate Investment Trust Either a corporation or a business trust which has certain tax attributes prescribed by Federal legislation, the most important of which is that the entity does not pay Federal taxes on its income if certain requirements (such as the obligation to pay at least 95% of its net income each year to the shareholders) are satisfied.

Resolution Trust Corporation A public corporation organized by Congress, in response to the banking and savings & loan crisis of the early '90s, to acquire and re-sell real estate and real estate loans from bankrupt (and near-bankrupt) lenders.

Retail REITs Retail REITs normally include REITs which specialize in any one or more of several different property types, including neighborhood (or "strip") shopping centers, malls and factory outlet stores.

Same-store Sales This concept, which is used to analyze retail companies, means sales from stores open for at least one year and excludes sales from stores which have been closed and from new stores (which often have unusually high sales growth). The "same-store" concept is applied to REITs' rental income, operating expenses and/or net operating income from those of its properties which have been owned and operated in the same fiscal period of the prior year.

Securitization or Equitization The process by which the economic benefits of ownership of a tangible asset, such as real estate, are divided among numerous investors and represented in the form of publicly-traded securities.

Total Return A stock's dividend income plus capital appreciation, before taxes and commissions. For example, if a stock rises 6% in price and provides a 7% yield during the measurement period, the investor's total return would have been 13%.

Triple Net Type of lease which requires the tenant to pay its pro rata share of all recurring maintenance and operating costs of the property, such as utilities, property taxes and insurance.

UPREIT A REIT which does not own its properties directly, but owns a controlling interest in a limited partnership which owns the REIT's real estate; other partners (besides the REIT itself) might include management and other private investors. See also "DownREIT" in this Glossary.

Volatility The extent to which the market price of a stock tends to fluctuate from day to day, or even hour to hour.

The Essential REIT:
A Guide to Profitable Investing in Real Estate Investment Trusts

By Ralph L. Block

Order by phone, toll free: 1-888-705-8844
or
Order by fax: 1-415-705-7775

Name _____ Phone _____

Address _____

City _____ State ____ Zip _____

#_____ copies of **The Essential REIT** @ $19.95
each: $ _____

CA residents add 8.5% sales tax: _____

Add $2.95 S&H for first book: _____

$1.00 S&H each additional book: _____

TOTAL PAYMENT: $ _____

☐ Check or Money Order enclosed (Payable to: Brunston Press)
☐ American Express
☐ Visa
☐ Master Card

Card No. _____ Exp. Date _____

Signature _____

For mail orders: Brunston Press
160 Sansome Street, Suite 1700
San Francisco, CA 94104
(Allow 2-3 weeks for delivery.)

Notes

Notes

Notes

Notes

Notes

Notes